FUNDAMENTAL ISSUES IN EVALUATION

EDITED BY

NICK L. SMITH
PAUL R. BRANDON

THE GUILFORD PRESS
New York   London

© 2008 The Guilford Press
A Division of Guilford Publications, Inc.
72 Spring Street, New York, NY 10012
www.guilford.com

Printed in the United States of America

This book is printed on acid-free paper.

Last digit is print number: 9 8 7 6 5 4 3 2 1

Library of Congress Cataloging-in-Publication Data

Fundamental issues in evaluation / edited by Nick L. Smith, Paul R. Brandon.
    p. cm.
  Includes bibliographical references and index.
  ISBN-13: 978-1-59385-342-6 (pbk. : alk. paper)
  ISBN-10: 1-59385-342-4 (pbk. : alk. paper)
  ISBN-13: 978-1-59385-604-5 (hardcover : alk. paper)
  ISBN-10: 1-59385-604-0 (hardcover : alk. paper)
  1. Evaluation research (Social action programs) I. Smith, Nick L. II.
Brandon, Paul R.
  H62.F84 2008
  001.4—dc22

                                                    2007035948

For Karen and Susan

Preface

FOCUS OF THE BOOK

There is an old adage that civilization must continually find new solutions to the persistent underlying problems of food, shelter, health, and communication. Similarly, in evaluation there are recurring themes, problems, and issues that periodically resurface in new forms to demand our attention.

- Why should evaluation be done? To improve programs? To influence decision making? To protect the public? To solve social problems? To promote social diversity?
- What are the proper social role(s) for the evaluator as a professional? As a researcher? As a teacher? As an advocate? As a facilitator? As a judge?
- How can stakeholders best be involved in evaluation studies? As served clients? As participants? As collaborators? As empowered citizens?
- What should we consider acceptable evidence for making evaluative decisions? Causal claims? Moral conclusions? Expert opinion? Aesthetic judgments? Stakeholder consensus?
- How do we arrive at the most valid understandings of quality? Controlled experiments? Moral deliberation? Phenomenological renderings?
- What is the most effective way to ensure the quality of evaluation practice? Advanced training? Accreditation and licensing? Consensual professional standards? Mandatory metaevaluation?

Fundamental issues are therefore those *underlying concerns, problems, or choices that continually resurface in different guises* throughout evaluation work. By their very nature, these issues can never be finally solved but only temporarily resolved. Fundamental issues underlie all areas of evaluation, whether it be communication with clients, ethical dilemmas, cultural differences, preparation of new evaluators, work with special populations, governmental service, methodological difficulties, social justice, evaluation influence, or economic survival as a professional. In this volume, we examine the nature and importance of issues such as these, issues that influence the character of evaluation theory, method, practice, and, indeed, the profession itself.

The chapter authors in this volume identify such issues in evaluation work, examine their importance, reflect on how they impact the nature of evaluation, and consider effective means of dealing with them. Such examinations help keep current problems in evaluation in better historical perspective, provoke thoughtful consideration of present options, and enable us to create more effective alternatives for the future. The considerations of fundamental issues in evaluation that are raised in this volume provide lively topics for analysis, disagreement, and discussion. They include issues that will continue to shape the nature and future of the evaluation profession.

DEVELOPMENT OF THE BOOK

"Fundamental Issues in Evaluation" was the conference theme of the 2004 annual meeting of the American Evaluation Association (AEA). This theme was the topic of plenary presentations made at the conference as well as the focus of a collection of Presidential Strand presentations featured throughout the meeting. Smith, as the 2004 AEA president, and Brandon, as the presidential strand chairperson, collaboratively developed the theme and invited a wide range of conference presentations on the topic. A few of the best of these presentations were solicited for inclusion in the present volume. Additional chapters were subsequently solicited to ensure a balanced coverage of the overall topic.

The initial conference presentations have been substantially reworked and expanded. Critical reviews of interim drafts were provided by the volume editors as well as by independent reviewers selected for their expertise in the respective topics of each chapter. These reviewers were selected mutually by the chapter authors and the volume editors. We are pleased to acknowledge below the important contributions of these independent reviewers. The result of this careful attention to quality is this impressive collection of chapters examining a range of issues that have played, and will continue to play, a central role in the profession of evaluation.

ORGANIZATION OF THE BOOK

In order to understand better the different foci of fundamental issues in evaluation, we have identified four general overlapping categories: theory, method, practice, and profession. These categories were used in scheduling the AEA conference presentations and are included here as an organizing structure for the volume. These four aspects encompass the world of evaluation, but they are simultaneously separate and interconnected. Some fundamental issues may be primarily problems of theory or practice, but many are entangled across several or all of these aspects. A category description focuses attention on a dominant aspect of the fundamental issue, but fundamental issues are often enmeshed across two or more categories.

Theory is that aspect reflecting our thinking about how and why we engage in evaluation; whether evaluation is done for purposes of validation, accountability, monitoring, or improvement and development; whether evaluation is a form of knowledge production, client service, social reform, or political control.

Method reflects our tools, the means by which we accomplish our intended purposes; tools of inquiry, of resource management, of interpersonal engagement, of social reform.

Practice reminds us of the immediate world of politics, clients, resources, role ambiguity, and changing field conditions; the practical concerns of getting the work done well and of making a difference.

Profession is about evaluation as a socially defined guild of practitioners and colleagues; the definitions of our work, our ethics, our responsibilities, and our livelihoods.

Because fundamental issues are, well, fundamental, any specific issue tends to have implications across all four aspects. For example, whether to employ a particular strategy for involving stakeholders in an evaluation might raise considerations of (1) whether the strategy is, in principle, well designed (method), (2) whether it can be effectively implemented in the current situation (practice), (3) whether its use is consistent with what is considered to be the proper role of stakeholder involvement in this particular evaluation (theory), and (4) the extent to which its use might benefit or harm society (profession). Which aspect is considered most salient depends, of course, on how one frames the issue—a methodologist may see the issue as one of designing an effective strategy (method), while a social critic may see the issue as whether use of the strategy promotes social justice (profession).

The fundamental issues discussed in this volume could similarly be classified across several or all four aspects, depending on one's point of view. For example, some issues that arise as concerns of method, such as in Chapter 4, "Multiple Threats to the Validity of Randomized Studies," can be shown to have profound implications for the profession of evaluation itself, as seen in Chapter 10, "The Impact of Narrow Views of Scientific Rigor on Evaluation Practices for Underrepresented Groups."

Each of the chapters in this volume alludes to multiple fundamental issues, issues that reflect complex, interwoven concerns that evolve over time. The grouping of the chapters in this volume reflects in part, therefore, how the present authors are currently dealing with these fundamental concerns, and what we, as editors, see as important interconnections. The fundamental issues represented here, however, will likely resurface in the future with possibly some other aspect seen as more salient at that moment in time. Although we have placed the chapters into sections of theory, method, practice, and profession according to what we judge to be the dominant perspective in each chapter, we invite the reader to consider the implications of each chapter for the other aspects of evaluation.

After an opening chapter, the book is divided into four parts. Part introductions are included in the volume to introduce the chapters and to highlight how each contributes to understanding of the relevant aspect of theory, method, practice, or profession considered in that part. There are, of course, scores of fundamental issues possible under each aspect; those included in this volume are but a sample of some of the fundamental issues currently of most concern in the evaluation profession.

CONTENTS OF THE BOOK

In "Fundamental Issues in Evaluation" (Chapter 1), Nick L. Smith introduces the topic of fundamental issues in evaluation. He presents an overview, identifies a variety of examples, considers the characteristics of fundamental issues, and discusses why and how such issues are fundamental in evaluation. This chapter explains why the concept of fundamental issue is a productive way to examine recurring themes and problems in evaluation, and it provides a conceptual framework within which to consider subsequent chapters of the volume. Each chapter treats one or more fundamental issues, grouped according to the aspects of theory, method, practice, and profession.

Part I: Issues of Theory includes two chapters. In "The Relevance of Practical Knowledge Traditions to Evaluation Practice" (Chapter 2), Thomas A. Schwandt raises the question, What is the nature of practical knowledge and how does it influence our understanding and practice of evaluation? He argues that good practice in evaluation "depends in a significant way on the experiential, existential knowledge we speak of as perceptivity, insightfulness, and deliberative judgment" (p. 37). In considering the fundamental issue, What is the nature of expertise in evaluation?, Schwandt contrasts the role of practical knowledge with more technicist interpretations.

In her chapter, "Stakeholder Representation in Culturally Complex Communities: Insights from the Transformative Paradigm" (Chapter 3), Donna M. Mertens raises the difficult recurring issues of how to deal with cultural competence and the treatment of diversity within evaluation practice. She proposes the use of a transformative paradigm that seeks to ensure that stakeholders are fairly represented, that the diversity of stakeholder groups is considered adequately, and that differences in power among these groups are addressed in evaluations.

Both chapters in Part I illustrate how selecting a particular theoretical position about the nature of evaluation subsequently shapes the way we think about the profession itself and therefore which methods and forms of practice we consider appropriate.

"Multiple Threats to the Validity of Randomized Studies" (Chapter 4) by Judith A. Droitcour and Mary Grace Kovar leads off *Part II: Issues of Method.* The authors address the fundamental issue, How can experimental studies best be designed for practical use in the field?, by focusing on two threats to validity when using experiments: differential reactivity and biasing social interactions. Using numerous examples, they present a clear, succinct summary of the literature on these threats, with the valuable addition of suggesting means for prospective identification of the two forms of bias.

The second of the three chapters in Part II is "Research Synthesis: Toward Broad-Based Evidence" (Chapter 5). In this chapter, Susan N. Labin presents an overview of types of research syntheses including traditional literature reviews, qualitative reviews, and broad-based research syntheses; meta-analyses; evaluation syntheses and retrospective evaluation syntheses; and the synthesis method presented in the *Guide to Community Preventive Services*, as well as others. Her critical review of the advantages, disadvantages, and selection criteria of these methods provides important insights about the fundamental issue, What is the proper way to synthesize evaluation and social science research findings in evaluation?

"Building a Better Evidence Base for Evaluation Theory: Beyond General Calls to a Framework of Types of Research on Evaluation" (Chapter 6), by Melvin M. Mark, completes Part II. Mark provides a taxonomy of types of studies for researching evaluation, including descriptive studies, classification studies, causal analyses, and values inquiries. The taxonomy serves as a guide for the design, classification, and interpretation of research on evaluation. As Mark points out, a stronger empirical understanding of prior evaluation work can contribute to better responses to questions about other fundamental issues, such as What are the best approaches and methods for a given evaluation?, How have those choices been manifested in previous studies?, and What have been the consequences of those choices?

All three chapters in Part II provide theoretical arguments concerning which methods will most improve evaluation practice. Collectively they portray the profession of evaluation as an empirically based, inquiry-focused enterprise, and they each make important contributions to technical issues of evaluation method.

Part III: Issues of Practice begins with "Complexities in Setting Program Standards in Collaborative Evaluation" (Chapter 7) by J. Bradley Cousins and Lyn M. Shulha. Cousins and Shulha address the fundamental issue, What level of performance must an evaluand achieve for its performance to be considered adequate or satisfactory? They discuss aspects of selecting bases for comparison, determining values, setting standards, and ensuring cultural sensitivity when stakeholders and evaluators work together to conduct formative collaborative evaluations. In such evaluations, power over evaluation decision making is shared equally among the evaluators, who have technical skills, and program personnel, whose understanding of the substance, organization, and daily operations of the program is far greater than that of the program's evaluators. Such evaluations should be ideal for explicitly and carefully deciding how well the evaluated program has to perform.

Carlos C. Ayala and Paul R. Brandon continue the focus on formative evaluation in Chapter 8, "Building Evaluation Recommendations for Improvement: Insights from Student Formative Assessments." They consider the case of K–12 student formative assessment that is conducted by the classroom teacher for the purpose of providing immediate feedback to students about how to improve their learning. Ayala and Brandon present a formal approach to assessment called the Assessment Pedagogy Model, which uses assessment as an integral part of teaching.

They describe the several components of the model and review implications of the model for formative program evaluation in general.

Both these chapters illustrate how difficulties in evaluation practice not only have resulted in subsequent improvements to that practice but also have led evaluators to reconsider issues of theory and method. These chapters illustrate the essential contribution of self-reflective practice in producing an effective and useful profession.

Part IV: Issues of the Profession consists of three chapters. In "What Is the Difference between Evaluation and Research—and Why Do We Care?" (Chapter 9), Sandra Mathison provides new insights on the perennial questions of how social research and evaluation differ: What is the overlap of the purposes and methods of these two forms of inquiry? What knowledge and skill sets are required of evaluators versus social science researchers? Mathison's analysis of the depictions of the differences between these two forms of inquiry, such as the extent to which the findings of studies result in decisions (vs. generalizations), shows that the differences depend on the context and the purpose of particular studies. Her chapter will help readers move from the overly simple question, What is the difference between research and evaluation?, to a more sophisticated consideration of the conditions under which research and evaluation share both similarities and differences.

The two remaining chapters in Part IV address important fundamental issues that have received increasing attention in recent years. With greater appreciation for the diversity within society and the increasing globalization of evaluation, evaluators are now more explicitly dealing with such fundamental issues as What is the nature of a culturally competent evaluation? and What are the proper role and means for evaluation in contributing to social justice?

In Chapter 10, "The Impact of Narrow Views of Scientific Rigor on Evaluation Practices for Underrepresented Groups," Elmima C. Johnson, Karen E. Kirkhart, Anna Marie Madison, Grayson B. Noley, and Guillermo Solano-Flores argue that rigorous studies, although internally valid, are often not sufficiently robust, because they do not arrive at conclusions that properly take into account program and evaluation context, particularly the contextual factors that affect communities of peoples of color. They argue that the primary purposes of program evaluations and assessments should be to ensure social justice, enhance fairness, and address inequities in access to power. They illustrate how robustness can be increased by focusing on three issues: (1) how definitions of validity determine the operationalization of rigor, (2) how language theory can inform the assessment of second-language learners, and (3) how evaluations can advance social justice by using multiple measures of accountability. Their discussion speaks to fundamental issues of the proper purposes, roles, and uses of evaluation.

The third chapter in Part IV is "Improving the Practice of Evaluation through Indigenous Values and Methods: Decolonizing Evaluation Practice—Returning the Gaze from *Hawai'i* and *Aotearoa*" (Chapter 11), by Alice J. Kawakami, Kanani Aton, Fiona Cram, Morris K. Lai, and Laurie Porima. The authors make a strong case that many evaluations in Polynesian settings have adapted a "Western approach" that has ignored or disrespected the role of community elders as the arbiters of quality, has failed to acknowledge and incorporate indigenous spiritual values, and has disregarded cultural practices such as valuing lineage. They demonstrate that these evaluations typically have not benefited the communities in which the programs have occurred. They argue that indigenous peoples have a right to evaluation methods that are culturally relevant, not simply because the results will be more culturally and epistemologically valid, or because such methods will lead to greater stakeholder support of the resultant findings, but because indigenous peoples have a moral right to self-determination, a right to influence the choice of methods for evaluating the programs that affect their lives.

All three chapters in Part IV illustrate how our understanding of the nature of evaluation as a profession continues to evolve. The latter two chapters draw our attention to especially serious issues about what the generative principles should be that define who evaluators are, what they do, and how they operate—fundamental issues of the evaluation profession.

We offer here a note on how to read this volume. Chapter 1 provides an overview and general discussion of the nature and importance of fundamental issues in evaluation. It might be a useful starting point. Used as a text, one might read this volume sequentially, moving from theory through method, practice, and profession; this pattern reflects the sequence in which one typically learns about evaluation. Those readers with specific interests in a given aspect, say method or practice, might proceed immediately to those sections. Or, the volume can be used as a general resource, with the reader focusing just on the specific topics of interest. We encourage the reader to review each of the chapters in the volume. We have worked hard with each author to ensure that the material is accessible to all readers, not just to those with a prior background or interest in the specific topic. We believe that an important value of this book is that all readers can gain a new appreciation for the significance and long-term impact on evaluation of fundamental issues that lie outside their usual areas of interest.

ACKNOWLEDGMENTS

This volume reflects a novel way of examining recurring themes in evaluation. We are most grateful to the contributing authors for their patience and goodwill in helping us draw out the fundamental issues in their own work. To assist the authors, we collaboratively selected independent reviewers who provided insightful, constructive, and in some cases extensively detailed comments on earlier chapter drafts. This volume is much stronger because of their collective efforts, and we wish to thank them for their professional diligence and collegial support. Our grateful thanks to:

Gary Bond
Indiana University–Purdue University Indianapolis

Christina Christie
Claremont Graduate University

David Cordray
Vanderbilt University

Lois-ellin Datta
Datta Analysis

Lorna Earl
Ontario Institute for Studies in Education / University of Toronto

Leslie Goodyear
Education Development Center, Inc.

Robin Miller
Michigan State University

Hallie Preskill
Claremont Graduate University

Darlene Russ-Eft
Oregon State University

Mary Ann Scheirer
Scheirer Consulting

Elizabeth St. Pierre
University of Georgia

Veronica Thomas
Howard University

Elizabeth Whitmore
Carleton University

Susan Kistler, Executive Director of the American Evaluation Association (AEA), provided invaluable assistance in planning and conducting the 2004 AEA conference, during which early drafts of most of the chapters in this volume were presented. Her technical staff produced the excellent renderings of our concept of the mandala of overlapping nautilus shells. Without her outstanding organizational skills and professional support, this volume would not have been possible.

Finally, we offer our sincere thanks to C. Deborah Laughton of The Guilford Press for her unwavering support of this project. Her patience, thoughtful guidance, and good humor were key to our ultimately finishing this volume. Any remaining limitations are, of course, our own responsibility.

NICK L. SMITH
PAUL R. BRANDON

Contents

Contents

FUNDAMENTAL ISSUES
IN EVALUATION

CHAPTER 1

Fundamental Issues in Evaluation

NICK L. SMITH

Build thee more stately mansions, O my soul,
As the swift seasons roll!
Leave thy low-vaulted past!
Let each new temple, nobler than the last,
Shut thee from heaven with a dome more vast,
Till thou at length art free,
Leaving thine outgrown shell by life's unresting sea!
—OLIVER WENDELL HOLMES (1858)

The title and topic of this book is *Fundamental Issues in Evaluation*. Fundamental issues are those underlying concerns, problems, or choices that continually resurface in different guises throughout our evaluation work. By their very nature, they are never finally solved, only temporarily resolved. In this chapter, I invite you to consider the nature and importance of these issues that influence the character of evaluation theory, method, practice, and, indeed, the profession itself. There are numerous such fundamental issues in evaluation, and I present a sampling. I also discuss a particularly salient example of a fundamental issue, the role of randomized controlled trials in evaluation, a topic that is being very actively debated in evaluation at present.

MANDALA OF NAUTILUS SHELLS

An essential defining characteristic of a fundamental issue is that, while the issue itself is ever a part of evaluation, its form is continually transitory and changing, reflecting contemporary concerns and circumstances. To represent the impermanent form of these never-ending issues, I have chosen a mandala of nautilus shells.

The word *mandala* is from Sanskrit, meaning circle. It represents wholeness. The mandala pattern appears in many traditions and in Buddhist, Muslim, and Christian architecture. Groups as diverse as Tibetan monks and Navajo Indians create sand mandalas as a way to illustrate the impermanence of life. Tibetan monks ceremonially destroy the sand mandala to symbolize the cycle of life. Tibetan Buddhists say that a mandala consists of five "excellencies": The Time, The Site, The Audience, The Teacher, and The Message. A particular resolution of a fundamental issue, then, can be thought of as a current temporary form (The Message) constructed by someone in the profession (The Teacher) for others in the profession (The Audience) in a given time and context (The Time and The Site) (Mandala Project, n.d.).

Whenever a center is found radiating outward and inward, there is a wholeness—a mandala. The spiraling of a nautilus shell itself reflects a mandala pattern, and so each of the four shells is itself a mandala, each representing a different aspect of the world of evaluation that continues to grow and change. In the figure on page 1, notice also that the positioning of the shells, Theory under Method under Practice under Profession, further creates a spiraling mandala pattern of the world of evaluation.

Why is it useful to have a visual representation of fundamental issues? To help us remember that heated arguments of proper method or best practice or strongest theory are just today's debates about much older fundamental concerns. Agreement on an issue can lead us to a resolution that is useful for the moment, but it is the cumulative growth of our understanding that is the important result of these interchanges—not the ultimate resolution of the issues, since, as the mandala reminds us, there is no ultimate resolution. We will need to revisit each of these fundamental issues time and time again in the future as our circumstances and problems change.

Aspects of Evaluation

I have selected the four aspects of theory, method, practice, and profession to encompass the world of evaluation. These aspects are simultaneously separate and interconnected. Some fundamental issues are primarily problems of theory or practice, but many are entangled across several or all of these aspects. The shells focus our attention on a dominant aspect, but fundamental issues are often enmeshed across them.

Theory is that aspect reflecting our thinking about how and why we engage in evaluation. Is the purpose of evaluation validation, accountability, monitoring, or improvement and development? Is evaluation a form of knowledge production, client service, social reform, or political control? *Method* reflects our tools, the means by which we accomplish our intended purposes; tools of inquiry, of resource management, of interpersonal engagement, of social reform. *Practice* reminds us of the immediate world of politics, clients, resources, role ambiguity, and changing field conditions; the practical concerns of getting the work done well and of making a difference. *Profession* is about evaluation as a socially defined guild of practitioners and colleagues; the definitions of our work, our ethics, our responsibilities, and our livelihoods.

Throughout history, problems of food, shelter, and health have periodically required updated solutions. Similarly, in evaluation there are recurring problems and issues that periodically resurface in new forms to demand our attention.

Examples

- Why should evaluation be done? To improve programs? To influence decision making? To protect the public? To solve social problems? To promote social diversity?
- What are the proper social roles for the evaluator as a professional? Researcher? Teacher? Advocate? Facilitator? Judge?
- What should we consider acceptable evidence for making evaluative decisions? Causal claims? Moral conclusions? Expert opinion? Aesthetic judgments? Stakeholder consensus?

- How do we arrive at the most valid understandings of quality? Controlled experiments? Moral deliberation? Phenomenological renderings?
- How can stakeholders best be involved in evaluation studies? As served clients? As participants? As collaborators? As empowered citizens?
- What is the most effective way to ensure the quality of evaluation practice? Advanced training? Accreditation and licensing? Consensual professional standards? Mandatory metaevaluation?

Fundamental issues underlie all areas of evaluation theory, method, practice, and the profession, whether it be communication with clients, ethical dilemmas, cultural differences, preparation of new evaluators, work with special populations, governmental service, methodological difficulties, social justice, evaluation influence, or economic survival as a professional. Fundamental issues are essential considerations of the evaluation enterprise that recur over time. They are periodically encountered, struggled with, and resolved, reflecting contemporary values, technical considerations, political forces, professional concerns, emerging technologies, and available resources. There can never be a final "once-and-for-all" resolution to a fundamental issue. The resolution of such issues is often a point of contention and debate as the profession struggles to shed old ways of dealing with the issue and adopt a newer, more effective, position. The attention and effort generated during these struggles attest to the fundamental importance of these concerns to the identity and livelihood of professional evaluation.

Why Are Fundamental Issues Important?

Often, current disagreements or tensions in evaluation are actually manifestations of more fundamental issues. If we can identify such issues in our work, we can then better examine their importance, reflect on how they impact our work, and develop more effective ways of dealing with them. Such examinations may help us keep our current problems in better historical perspective, support more thoughtful considerations of our present options, and enable us to create more effective alternatives for the future.

As the words suggest, fundamental issues are problematic, underlying, ongoing concerns or options. By definition, there is no single long-term answer to a fundamental issue; rather, the resolution to such issues is inevitably temporary, contextual, situational, and conditional. Just as in addressing the fundamental issue of meeting our energy needs, where we have moved from wood, to coal, to oil, to electricity, to nuclear, to wind, and back again, so with the issue of evaluation purpose, we have moved from research to client service to social reform and back to research. Which fundamental issue is most important at any given time reflects factors both internal and external to the profession; which resolution is favored by particular groups reflects values, collective experience, resources, and the options available.

Thus, one approach to dealing with problems in evaluation is to ask: What are the fundamental issues underlying the current situation? How have these fundamental issues been addressed previously? What do we know about their nature, constraints, and effective resolution that would help us deal with the current situation?

A first step is to consider how to examine fundamental issues, including the way their elements may touch upon all four aspects of evaluation, namely, theory, method, practice, and profession. In this chapter, I examine the highly visible debate about scientific-based or evidence-based evaluation and the use of randomized controlled trials (RCTs). Initially, this may appear to be an argument about evaluation method, but the case actually incorporates a variety of fundamental issues across all four aspects of evaluation.

EXAMPLE: THE ROLE OF RCTs IN EVALUATION

Personal

When discussions of the role of experimental designs in evaluation became increasingly public a few years ago, I thought, "Didn't we already settle this?" Almost 25 years ago, I organized and moderated a debate at the 1981 joint meeting of the predecessor organizations of the American Evaluation Association (AEA): the Evaluation Network and the Evaluation Research Society. The title of the debate was "Should the federal government mandate the use of experimental methods in evaluation?" The participants were Milbrey McLaughlin of Stanford University and Bob Boruch who currently is principal investigator of the What Works Clearinghouse and cochair of the international Campbell Collaboration Steering Group. At the time, I published a couple of articles on the desirability of experimental methods and on noncausal alternatives (Smith, 1980, 1981).

But that is the nature of fundamental issues; they may be temporarily resolved, but they will resurface later, in a different form, requiring a new, hopefully more thoughtful and sophisticated, resolution. I once commented to a senior colleague, David Krathwohl, that I thought I discerned a particular trend happening in evaluation. He observed that, if you lived long enough, you realized there were no trends, only cycles. So, I have lived long enough to see this fundamental issue return to our attention—indeed, if it ever left. And the nautilus seems like a relevant image—a shell continually expanding its chambers to house our growing understanding of a recurring issue.

Historical Perspective

Of course, experimental methods have always been of interest in evaluation. Before it was claimed that RCTs were the "gold standard" for evaluation practice, their use was justified by using a religious metaphor. Recall, for example, this often cited observation by Rossi and Wright in 1977:

> There is almost universal agreement among evaluation researchers that the randomized controlled experiment is the ideal model for evaluating the effectiveness of a public policy. If there is a Bible for evaluation, the Scriptures have been written by Campbell and Stanley (1966), along with a revised version by Cook and Campbell (1975). The "gospel" of these popular texts is that all research designs can be compared more or less unfavorably to randomized controlled experiments, departures from which are subject to varying combinations of threats to internal and external validity. (p. 13)

Eminent colleagues have worked for decades to improve our understanding and use of experimental approaches in evaluation, from early work published in the first *Handbook of Evaluation Research* (Struening & Guttentag, 1975) to the recent major contribution by Shadish, Cook, and Campbell (2002).

These researchers continue to work on the development and application of experimental approaches in evaluation. Issues such as the following continue to be addressed:

- Role of causal versus noncausal questions in evaluation
- Conditions under which experimental approaches are preferable
- Alternative ways to establish causality
- Problems of context–question–method match
- Differences in levels of evidence required
- Local variations within large-scale studies
- Match of evaluation design to developmental stage of evaluand
- Generalizability and the need for multiple replications

- Practical considerations of cost, intrusion, and control
- Concerns of cultural relevance
- Ethical concerns of risk and responsibility

The Recent Debate

Although many evaluators would agree that experimental designs are the best choice in certain cases, fewer would agree that they are the best method in every case. The fundamental issue of concern here, however, is not simply the method problem of whether experimental approaches are always the best design but, in part, the attempt to have that position become a national mandate.

The terms *scientifically based* and *evidence-based* appear widely in today's popular and professional media, from "evidence-based medical practice" to "scientifically based educational research." Perhaps as part of an attempt to strengthen the quality of evidence used to make program and policy decisions, the federal government has been systematically passing legislation that mandates particular methodological approaches to the problems being addressed. Eisenhart and Towne (2003), for example, chart the evolution of the federal concept of "scientifically based education research" as written into law in the No Child Left Behind Act of 2001, the Education Sciences Reform Act of 2002, and the National Research Council's 2002 publication *Scientific Research in Education* (Shavelson & Towne, 2002). They conclude that, as one might expect, there are differences in interpretation across the federal scene. There does seem to be, however, a concerted effort to restrict the range of what are to be considered acceptable evaluation approaches.

Over the past decades, evaluation methods have ostensibly shifted from the dominance of narrow experimental approaches to include a wider range of quantitative designs, the development of more client-centered consultative models, and the application of more sophisticated qualitative and interpretive approaches. And yet recently one of our most heated debates has concerned the U.S. Department of Education's proposed priority to establish experimental methods as the gold standard for certain educational evaluations.

THE U.S. DEPARTMENT OF EDUCATION'S PROPOSED PRIORITY

On November 4, 2003, the U.S. Department of Education (2003a) issued a notice of proposed priority titled "Scientifically Based Evaluation Methods" that read in part:

The Secretary proposes a priority for program projects proposing an evaluation plan that is based on rigorous scientifically based research methods to assess the effectiveness of a particular intervention. The Secretary intends that this priority will allow program participants and the Department to determine whether the project produces meaningful effects on student achievement or teacher performance.

Evaluation methods using an experimental design are best for determining project effectiveness. Thus, the project should use an experimental design under which participants—e.g., students, teachers, classrooms, or schools—are randomly assigned to participate in the project activities being evaluated or to a control group that does not participate in the project activities being evaluated.

If random assignment is not feasible, the project may use a quasi-experimental design with carefully matched comparison conditions. . . .

In cases where random assignment is not possible and an extended series of observations of the outcome of interest precedes and follows the introduction of a new program or practice, regression discontinuity designs may be employed. . . .

Proposed evaluation strategies that use neither experimental designs with random assignment nor quasi-experimental designs using a matched comparison group nor regression discontinuity designs will not be considered responsive to the priority when sufficient numbers of participants are available to support these designs. . . . (p. 62446)

THE AEA RESPONSE

The public was given 1 month to respond to the Department of Education's request for public comment, which was issued while the AEA was having its 2003 annual conference. On November 25, 2003, the AEA (2003) issued a response to the proposed priority that included the positions that:

- Randomized control group trials are not the *only* means of establishing causality.

- Randomized control group trials are not always the *best* way to establish causality.

- Randomized control group trials sometimes should not be used for *ethical* reasons.

- Randomized control group trials sometimes should not be used because data sources are insufficient.

- Evaluators should employ a repertoire of methods.

- Conditionality of effectiveness, not just causality, should be considered.

- "Fettering evaluators with *unnecessary and unreasonable con-straints* would deny information needed by policy-makers. . . . We believe that the constraints in the proposed priority would deny use of other needed, proven, and scientifically credible evaluation methods, resulting in fruitless expenditures on some large contracts while leaving other public programs unevaluated entirely;" emphasis in original.

Other professional associations such as the American Educational Research Association and the National Education Association also responded with criticism and suggestions for revising the proposed priority. All of these statements are available on the AEA website (*www. eval.org/doepage.htm*).

REACTION TO THE AEA RESPONSE

AEA members responded immediately to the AEA statement and debated the statement on EVALTALK (the AEA listserv) for some time under the subject heading of "The Causal Wars." The AEA was both praised and condemned for making the statement. Some members charged that the AEA leadership had no right to issue any such statement; others claimed that the association had a professional responsibility to do so. The AEA was criticized for not vetting the statement through the entire membership. The association has subsequently established procedures and a formal committee for future cases.

In January 2005, the U.S. Department of Education (2005) posted its final priority statement related to scientifically based evaluation methods. Almost 300 parties submitted comments on the proposed priority, which were summarized into 11 primary issues, of which the major ones were similar to those raised by the AEA. The U.S. Department of Education (ED) responded that it did not agree with many of the concerns raised and did not feel that implementation of the proposed priority would be as problematic as others feared. In short, the ED chose not to change the priority statement in response to received comments:

Although we received substantive comments, we determined that the comments did not warrant changes. However, we have reviewed the notice since its publication and have made a change based on that review. . . . Except for a technical change to correct an error in the language of the priority, one minor clarifying change, and the addition of a definitions section, there are no differences between the notice of proposed priority and this notice of final priority. (U.S. Department of Education, 2005, p. 3586)

That this has been a very influential statement of priority has been noted by one congressional report that stated:

> At a minimum, the priority has influenced the use of hundreds of millions of research dollars controlled by ED [the Department of Education] and arguably education policy, as implemented by ED. For example, ED's department-wide strategic planning documents and activities appear to reflect the priority. The ED strategic plan established a goal of 75% of "new research and evaluation projects funded by the Department that address causal questions . . . employ randomized experimental designs." (Brass, Nuñez-Neto, & Williams, 2006, p. 24)

The authors went on to conclude that

> In effect, as demonstrated through ED policy and strategic planning documents, the ED priority appears in some respects to be extending ED's interpretation of ESRA [Education Sciences Reform Act of 2002] definitions and preferences for certain types of evaluations (especially RCTs) beyond IES [Institute of Education Sciences] to the entire Education Department, notwithstanding the apparently differing definitions and preferences expressed in NCLB [No Child Left Behind Act of 2001]. . . . In 2004, the Bush Administration elevated RCTs as the preferred way to evaluate federal executive branch "programs" under portions of its Program Assessment Rating Tool (PART) initiative. (Brass et al., 2006, pp. 27–28)

THE ONGOING FUNDAMENTAL CONCERNS

An examination of this debate draws our attention to a number of fundamental issues in evaluation theory, method, practice, and the profession. This proposed priority and similar statements on acceptable evaluation methods have resulted in widespread efforts to clarify and improve evaluation. Some efforts have been beneficial to the profession, others divisive. It is important, therefore, to understand the implications of these positions and how these events reflect fundamental disagreements about the purpose and method of the evaluation profession— disagreements not just within the federal government or society but within the evaluation profession itself.

The fundamental issue of the quality of evaluation methods continues to be a widely discussed topic, including public claims of evaluation's failure. In the June 11, 2004, issue of *Science* Judith Ramaley, head of the education directorate at the National Science Foundation (NSF), was quoted as saying that "the entire discipline of rigorous evaluation is just emerging" (Mervis, 2004, p. 1583). The article noted that there was a "dirty little secret" behind the requirement of the No Child Left Behind legislation that programs be shown to be effective through scientifically based research, namely, that "No program has yet met that rigorous standard, because none has been scientifically evaluated and shown to be effective. (A related secret is that there's no consensus on the type of evaluation studies that are needed.)" (Mervis, 2004, p. 1583).

The NSF funded a National Research Council (NRC) study *On Evaluating Curricular Effectiveness*, (Mathematical Science Education Board, 2004) of 19 elementary and secondary school mathematics curricula, and found their evaluations inadequate. The NSF also funded a study by a public–private consortium, Building Engineering and Science Talent (BEST), of programs designed to increase the number of minorities, women, and low-income students in mathematics and science. Of 200 programs, only 34 could be analyzed, and, of those only 20 could be rated; 11 warranted more research, 7 were notable, 2 were probably effective, and none was verifiably effective—the requirement being five studies conducted by independent evaluators that showed substantially positive results (Mervis, 2004). An American Institutes for Research contractor that worked for NSF on the BEST study claims that "NSF is now asking for multivariate and controlled studies" (Mervis, 2004, p. 1583).

To some extent, these experimental positions reflect the values of influential segments of current society, both within the United States and elsewhere. These policies are not simply the work of a small cabal of conservatives at the federal level but reflect widely held and supported beliefs. For some, the insistence on RCTs reflects a belief in the importance of causal questions as a primary focus of evaluation and the judgment that RCTs are the strongest method for answering such questions. That is, support for experimental approaches to evaluation reflects a complex combination of national politics, social context, political values, and technical methodological analyses and commitments.

We must see this conflict concerning methodological superiority as just the latest skirmish in an ongoing long-term struggle to create a useful and viable profession of evaluation. Viewed this way, the current debate helps us to acknowledge our reasonable differences and to use these contentious issues to energize our work. I propose more than just a revisiting of the "paradigm wars" of earlier years in which evaluators pitted one method or approach against another to determine methodological dominance. I propose we attempt to look more deeply at the fundamental differences that give rise to these disagreements in the first place and that still fuel debates about proper methodology. Understanding better the fundamental issues underlying these methods choices can help evaluators make more thoughtful selections from present options and create more effective alternatives for future use.

For example, the federal initiatives have been posed largely in terms of method superiority. Evaluators have been quick to respond in a similar vein, probably in part because evaluators frequently define their own view of evaluation in terms of method. Further, a large majority of evaluators also see their work as assessing the impact of treatments or interventions, including the identification of causal influences, just as the federal positions presuppose.

Thus, some evaluators have accepted the federal construction of the situation without stopping to consider the full range of underlying fundamental issues. Much less attention has been given to alternative interpretations, to the identification of other important issues at stake, such as:

- *Theory*—doesn't defining evaluation primarily as providing empirical evidence of intervention impact preclude many other useful forms of evaluation?

- *Method*—doesn't selecting any method as a gold standard corrupt the accepted logic of problem-driven methods choices? (see Patton, 2004)

- *Practice*—won't the strict requirements of experimental studies, and the difficulty in mounting such studies, result in a dramatic decline in the number of evaluations being conducted?

- *Profession*—shouldn't professionals make context and problem-based design decisions instead of such choices being federally mandated? Don't federal mandates increasingly restrict the professional latitude of evaluators?

Those evaluators who have engaged in this debate as an issue of the superiority of certain methods may have implicitly conceded resolutions on such fundamental issues as what the proper purpose of evaluation is and who has the right and responsibility for determining such professional matters as evaluation methods.

Let us consider in more detail some of the other fundamental issues hidden within the ongoing debate about the superiority of experimental methods in evaluation.

Theory

Theory, in part, provides a rationale for why an evaluation should be done. It concerns the purposes of evaluation.

- Why should evaluation be done? To test program effectiveness? To improve programs? To influence decision making? To protect the public? To solve social problems? To promote social diversity?
- What should we consider acceptable evidence for making evaluative decisions? Causal claims? Moral conclusions? Expert opinion? Aesthetic judgments? Stakeholder consensus?

Federal policy that requires the use of experimental methods resolves these issues by mandating that, for the programs in question, the proper purpose of evaluation is to provide conclusive empirical evidence of the causal effects of treatments and interventions. None of the other options suggested in these two sets of questions is considered acceptable, or at least not worth federal financial support under such a policy.

This policy interprets questions of program value, as well as stakeholder concerns, as questions of causal impact. Perhaps many evaluators are not likely to notice or complain too much about this. An empirical study of over 60 exemplary national-level evaluations in education and health conducted between 1976 and 1987 suggested that it was common for evaluators to interpret questions of value as questions of causation when designing evaluation studies (Smith & Mukherjee, 1994).

How do theoretical perspectives of evaluation as client service, or as assessment of quality, or as social reform, influence which methods are considered appropriate and acceptable? Or, alternately, what happens to these forms of evaluation if only RCTs are seen as exemplary in evaluation? Doesn't the choice of a preferred method, in fact, presuppose the purpose and theoretical basis for evaluation itself? For example, I have argued elsewhere (Smith, 2007) that construing methods choices as purely technical issues overlooks other potentially serious theoretical considerations such as:

- Could certain methods choices have wide-ranging negative consequences for society?
- Could certain methods choices be discriminatory, if not by design or intent, perhaps through the nature of their application and effect?
- Could certain methods choices violate the rights of democratic participation and self-determination?

Methods choices may be driven, in part, by theoretical considerations, but they also have theoretical implications.

Method

Issues of method most often concern how we conduct a study, how we provide relevant evidence.

- How do we arrive at the most valid understandings of quality? Controlled experiments? Moral deliberation? Phenomenological renderings?
- What influences shape decisions about choice of evaluation methods? Technical considerations? Client wishes? Contextual relevance? Political considerations?

Datta (2007) and Chelimsky (2007) have recently provided excellent discussions of how context, policy rationale, accumulated experience, and political pressure have shaped methods choices made by various federal agencies.

Many of the current federal initiatives, and the Department of Education proposed priority in particular, have insisted that experimental designs are superior in evaluation. In December 2003, for example, the U.S. Department of Education, Institute of Education Sciences, National Center for Education Evaluation and Regional Assistance, published a document titled *Identifying and Implementing Educational Practices Supported by Rigorous Evidence: A User Friendly Guide* (U.S. Department of Education, 2003b). (Note that this appears to already have been in development, if not finished, at the time Secretary of Education Rod Paige issued the proposed funding priority discussed above.) According to the *User Friendly Guide*, only two types of evaluation evidence are acceptable: "strong" and "possible."

- To establish "strong" evidence, one needs "randomized controlled trials that are well-designed and implemented" plus "trials showing effectiveness in two or more typical school settings, including a setting similar to that of your schools/classrooms" (p. v).
- To establish "possible" evidence, one needs "randomized controlled trials whose quality/quantity are good but fall short of 'strong' evidence; and/or comparison-group studies . . . in which the intervention and comparison groups are *very closely matched* in academic achievement, demographics, and other characteristics" (p. v, emphasis in original).
- Types of studies that do not comprise even "possible" evidence include pre–post studies, non closely matched comparison group

studies, and meta-analyses that include the results of lower quality studies.

- If, according to these criteria, one does not have either "strong" nor "possible" evidence, then, "one may conclude that the intervention is not supported by meaningful evidence" (p. v).

Notice the rhetorical move from lack of strong or possible evidence to *no meaningful* evidence. Qualitative studies, reviews on moral or cultural grounds, user values, etc.—presumably none of these is considered to provide meaningful evidence.

As Eisenhart and Towne (2003) have noted, however, there is a diversity of opinions at the federal level. Contrast, for example, the Department of Education *User Friendly Guide*, with the National Science Foundation's *2002 User Friendly Handbook* (Frechtling, 2002). "Randomized controlled trials" and "experiments" are not even in the glossary of the NSF *Handbook*. The NSF *Handbook* stresses the assessment of the strengths and weaknesses of alternative approaches with choices made within a mixed-method approach, based on the nature of the program and local context. This results in the possibility of a wide range of alternate designs, depending on the case being dealt with. The NSF emphasis is similar to the position taken by the AEA in its Department of Education response. Michael Patton argued in a National Cancer Institute videocast that if the AEA has a gold standard it is methodological appropriateness: "matching the evaluation design to the evaluation's purpose, resources, and timeline to optimize use" (Patton, 2004).

In 2002 the Institute of Education Sciences (IES) of the U.S. Department of Education (ED) established the What Works Clearinghouse (WWC) to

> provide educators, policymakers, researchers, and the public with a central and trusted source of scientific evidence of what works in education. The WWC aims to promote informed education decision making through a set of easily accessible databases and user-friendly reports that provide education consumers with high-quality reviews of the effectiveness of replicable educational interventions (programs, products, practices, and policies) that intend to improve student outcomes. (What Works Clearinghouse, n.d.)

As of April 2007, the WWC website listed 35 reports across seven categories of interventions.

Only a narrow range of experimental methods is considered acceptable under the WWC review process: randomized trials, regression discontinuity designs, and quasi experiments with equating of pretest differences. In reviewing WWC methods, Brass et al. (2006) conclude: "Therefore, it appears that ED and IES determinations of "what works" might be drawn primarily, or only, from studies that include RCTs, certain quasi-experiments, and the exceptions allowed for in the ED priority, and not other kinds of program evaluation" (p. 27). This reliance on such a narrow range of acceptable methods has been criticized by many, including Confrey (2006), who contrasts WWC studies of middle school mathematics with National Research Council work on the same topic. She concludes that the differences between the two approaches are "profound. WWC has selected a more narrow emphasis on one type of idealized comparative study, whereas the NRC report argues that multiple methodologies with potentially conflicting or divergent information must be summarized by integrated judgment" (Confrey, 2006, p. 211). This comparison illustrates the inextricable connection between method and practice, and the need for comparative studies of methods in practice. Judgments of the utility of a proposed method rest as much on how well it performs in practice as on the logic of its operation. Issues of practice and method necessarily intersect.

In a related event, Schoenfeld (2006a, 2006b) charged that excessive governmental intervention and control by the Institute of Education Sciences resulted in suppression of research that was critical of WWC work and methods. The WWC response (Herman, Boruch, Powell, Fleischman, & Maynard, 2006) posed the disagreement more in terms of the extent to which the federal government has the right not to release information obtained under contractual (rather than grant) arrangements. This case provides further illustration of how methods choices can be influenced by governmental pressures and raises fundamental issues about the proper relationships among government agencies, individual researchers, and the evaluation profession.

Practice

Issues of practice frequently concern how an evaluation activity can be accomplished, the procedures for actually getting the work done.

- What are the best feasible, practical, and cost-effective procedures for conducting evaluations?
- How can and should considerations of local context and practical constraints shape choices of theory and method?

Federal initiatives promoting experimental approaches say little about the practical problems of conducting randomized controlled trials in the field.

Indeed, it has been the practical difficulties that have often impeded the more widespread use of experimental approaches. Fundamental issues of concern in the area of practice include such things as operational feasibility of alternative designs, client acceptance of approaches that are intrusive or disruptive to daily operations, and tradeoffs among rigor, cost, and utility in designing and conducting studies. Selecting and implementing feasible and acceptable methods are among the most difficult tasks for evaluators.

An analysis of RCTs by the Congressional Research Service, for example, notes the difficulty of designing and implementing RCTs well. Difficulties include problems with small sample sizes, generalizing program impact to broader or different populations (i.e., limitations of external validity), being impractical or unethical, requiring too much time or resources, and not providing information on causal mechanisms, cost effectiveness, or unintended side effects. (Brass et al., 2006, pp. 16–17)

Schwandt (2004) has argued that viewing methods choices as purely a technical consideration overlooks the fact that such choices involve synthesis judgments based in part on practical knowledge:

> . . . the answer is a practical argument, contextual, dialectical, a matter of both persuasion and inquiry, and (sometimes) political. There is no universal set of criteria or standards that can be used to definitively answer the question of how best to support evaluative judgments as defined here, precisely because they have the character of being synthetic, practical, and contextual. (Schwandt, 2004, p. 7)

Perhaps from the standpoint of the practitioner dealing with myriad local conditions and influences, the final answer has been provided by Trochim (2004, p. 1): "The question that has been raised . . . Which methods best support evaluative judgments?—is at the same time both easy and impossible to answer. The easy answer is, of course, 'It all depends.' "

Profession

Professional issues encompass concerns of ethical practice, societal benefit, and the control and improvement of the profession.

- What does society and the evaluation profession gain and lose from conducting evaluation through exclusive reliance on experimental approaches?
- What should the policy of the profession be with regard to evaluative evidence?
- What is the proper role of government and society in shaping the nature of the evaluation profession?

When the Department of Education proposed priority was issued, some suggested that AEA should not issue a formal response and that such a response should be the prerogative of individual AEA members. Some objected that the AEA response was antiquantitative and too pro-qualitative. Others argued that, even if the Department of Education proposed priority had been blatantly proqualitative, that AEA should respond. The important issue was not the superiority of experimental methods but whether professional decisions of proper evaluation methods should be made by professional evaluators or by the federal government. The section of the AEA statement arguing for a "repertoire" of evaluation methods reflects that concern.

Governmental resources can play a significant role in shaping professional activities. For example, in 2004 the Institute of Education Sciences provided a grant for the founding of a new professional society, the Society for Research on Educational Effectiveness (SREE), whose stated mission is "to advance and disseminate research on the causal effects of education interventions, practices, programs, and policies" (Society for Research on Educational Effectiveness, 2007). This new society is an evaluation-related organization reflecting the federal government's interest in causal studies of educational effectiveness, and created "to serve constituents interested in developing empirically credible answers to questions of educational effectiveness" (Society for Research on Educational Effectiveness, 2007).

Societal values also shape professional activities and methods (Smith, 1995), and "evidenced-based practice" is clearly a dominant theme of modern U.S. society. Its influence can be seen in fields allied with evaluation, such as psychology. For example, in 2006, the American Psychological Association Presidential Task Force on Evidence-Based Practice issued a statement of the professional organization's official position:

> In an integration of science and practice, the Task Force's report describes psychology's fundamental commitment to sophisticated EBPP [evidence-based practice in psychology] and takes into account the full range of evidence psychologists and policymakers must consider. (p. 271)

The operation of this stated policy was evident when a new editorial board assumed control of *Professional Psychology: Research and Practice (PPRP)*:

> The intent of the new editorial team is to make *PPRP* a forum for the discussion of how evidence-based practice is fulfilled . . . The editorial team intends to publish articles that are founded on the literature that is based within the scientific tradition of psychology, where applicable, and on the

integration of science and practice to advance evidence-based practice. (Roberts, 2007, p. 1)

Although neither the Task Force report nor the editorial policy of *PPRP* restrict acceptable evidence to experimental designs, their policy statements force them to consider just what does constitute acceptable evidence. This question is being intensively examined within the profession of evaluation as well; for example, the topic of the Claremont Graduate University Stauffer Symposium in 2006 was "What constitutes credible evidence in evaluation and applied research?" (Claremont Graduate University, 2006). The Symposium drew a large number of senior evaluation theorists and methodologists.

It is important, therefore, to recognize how governmental and societal influences are shaping the evaluation profession and consequently the manner in which it is dealing with these fundamental issues of what constitutes proper evaluation evidence and what is the proper role of RCT methodology. Whatever resolutions are reached will, therefore, reflect the current nature of society and its present "evidence-based" preoccupation.

CONCLUSION

Evaluators have been arguing about proper methods since the 1960s. The disagreements have motivated the creation of alternative theories and the development of new methodological approaches, have led to improved practice, and, ironically, have provided an increased sense of professional identity. Even during the "paradigm wars," which were seen by some as a culture clash between qualitative and quantitative advocates, the struggle within evaluation seemed to be played out within the profession, with a shared intent to improve the profession. (Of course, as a fundamental issue, the qualitative vs. quantitative debate continues in evaluation as elsewhere; for a recent contribution in educational research, see Ercikan & Roth, 2006.)

The current struggle in evaluation seems more strident and divisive. The involvement of the federal government has broadened the playing field and raised the stakes. Decisions are increasingly made as much on the basis of political, ideological, and economic influences as they are based on theoretical, technical, and professional considerations. These dynamics can have either a positive or negative impact on the evaluation profession and the AEA.

For example, the professional efforts of such groups as the Campbell Collaboration and the What Works Clearinghouse to improve the quality of information used to make program and policy decisions should be supported. Their work to improve experimental methods and evidence will lead to improvements in our profession and make important contributions to society. To do this work at the expense and denigration of other legitimate forms of evaluation, however, can lead to alienation within the profession. For example, to be listed in the What Works Clearinghouse *Registry of Outcome Evaluators*, the purpose of which is to provide a public listing of evaluators who have experience in conducting causal inference studies of the effectiveness of educational interventions, one must sign a "Letter of Commitment" that states, in part: "(I/We) commit to using the highest standards of scientific evidence, as defined by the WWC, for answering questions on the effectiveness of educational interventions" (What Works Clearinghouse, n.d.). Although perhaps intended as a quality-control measure, such loyalty oaths are likely to be seen as exclusionary and elitist.

Disagreements about the relative dominance of scientific versus public policy and practice issues have fractionated other professional organizations, as when a group left the APA in the late 1950s to form the Psychonomic Society, and a similar exodus from APA later formed the American Psychological Society. These departures illustrate the important implications of such debates and the potentially divisive outcomes that can result.

Alternatively, evaluators can actively engage their differences of opinion and use them to energize their work. Examining the important fundamental issues underlying these differences can keep evaluators aware of the fact that they are all working on the same set of underlying generic problems and keep them better attuned to the social and political contexts within which they work. The study of such fundamental issues can, therefore, not only deepen our understanding of the evaluation profession but also keep our work timely, responsive, and more balanced. What may appear on the surface to be a technical issue of the proper use of RCT methods in evaluation studies can be seen to have serious connections to related fundamental issues of evaluation theory, and practice, and the profession.

Space does not permit the exploration here of the many fundamental issues that are raised in the ongoing debate about RCTs. As was noted earlier, the purpose of this chapter is not to resolve these issues but rather to illustrate how the aspects of theory, method, practice, and profession are intertwined when such issues are encountered and to remind us that the current struggle can profitably be seen as just the latest effort to provide a current resolution to an old problem. The resolution we reach today to such complex problems will suffice for a while and then serve as a basis for our inevitable reconsideration of this problem at a later point in time. As the mandala of nautilus shells reminds us, the resolutions attending our fundamental issues are forever impermanent, our understandings ever increasing.

The chapters that follow each deal with significant complex fundamental issues of theory, method, practice, and the profession. Drawing on our collective prior understanding of these issues, they offer insights about the importance and possible shape of the new resolutions we struggle with today.

REFERENCES

American Evaluation Association. (2003). American Evaluation Association response to U.S. Department of Education notice of proposed priority. Federal Register RIN 1890–ZA00, November, 2003, "Scientifically based evaluation methods." Retrieved June 10, 2007, from *http://www.eval.org/doestatement.htm*

American Psychological Association Presidential Task Force on Evidence-Based Practice. (2006). Evidence-based practice in psychology. *American Psychologist, 61*(4), 271–285.

Brass, C. T., Nuñez-Neto, B., & Williams, E. D. (2006). *Congress and program evaluation: An overview of randomized controlled trials (RCTs) and related issues.* Washington, DC: Congressional Research Service, U.S. Library of Congress.

Campbell, D. T., & Stanley, J. C. (1966). *Experimental and quasi-experimental designs for research.* Chicago: Rand McNally.

Chelimsky, E. (2007). Factors influencing the choice of methods in federal evaluation practice. In G. Julnes & D. J. Rog (Eds.), *Informing federal policies on evaluation methodology: Building the evidence base for method choice in government sponsored evaluation* (New Directions for Evaluation no. 113, pp. 13–33). New York: Wiley.

Claremont Graduate University. (2006). *What constitutes credible evidence in evaluation and applied research?* Retrieved April 2, 2007, from *www.cgu.edu/pages/4085.asp#videos.*

Confrey, J. (2006). Comparing and contrasting the National Research Council report *On Evaluating Curricular Effectiveness* with the What Works Clearinghouse approach. *Educational Evaluation and Policy Analysis, 28*(3), 195–213.

Cook, T. D., & Campbell, D. T. (1975). The design and conduct of quasi-experiments and true experiments in field settings. In M. D. Dunnette (Ed.), *Handbook of industrial and organizational research* (pp. 223–326). Chicago: Rand-McNally.

Datta, L. (2007). Looking at the evidence: What variations in practice might indicate. In G. Julnes & D. J. Rog (Eds.), *Informing federal policies on eval-*

uation methodology: Building the evidence base for method choice in government sponsored evaluation (New Directions for Evaluation no. 113, pp. 35–54). New York: Wiley.

Eisenhart, M., & Towne, L. (2003). Contestation and change in national policy on "scientific based" education research. *Educational Researcher, 32*(7), 31–38.

Ercikan, K., & Roth, W.-M. (2006). What good is polarizing research into qualitative and quantitative? *Educational Researcher, 35*(5), 14–23.

Frechtling, J. (2002, January). *The 2002 user-friendly handbook for project evaluation.* Arlington, VA: National Science Foundation.

Herman, R., Boruch, R., Powell, R., Fleischman, S., & Maynard, R. (2006). Overcoming the challenges: A response to Alan H. Schoenfeld's "What doesn't work." *Educational Researcher, 35*(2), 22–23.

Holmes, O. W. (1858). *The chambered nautilus.* Retrieved October 11, 2004, from *www.pddoc.com/poems/the_chambered_nautilus_oliver_wendel_holmes.htm.*

Mandala Project. (n.d.). *What is a mandala?* Retrieved April 1, 2007, from *www.mandalaproject.org/What/Index.html.*

Mathematical Science Education Board. (2004). *On evaluating curricular effectiveness: Judging the quality of K–12 mathematics evaluations.* (National Research Council). Washington, DC: National Academy Press.

Mervis, J. (2004). Meager evaluations make it hard to find out what works. *Science, 304*(5677), 1583.

Patton, M. Q. (2004). *The debate about randomized controls as the gold standard* (videocast). Retrieved October 21, 2004, from *videocast.nih.gov/PastEvents.asp.*

Roberts, M. C. (2007). Editorial. *Professional Psychology: Research and Practice, 38*(1), 1–2.

Rossi, P. H., & Wright, S. R. (1977). Evaluation research: An evaluation of theory, practice, and politics. *Evaluation Quarterly, 1,* 5–52.

Schoenfeld, A. H. (2006a). Replying to comments from the What Works Clearinghouse on "What doesn't work," *Educational Researcher, 35*(2), 23.

Schoenfeld, A. H. (2006b). What doesn't work: The challenge and failure of the What Works Clearinghouse to conduct meaningful reviews of studies of mathematics curricula. *Educational Researcher, 35*(2), 13–21.

Schwandt, T. A. (2004, November). *On methods and judgments in evaluation.* Plenary presentation at the meeting of the American Evaluation Association, Atlanta, GA.

Shadish, W. R., Cook, T. D., & Campbell, D. T. (2002). *Experimental and quasi-experimental designs for generalized causal inference.* Boston: Houghton Mifflin.

Shavelson, R. J., & Towne, L. (Eds). (2002). *Scientific research in education.* (National Research Council). Washington, DC: National Academy Press.

Smith, N. L. (1980). The feasibility and desirability of experimental methods in evaluation. *Evaluation and Program Planning, 3*(4), 251–256.

Smith, N. L. (1981). Non-causal inquiry in education. *Educational Researcher, 10*(3), 23.

Smith, N. L. (1995). The influence of societal games on the methodology of evaluative inquiry. In D. M. Fournier (Ed.), *Reasoning in evaluation: Inferential links and leaps* (pp. 5–14). San Francisco, CA: Jossey-Bass.

Smith, N. L. (2007). Judging methods. In G. Julnes & D. J. Rog (Eds.), *Informing federal policies on evaluation methodology: Building the evidence base for method choice in government sponsored evaluation* (New Directions for Evaluation no. 113, pp. 119–123). New York: Wiley.

Smith, N. L., & Mukherjee, P. (1994). Classifying research questions addressed in published evaluation studies. *Educational Evaluation and Policy Analysis, 16*(2), 223–230.

Society for Research on Educational Effectiveness. (2007). *Mission statement.* Retrieved June 10, 2007, from *www.educationaleffectiveness.org/pages/pressrelease/mission.shtml.*

Struening, E. L., & Guttentag, M. (Eds.). (1975). *Handbook of evaluation research, Vol. 1.* Beverly Hills, CA: Sage.

Trochim, W. M. (2004, November). *Randomized experiments: Lessons from the system of clinical trials in medical research.* Plenary presentation at the annual meeting of the American Evaluation Association, Atlanta, GA.

U.S. Department of Education. (2003a, November 4). Scientifically based evaluation methods. *Federal Register, 68*(213), 62445–62447. RIN 1890-ZA00.

U.S. Department of Education, Institute of Education Sciences, National Center for Education Evaluation and Regional Assistance. (2003b, November). *Identifying and implementing educational practices supported by rigorous evidence: A user friendly guide.*

U.S. Department of Education. (2005, January 25). Scientifically based evaluation methods. *Federal Register, 70*(15), 3586–3589. RIN 1890-ZA00.

What Works Clearinghouse (n.d.). *Registry of outcome evaluators.* Retrieved April 3, 2007, from *www.whatworks.ed.gov/.*

PART I

ISSUES OF THEORY

Considerations of theory have long played a major role in shaping the nature and direction of evaluation. The federal funding that created a growth industry in program evaluation in the United States in the early 1960s led to wave after wave of theoretical writings designed to define properly the profession, to sharpen evaluation thinking, to sort out problems of method, and to shape evaluation practice. Issues of evaluation theory have dominated some sectors of evaluation to such an extent that, in 1997, Will Shadish, then president of the American Evaluation Association (AEA), titled his presidential address "Evaluation Theory Is Who We Are" (Shadish, 1998). Indeed, many former presidents of the AEA have been known principally for their writings in evaluation theory.

The two chapters in Part I both illustrate how the principles we may select as defining our profession—that is, the theory of evaluation—

subsequently shape both our methods and our practice; form follows function in evaluation, as elsewhere. In different ways, both chapters illustrate how selecting a particular theoretical position about the nature of evaluation subsequently shapes how we think about the profession itself and therefore which methods and forms of practice are considered appropriate.

In Chapter 2, "The Relevance of Practical Knowledge Traditions to Evaluation Practice," Thomas A. Schwandt raises the question, What is the nature of practical knowledge and how does it influence our understanding and practice of evaluation? He characterizes practical knowledge as tacit knowledge that evaluation practitioners routinely manifest and yet cannot necessarily articulate readily. Practical knowledge does not stem from technical knowledge or instrumental skills; it is founded in the personal characteristics that practitioners develop and refine as they work to understand the day-to-day organizational, political, and social aspects of being an evaluator.

Just as theorists attempt to theorize the practice of those whose programs, processes, or products are evaluated, Schwandt is concerned that evaluation theorists and those who teach evaluation in universities will theorize evaluation practice, or, even worse, that they will attempt to characterize evaluation expertise solely as knowledge of what techniques to use in what situations. A fundamental issue of concern here, then, is: What is the nature of evaluation expertise, and how should we think about it? If evaluation expertise depends, in part, on the practical knowledge of the evaluator that is gained and cultivated through evaluation practice, then to disregard practical knowledge is to misunderstand fundamentally what it means to conduct an evaluation. It casts evaluation as a purely technical act.

This theoretical issue of the nature of practical knowledge has clear implications for how we think about and conduct evaluation practice, what methods are relevant to the conduct of that practice, and even what it means to be a professional evaluator.

Donna M. Mertens similarly adopts a particular theoretical position from which she then derives implications for appropriate methods and forms of practice. In Chapter 3, "Stakeholder Representation in Culturally Complex Communities: Insights from the Transformative Paradigm," Mertens raises the difficult recurring issues of how to deal with cultural competence and the treatment of diversity within evaluation practice. To deal with these issues, she proposes the use of a transformative paradigm that seeks to ensure that stakeholders are fairly represented, that the diversity of stakeholder groups is considered adequately, and that differences in power among these groups are addressed in evaluations. Through the use of case studies, she suggests methods and approaches for dealing with stakeholder diversity in terms of gender, disability, and political, racial, and ethnic differences.

Taken together, these two chapters raise such provocative questions as: How does one acquire the practical knowledge required to deal adequately with issues of cultural competence and diversity in evaluation practice? Can evaluation case studies be used to provide a kind of archival record of evaluator practical knowledge? Are collaborative evaluation approaches more conducive to evaluators' developing practical knowledge because of their closer engagement with stakeholders? How do evaluations that adopt the transformative paradigm differ from forms of collaborative evaluation, such as transformative participatory evaluation (as described by Cousins and Shulha in Chapter 7)?

An enduring fundamental issue in evaluation is: What is the nature of good evaluation practice? Schwandt notes that "Yet, the idea that 'good' practice depends in a significant way on the experiential, existential knowledge we speak of as perceptivity, insightfulness, and deliberative judgment is always in danger of being overrun by (or at least regarded as inferior to) an ideal of 'good' practice grounded in notions of objectivity, control, predictability, generalizability beyond specific circumstances, and unambiguous criteria for establishing accountability and success" (Chapter 2, p. 37). These chapters by Schwandt and Mertens offer theoretical arguments that good evaluation practice is marked as much by experience, judgment, and insight as it is by proper methods and procedures in the field. This seems especially true when dealing with the fundamental issues of: What is the nature of cultural competence in evaluation? and, What is the proper form of stakeholder participation in evaluation? These latter two fundamental issues are treated not only here in Part I but also in Chapters 7, 10, and 11.

REFERENCE

Shadish, W. R. (1998). Evaluation theory is who we are. *American Journal of Evaluation, 19*, 1–19.

CHAPTER 2

The Relevance of Practical Knowledge
Traditions to Evaluation Practice

THOMAS A. SCHWANDT

It is primarily through what we do that we learn about the world.
—BENGT MOLANDER

We do not experience our practice as knowledge. Rather, we
experience our practice as experience.
—MAX VAN MANEN

Discussions of knowledge in practices like evaluation, management,
teaching, nursing, and so on are often limited by an intellectualized
theory–practice distinction from which it is difficult to shake loose (Van
Manen, 1995). We routinely think in terms of a general theoretical
knowledge base, on the one hand, and craft knowledge or skill, on the
other. This is another way of making the distinction that Gilbert Ryle
labeled "knowing that" and "knowing how." Theory is regarded as the
realm of contemplation and reflection, and the territory of practice as
the domain of doing and action. It is not at all uncommon to equate the
practical with the use of instruments and procedures, as evident, for
example, in the many step-by-step manuals and guides to doing evaluation that one can readily find in searching the Web (a recent search on
Google yielded 545,000 results for the phrase "evaluation toolkits").
Moreover, the current dominance of output-oriented thinking in society
in general leads us to further associate practice with performativity and
practical knowledge solely with instrumentality and the successful exe-

cution of specialized techniques. It is widely recognized that the dualism reflected in distinguishing theory from practice and knowledge from action (as well as mind from body, fact from value, etc.) in this way is broadly characteristic of the whole of the Western theoretical and scientific tradition of knowledge.

There have been notable attempts to reject, or at least bridge, this dualism in our thinking about knowledge, including Dewey's theory of learning (which interweaves doing and reflection), Schön's idea of the reflective practitioner, and Joseph Schwab's efforts to develop a language of the practical. More recent developments, particularly in sociology and philosophy, aim to explicate the very idea of practice as a distinctive social phenomenon with its own structure and epistemology. Referred to as theory of practice or the practical turn in the social sciences (Reckwitz, 2002; Schatzki, Knorr Cetina, & von Savigny, 2001; Stern, 2003), this development encompasses several issues surrounding the ideas of practice and practical knowledge, including (1) how to define what constitutes a practice; (2) what structures or organizes practice (e.g., habitus, discursive moves/language games, moral vocabularies); (3) how one learns a practice and acquires practical knowledge; (4) the unique character and nature of practical reasoning and practical knowledge; (5) how recovering the significance of practical knowledge serves as an antidote to a near exclusive concern with technical rationality; (6) how the notion of practical reasonableness (individual capacities for discernment, deliberation, and good judgment) is centrally implicated in public democratic participation in decision making; and (7) how the cultivation of practical reason relates to aims of education and learning (e.g., see Bourdieu, 1997; Dunne, 1993; Dunne & Pendlebury, 2003; Forester, 1999; Kemmis, 2004; Lave & Wenger, 1991; Molander, 1992; Pendlebury, 1990; Schön, 1983; Schwandt, 2002; Taylor, 1995; Toulmin, 1988, 2001; Wagenaar & Cook, 2003; Wenger, 1998; Wiggins, 1980). This chapter singles out one aspect of this recent development, namely, the nature of practical knowledge, and then suggests what a focus on this might mean for evaluation practice. I hope to show that practical knowledge scaffolds the activity of evaluation and yet is in danger of being discounted and discarded in the press for ever more scientific and technical ways of understanding and evaluating human activities of teaching, providing health care, doing social work, and the like.

THE NATURE OF PRACTICAL KNOWLEDGE

In social phenomenology, the notion of *practical knowledge* refers to what an actor knows in relation to his or her own actions and social situation, but cannot necessarily state (*Collins Dictionary of Sociology,* 2000). This knowledge is often more tacit and "silent" than stated in propositions. It is neither necessarily consciously reflective (i.e., we do not routinely stand back from our involvement with the world and say to ourselves, "See, this is why I am acting the way I am"), nor is it fully capable of articulation in a direct conceptual and propositional manner; yet, it constitutes a distinctive kind of competence in acting in both general and specific ways (Van Manen, 1995). We might say, following an idea championed by Wittgenstein, that practical knowledge is something expressed by "showing" (acting) rather than by "saying." This kind of knowledge is shown or demonstrated via the kind of prereflective familiarity one has with ideas and concepts used to express oneself, one's ability to be present in and handle a situation, and one's capacity to exercise judgment of when to apply, or not apply, a particular kind of understanding of a situation.

To take one everyday example, consider all that I must know in order to interact appropriately and effectively with my octogenarian neighbors when they are sitting on their porch and call over to me when they see me outside of my condo. I must know the differences between what is called for in interacting with strangers, friends, family, acquaintances, and neighbors. I must be able to read the situation and decide whether they simply want to engage in everyday chat or they are interested in a more substantive conversation. I must be able to recognize and perform the kinds of conversational moves, so to speak, that are appropriate in a "backyard chat" (as opposed, for example, to a conversation with a colleague in the hallway of my building or a conversation with a student in a classroom). I must know what their different facial expressions and gestures mean as they talk. I must know when it is proper at various times in our conversation to be serious, humorous, considerate, thoughtful, inquisitive, and the like. I must understand the rhythm of the conversation in order to know when it is appropriate to end the conversation without offending them. And I must bring all of this knowledge to bear simultaneously in my interaction with them on this occasion. There is no (and can never be) a manual of procedures that I can follow to learn how to act appropriately and effectively in this situation; nor is the knowledge required here simply a matter of being familiar with which means are most effective to given ends.

This is a brief example of the general kind of practical knowledge that belongs to our everyday shared worlds of social interactions such as shopping, banking, meeting friends and strangers, and so forth. In everyday life we are often unaware of this practical knowledge and only recognize it when something happens to startle us or confuse our habituated and confident practices of being with one another. (This is the point of the breaching experiments conducted in ethnomethodological studies.)

The following features noted by Molander (2002, p. 370) further characterize practical knowledge (or, more broadly, the practical knowledge tradition):

- In contrast to knowledge regarded as "in the head" of an individual, knowledge is based on participation and dialogue with other people as well as living with materials, tools, and the physical circumstances of a situation.
- Knowledge and application form a unity; in other words, knowing and doing are not two separate steps in a process.
- Knowledge is knowing-in-action, living knowledge *in* the world. That is, practical knowledge does not depict or represent reality, but instead it leads rather seamlessly from question to answer and from task to execution within various human activities.

Van Manen (1999) adds that practical knowledge is a form of noncognitive knowing inhering in a person; it is agentive knowing, and it resides in several forms:

- In action as lived, for example, as confidence in acting, style, and practical tact, as habituations and routine practices.
- In the body, for example, as an immediate corporeal sense of things, as gestures and demeanor.
- In the world, for example, as being with the things of our world, as situations of "being at home" with something or "dwelling" in it.
- In relations, for example, as encounters with others, as relations of trust, intimacy, and recognition.

The lived, active, or—better said—the "enacted" character of this kind of knowledge cannot be overemphasized. Practical knowledge is located

> not primarily in the intellect or the head but rather in the existential situation in which [a] person finds himself or herself. . . . [T]he practical active knowledge that animates [a given practice like teaching, evaluating, nursing, etc.] is something that belongs phenomenologically more closely to the whole embodied being of the person as well as to the social and physical world in which this person lives. (Van Manen, 1995, p. 12)

We intuitively recognize this kind of knowledge when, for example, we say of someone, "She really knows her way around that situation" or "He is very good at sizing up a situation and knowing what to do."

PRACTICAL KNOWLEDGE IN EVALUATION

Like all professional practices, evaluation has its own unique kind of practical knowledge, comprising the tact, dispositions, and considered character of decision making called for in various situations faced in "doing" the practice. The very act of coming to an interpretation of the value of a social or educational program or policy is a practical matter involving the exercise of judgment (House & Howe, 1999; Schwandt, 2002). Likewise, negotiating the terms of an evaluation contract, determining how best to generate useful data in view of limited time and resources, understanding when (and how) it is appropriate to share preliminary data with a client, and facing ethical dilemmas such as those posed in the ethics column of the *American Journal of Evaluation* are examples of situations that call for practical knowledge.

Current calls for multicultural awareness and cultural competence in evaluation (e.g., Smith & Jang, 2000; Thompson-Robinson, Hopson, SenGupta, 2004) also resonate well with an emphasis on the practical knowledge demanded in evaluation practice.[1] Cultural competence involves several considerations, including an evaluator's reflexive awareness of how he or she is socially located in a given evaluation—that is, how an evaluator's own culturally bound experiences, class background, racial and ethnic identity, gender, and so on shape assumptions and frames of reference for understanding an evaluand. It also entails sensitivity to the danger of ethnocentrism in interpreting value. Recognizing and honoring different understandings of the problems that are ostensibly to be remedied by social and educational interventions as well as different understandings of the success or failure of such interventions is also an aspect of being culturally competent. Cultural competence also means knowing how to attend in careful and thoughtful ways to the lived experience of program stakeholders and beneficiaries as a source of knowledge and evidence (Abma, 1999; Sanderson, 2003; Schwandt & Burgon, 2006; Simons, 2004).

Our experience tells us that the skilled evaluation practitioner is distinguishable in terms of his or her ability to appropriately and effectively move around in or navigate these situations as evident in the kinds of judgments he or she exercises. Judgment or practical wisdom is a both a cognitive ability and a way of literally being present in a situation. Recognizing what is meant by judgment holds the key to understanding the evaluation practitioner's practical knowledge, as Dunne and Pendlebury (2003) explain:

> The exercise of judgment . . . requires resourcefulness and a kind of fluency. It involves creative insight insofar as it has to prove itself afresh in being equal to the demands of each new situation. . . . Experience, and the intimate exposure to particulars that comes with it, seems to be a necessary condition for acquiring it. Still, raw experience is not a sufficient condition: crucially, one must learn from one's experience—perhaps especially from one's mistakes—so that one's experience is constantly reconstructed. Openness to learning brings in a reference point beyond experience to character: personal qualities and not just cognitive abilities are in play. There are virtues such as patience in sticking with a problem, a sense of balance that keeps both details and "big picture" in focus, a sobriety that keeps one from being easily swayed by impulse or first impressions, a courage that enables one to persist in a truthful though otherwise unprofitable or unpopular direction. (p. 198)

Of course, competence in doing evaluation also requires a cognitive knowledge base of concepts, models, and theories as well as craft knowledge in the form of skills and techniques (literally, for example, how to design a questionnaire, how to conduct an interview, how to write a contract, and so on). But being practically wise demands something more, most notably the capacity for perception or focused attention on the circumstances of the case at hand, that is, "the ability to see fine detail and nuance and the ability to discern the differences between this situation and others that to the inexperienced eye might seem the same" (Dunne & Pendlebury, 2003, p. 207). Thus, developing such aspects of character as insight and discernment is at least as much a part of becoming an evaluator as is exposure to relevant evaluation models and reliable research on methods choice, contract negotiation, ethical conduct, and cross-cultural behavior. Moreover, to listen well and to understand and interpret what one hears and sees is a practical task that Van Manen (1995, p. 10) calls an "active intentional consciousness of thoughtful human interaction." This is more than mere diplomacy or etiquette, but a kind of perception, discernment, and tact that is a moral concern. We are always tactful, he argues, for the good of the other, in this case for the good of genuinely understanding the other.

It seems fairly noncontroversial that cultivation of practical judgment is highly valued in the preparation of evaluators. It is commonly acknowledged that being a good evaluator entails more than familiarity with models, concepts, and methods and their successful translation into practice. To be a good evaluator also demands a unique kind of educated understanding involving discretion, discernment, and sensitivity to the matter at hand. Hence, professional preparation in evaluation, particularly at the university, almost always involves some kind of practicum or opportunities for internship or apprenticeship in which this kind of knowledge is developed under the tutelage of an experienced evaluator. It is through observing the skilled evaluator at work in an imitative and personal relation that the student learns about the kind of ability and confidence that arises from "active" knowledge. One also learns practical knowledge through engaging stories of practice, once these stories are recognized as something more than simply descriptive tales or pictures of events. As Forester (1999) suggests, we learn from stories when we regard them as prescriptive tales, unfolding practical and political judgments not in the abstract but in the deed, and revealing what is important, what matters, what should be paid attention to, what needs to be worried about, and what is at stake if one fails to act. Stories of practice also convey the emotional demands of work in an ambiguous politicized world; they reveal "nuances of plot and character; the dense meshing of insights and oversights, of convergent or contrary purposes, motivations, and interests; of unanticipated responses from . . . relevant agents, all conspiring to bring relative success or failure" (Dunne & Pendlebury, 2003, p. 203).

PRACTICAL VERSUS TECHNICAL KNOWLEDGE

It should be apparent thus far that practical knowledge is something other than the skillful performance of technique or the competent carrying out of procedures. In fact, practical knowledge is called for precisely in problematic situations not resolvable by solutions forthcoming from following procedures or "going by the book." Practical knowledge is called for especially in complex or novel situations that require "fitting practical strategies to unique situations to achieve good results" (Forester, 1999, p. 9). This is, more or a less, a noncontroversial understanding in evaluation. However, in one important sense, what makes practical knowledge a "fundamental issue" in evaluation (and in many other social practices as well) is that it is always in danger of being discredited by efforts to theorize a practice and absorbed into technical or instrumental rationality.

What theorizing a practice means here requires a bit of unpacking. In a rather open-ended sense, the term *theory* can mean any general or systematic way of approaching a subject matter, including such activities as providing models, developing conceptual categories or frameworks, or providing genealogies (Stern, 2003). This is the sense in which we usually speak of theory of evaluation practice, and it is readily reflected in attempts to systematically or historically recount evaluation theory, such as those by Shadish, Cook, and Leviton (1991) and more recently Alkin (2004). But my concern here is not the matter of theory of evaluation practice per se but theory of practices in which evaluation is implicated, such as the theory of teaching practice, nursing, providing mental health care, social work, and so on. To theorize these practices has traditionally involved attempts to remove or disembed the knowledge or skill implicit in the performance of the tasks of a practice "from the immediacy and idiosyncrasy of the particular situations in which those tasks are deployed, and from the experience and character of the practitioners in whom they reside" (Dunne & Pendlebury, 2003, p. 197).[2]

The effort to theorize practices is thought to be of value precisely because the assumption is that the practical knowledge required in dealing with situations in a case-by-case fashion is unreliable, makeshift, unaccountable, and based on intuition and habit. To eliminate reliance on "merely" practical knowledge as a guide to action, researchers and evaluators aim to distill from actual practice the knowledge, skills, and operations that constitute its core activities (e.g., teaching, nursing) and encapsulate and summarize them in explicit general categories, rules, or procedures. As Dunne and Pendlebury (2003) explain, the formulae or procedures then

> are to be applied to the various situations and circumstances that arise in the practice so as to meet the problems that they present. These problems are supposed to have nothing in them that has not been anticipated in the analysis that yielded the general formulae, and hence to be soluble by a straightforward application of the latter, without need for insight or discernment in the actual situation itself. Control—and efficiency—seems to be made possible here by the fact that the system is minimally dependent on the discretion or judgment of individual practitioners, with all the hazard and lack of standardization this might entail. The ideal to which [this notion of] technical rationality aspires, one might say, is a practitioner-proof practice. (p. 197)

Given the general social concern with ensuring, monitoring, and measuring the output of human service activities such as teaching, nursing, and providing mental health care, there is genuine danger that such activities are being theorized in this way. Instruments by means of which these social practices are ideally made practitioner-proof and standardized include evidence-based treatment systems, quality control and assurance routines, performance audits, and uniform indicators of practice outcomes.

To the extent that evaluation practice promotes the use of such instruments as the best means of evaluating human services, it is complicit in promoting the kind of technical rationality that is involved in theorizing human service undertakings and in fostering absorption of the practical into the technical. In other words, two related phenomena unfold here in a mutually reinforcing relationship: first, the general social interest in viewing human service programs solely in terms of their performativity, so to speak, is reinforced by a conception of evaluation practice as a technical undertaking—that is, one in which the task of evaluation is largely that of applying toolkits of various kinds to measure outcomes; second, a technical conception of evaluation arises as the natural accompaniment to society's interest in defining human service practices solely in terms of their output. As a result, we witness the disappearance of practical knowledge in two arenas—the practical knowledge that enables good teaching, nursing, and so forth is eliminated as those practices are made practitioner-proof, and the practical knowledge that enables good evaluation is done away with as that practice is transformed into largely an instrumental undertaking.

The fundamental distinction between instrumental reason as the hallmark of technical knowledge and judgment as the defining characteristic of practical knowledge is instinctively recognizable to many practitioners (Dunne & Pendlebury, 2003). Yet, the idea that "good" practice depends in a significant way on the experiential, existential knowledge we speak of as perceptivity, insightfulness, and deliberative judgment is always in danger of being overrun by (or at least regarded as inferior to) an ideal of "good" practice grounded in notions of objectivity, control, predictability, generalizability beyond specific circumstances, and unambiguous criteria for establishing accountability and success. This danger seems to be particularly acute of late, as notions of auditable performance, output measurement, and quality assurance have come to dominate the ways in which human services are defined and evaluated. Recovering an understanding of the uniqueness of practical reason and what it means to be practically wise can serve as one avenue for resisting the march of technical reason. No matter how well developed and sophisticated the scientific–technical knowledge base for a practice, the skillful execution of that practice is ultimately a matter of practical wisdom.

ACKNOWLEDGMENTS

My thanks to Paul Brandon, Jennifer Greene, and Leslie Goodyear for their helpful comments on an earlier draft.

NOTES

1. The recent emphasis on cultural competence in evaluation can be interpreted in two ways. On the one hand, it can be read as a call for greater socio-anthropological—that is, multicultural—sensitivity and understanding in evaluation practice. Evaluators, in much the same way as cultural anthropologists, ought to be competent in reading, interpreting, and navigating different cultural practices. These activities require practical knowledge as it is discussed here. Accordingly, an adequate evaluation of a social or educational program must be situated in and take account of the languages, understandings, and forms of life of stakeholders and beneficiaries of social programs. On the other hand, the call for cultural competence in evaluation can be situated within standpoint theory and methodology. Here, evaluation practice is regarded as representing the distinctive cultural view of the ruling group(s) of society, which in turn suppress cultural heterogeneity, control definitions of social problems, block differential understandings of value, and severely restrict the deployment of politics that increase the inclusiveness, fairness, and accountability of evaluation (Harding, 2003). The distinctiveness (and potential overlap) of these two interpretations requires a kind of attention that is beyond the purpose of this chapter.

2. Logic models used in evaluation can contribute to the theorizing of practice. A logic model is a representation of a program that is distilled from the actual operation of the program into some kind of underlying theory that explains how the program "works." As an abstraction of how the program operates, the model disassociates the actions of practitioners from the lived, embodied, contested reality in which such actions unfold and re-presents the workings of the program in terms of generalized notions of inputs, processes/actions, and results. This is not to say that logical models cannot in some way be useful to practitioners; however, logical models as well as program theory are closely related to attempts to theorize practice.

REFERENCES

Abma, T. (1999). Introduction: Narrative perspectives on program evaluation. In T. Abma (Ed.), *Telling tales: On evaluation and narrative* (pp. 1–27). Stamford, CT: JAI Press.

Alkin, M. (Ed.). (2004). *Evaluation roots: Tracing theorists' views and influences.* Thousand Oaks, CA: Sage.

Bourdieu, P. (1997). *Outline of a theory of practice* (R. Nice, Trans.). Cambridge, UK: Cambridge University Press.

Collins Dictionary of Sociology. (2000). "Practical knowledge or practical consciousness." Retrieved August 11, 2004, from *www.xreferplus.com/entry/1417477.*

Dunne, J. (1993). *Back to the rough ground: "Phronesis" and "techne" in modern philosophy and in Aristotle.* Notre Dame, IN: University of Notre Dame Press.

Dunne, J., & Pendlebury, S. (2003). Practical reason. In N. Blake, P. Smeyers, R. Smith, & P. Standish (Eds.), *The Blackwell guide to the philosophy of education* (pp. 194–211). Oxford: Blackwell.

Forester, J. (1999). *The deliberative practitioner.* Cambridge, MA: MIT Press.

Harding, S. (2003). How standpoint methodology informs philosophy of social science. In S. P. Turner & P. A. Roth (Eds.), *The Blackwell guide to the philosophy of the social sciences* (pp. 291–310). Oxford, UK: Blackwell.

House, E. R., & Howe, K. R. (1999). *Values in evaluation and social research.* Thousand Oaks, CA: Sage.

Kemmis, S. (2004, March). *Knowing practice: Searching for saliences.* Paper presented at the invitational conference "Participant Knowledge and Knowing Practice," Umeå University, Umeå, Sweden.

Lave, J., & Wenger, E. (1991). *Situated learning: Legitimate peripheral participation.* Cambridge, UK: Cambridge University Press.

Molander, B. (1992). Tacit knowledge and silenced knowledge: Fundamental problems and controversies. In B. Göranzon & M. Florin (Eds.), *Skill and education: Reflection and experience* (pp. 9–31). London: Springer-Verlag.

Molander, B. (2002). Politics for learning or learning for politics? *Studies in Philosophy and Education, 21,* 361–376.

Pendlebury, S. (1990). Practical reasoning and situated appreciation in teaching. *Educational Theory, 40,* 171–179.

Reckwitz, A. (2002). Toward a theory of social practices: A development in culturalist theorizing. *European Journal of Social Theory, 5,* 243–263.

Sanderson, I. (2003). Is it "what works" that matters? Evaluation and evidence-based policy making. *Research Papers in Education: Policy and Practice, 18,* 331–345.

Schatzki, T., Knorr Cetina, K., & von Savigny, E. (Eds.). (2001). *The practice turn in contemporary theory.* London: Routledge.

Schön, D. A. (1983). *The reflective practitioner.* New York: Basic Books.

Schwandt, T. A. (2002). *Evaluation practice reconsidered.* New York: Peter Lang.

Schwandt, T. A., & Burgon, H. (2006). Evaluation and the study of lived experience. In I. Shaw, J. Greene, & M. Mark (Eds.), *Handbook of evaluation* (pp. 98–117). London: Sage.

Shadish, W. R., Cook, T. D., & Leviton, L. (1991). *Foundations of program evaluation: Theories of practice.* Newbury Park, CA: Sage.

Simons, H. (2004). Utilizing evaluation evidence to enhance professional practice. *Evaluation 10,* 410–429.

Smith, N. L. & Jang. S. (2002). Increasing cultural sensitivity in evaluation practice: A South Korean illustration. *Studies in Educational Evaluation, 28*(1), 61–69.

Stern, D. G. (2003). The practical turn. In S. P. Turner & P. A. Roth (Eds.), *The Blackwell guide to the philosophy of the social sciences* (pp. 185–206). Oxford, UK: Blackwell.

Taylor, C. (1995). *Philosophical arguments.* Cambridge, UK: Cambridge University Press.

Thompson-Robinson, M., Hopson, R., & SenGupta, S. (Eds.). (2004). *In search of cultural competence in evaluation.* (New Directions for Evaluation no. 102). San Francisco: Jossey-Bass.

Toulmin, S. (1988). The recovery of practical philosophy. *American Scholar, 57,* 345–358.

Toulmin, S. (2001). *Return to reason.* Cambridge, MA: Harvard University Press.

Van Manen, M. (1995). On the epistemology of reflective practice. *Teachers and Teaching: Theory and Practice, 1,* 33–50. Retrieved August 11, 2004, from *www.phenomenologyonline.com/max/epistpractice.htm.*

Van Manen, M. (1999). The practice of practice. In M. Lange, J. Olson, H. Hansen, & W. Bÿnder (Eds.), *Changing schools/Changing practices: Perspectives on educational reform and teacher professionalism.* Luvain, Belgium: Garant. Retrieved August 11, 2004, from *www.phenomenologyonline.com/max/practice.htm.*

Wagenaar, H., & Cook, S. D. N. (2003). Understanding policy practices: Action, dialectic and deliberation in policy analysis. In M. Hajer & H. Wagenaar (Eds.), *Deliberative policy analysis: Understanding governance in the network society* (pp. 139–171) Cambridge, UK: Cambridge University Press.

Wenger, E. (1998). *Communities of practice: Learning, meaning and identity.* New York: Cambridge University Press.

Wiggins, D. (1980). Deliberation and practical reason. In A. O. Rorty (Ed.), *Essays on Aristotle's ethics* (pp. 221–240). Berkeley, CA: University of California Press.

CHAPTER 3

Stakeholder Representation in Culturally Complex Communities
Insights from the Transformative Paradigm

DONNA M. MERTENS

That the HIV/AIDS epidemic in Botswana is escalating amidst volumes of research may be an indication that ongoing research is dominated by Euro-centric research epistemologies and ethics that fail to address the problem from the researched's frame of reference. Creating space for other knowledge systems must begin by recognizing local language and thought forms as an important source of making meanings of what we research. . . . Given the HIV/AIDS epidemic in Sub-Saharan Africa, the need for diversity in research epistemologies has become not a luxury of nationalism of the African Renaissance, but rather an issue of life and death.
—CHILISA (2005, p. 678)

Early program evaluation models were rooted in applied social research that focused primarily on methodological rigor, with little attention to strategies to involve stakeholders in ways that might increase that rigor and enhance the probability of appropriate use of the findings (Alkin, 2004). Stufflebeam provided a major stimulus that shifted the focus to the provision of information for decision making rather than the more limiting use of experimental designs and standardized tests to confirm schools' success or failure to achieve (potentially dubious) objectives (Stufflebeam, 2001, 2004). Currently, intended users of the evaluation are recognized as central to the concept of utility; in the evaluation world, those intended users are called stakeholders. Thus, Stufflebeam's

41

concern for utility is reflected in *The Program Evaluation Standards: How to Assess Evaluation of Educational Programs* (Joint Committee on Standards for Educational Evaluation, 1994) and in the Guiding Principles that the American Evaluation Association (AEA) endorses (American Evaluation Association, 2005).

As evaluation grew from its infancy in which the focus of utility was primarily on decision makers, awareness increased as to the need to be responsive to the cultural complexity in communities in which evaluations are conducted. In this chapter, I explore those insights that arise from the use of the transformative paradigm for evaluators seeking to accurately and appropriately represent stakeholders in culturally complex communities. Using examples of evaluation studies, I make the argument that application of a transformative lens will provide guidance to evaluators with regard to culturally appropriate stakeholder representation and involvement as a means to manage cultural complexity and diversity, increase the accuracy of stakeholder representation, and enhance the probability of the use of evaluation work to further social justice.

THE TRANSFORMATIVE PARADIGM

Paradigms are a basic set of beliefs that guide action (Guba & Lincoln, 2005). Four basic beliefs help to define a paradigmatic stance as well as to distinguish one paradigm from another: axiology (what is the meaning of ethical behavior?), ontology (what is the nature of reality?), epistemology (what is the relationship between the inquirer and the known?), and methodology (what are the appropriate means for acquiring knowledge about the world?).

As cultural diversity is a fundamental issue in evaluation, no matter what the evaluator's paradigmatic stance or methodological approach, why position this chapter in the transformative paradigm? The core of the transformative paradigm rests on adherence to philosophical assumptions that directly and explicitly address cultural complexity and issues of power, privilege, and social justice. Evaluators who work from other stances may find disagreement with this as a primary focus. Nevertheless, the insights gained from scholars who position themselves within this framework have the potential to illuminate issues regarding cultural complexity and stakeholder representation that might otherwise not surface. The basic beliefs of the transformative paradigm are summarized in Table 3.1.

The transformative paradigm of research and evaluation provides an overarching theoretical framework to guide evaluators who wish to

TABLE 3.1. Basic Beliefs of the Transformative Paradigm

Ontology: assumptions about the nature of reality	Multiple realities are shaped by social, political, cultural, economic, ethnic, gender, and disability values
Epistemology: assumptions about the nature of the relationship between the evaluator and the stakeholders	Interactive link exists between evaluator and stakeholders; knowledge is socially and historically situated; power and privilege are explicitly addressed; development of a trusting relationship is critical
Methodology: assumptions about appropriate methods of systematic inquiry	Inclusion of qualitative (dialogic) is critical; quantitative and mixed methods can be used; contextual and historic factors are acknowledged, especially as they relate to oppression
Axiology: assumptions about ethics	Ethical considerations include respect for cultural norms of interaction; beneficence is defined in terms of the promotion of human rights and an increase in social justice

Note. Data from Mertens (2005, in press).

address issues of cultural complexity (Mertens, 2005). The transformative paradigm serves as a useful theoretical umbrella to explore philosophical assumptions and guide methodological choices. Although most evaluation approaches could benefit from an increased understanding of cultural complexity and competency, evaluation approaches such as those labeled inclusive (Mertens, 1999, 2005), human rights-based (Whitmore et al., 2006), democratic (House & Howe, 1999), or culturally responsive (Hood, Hopson, & Frierson, 2005) are most commensurate with this paradigm.

Transformative, culturally responsive, and deliberative democratic evaluations revolve around central questions and issues of social inequity and social justice where the lives and experiences of underrepresented groups and those pushed to the margins are included in the evaluation process in meaningful ways. The transformative paradigm extends the thinking of democracy and responsiveness by consciously including the identification of important dimensions of diversity in evaluation work and their accompanying relation to discrimination and oppression in the world (Mertens, 2005).

Ontologically, this paradigm explicitly interrogates the social and cultural forces that determine what is deemed to be real, how power and privilege play into the accepted definitions of reality, and the consequences of accepting one reality over another. Epistemologically, the transformative paradigm calls for a respectful and knowledgeable link between the evaluator and the stakeholders, with explicit recognition of the influence of power and privilege in human relations and trust building. Methodologically, decisions are guided by a deep understanding of the cultural norms and values in the program context and usually are associated with dialogue among the stakeholders, the use of mixed methods of data collection, and shared power in the use of the findings.

The philosophical principles underlying the transformative paradigm provide the theoretical framework for critically examining such issues as: What dimensions of diversity should be represented in the specific context of an evaluation? Who makes decisions regarding invitations for participation? What methods of invitation are appropriate, and what accommodations and support are necessary for authentic involvement of multiple stakeholders? How do issues of power and privilege influence decisions about the representation of stakeholders? What are the costs of not authentically engaging with the members of culturally complex communities? What are the benefits of doing so? What is the evaluator's role in uncovering that which has not been stated explicitly, especially as it relates to oppression and discrimination?

THE TRANSFORMATIVE PARADIGM AS A FRAMEWORK FOR CRITICAL ANALYSIS OF EVALUATION PRACTICE

Chilisa's (2005) critique of a needs assessment that served as the basis for the development of an HIV/AIDS prevention program in Botswana illustrates the application of the transformative paradigm to an evaluation study in a culturally complex community. The leader and several members of the evaluation team were from a U.S. university who were contracted to work in a collaborative relationship with in-country evaluators. (Chilisa is an indigenous Botswanan with a PhD from a U.S. university.) The contract explicitly stated that the lead evaluator was responsible for producing the final document and that all intellectual property including copyright in the final and other reports were to be the property of the U.S. university.

The needs sensing preceded program development and consisted of a literature review and a standardized survey. Chilisa provides numerous examples of ontological, epistemological, and methodological tensions that arose when indigenous knowledge was ignored by the evaluation and program development teams. For instance, the literature review included the statement "A high acceptance of multiple sexual partners both before marriage and after marriage is a feature of Botswana society" (p. 676). Working from a transformative framework, Chilisa recognized that realities are constructed and shaped by social, political, cultural, economic, and ethnic values, and that power is an important determinant of which reality will be privileged. When she saw this statement in the literature review regarding the sexual promiscuity of people in Botswana, she notified the U.S. evaluation team members that these statements were in conflict with her knowledge of the norms of the society. In response, the First World evaluators stated that they would not change the statement but that they would add additional literature citations to support it. Chilisa asks: "Which literature, generated by which researchers and using which research frameworks? . . . What if the researched do not own a description of the self that they are supposed to have constructed?" (p. 677). This example illustrates the depiction of reality when viewed from a transformative stance with that of a team of evaluators who choose to ignore the cultural complexity inherent in indigenous voices and realities.

The needs assessment survey was conducted using standardized procedures with a printed form that contained closed-ended questions, written in English, and using terminology based on Western scientific language about the disease. This provides a second example of tensions that arise when evaluators choose to ignore the assumptions of the transformative paradigm that accurate reflection of stakeholders' understandings needs to be implemented in ways that facilitate involvement of the participant community, with recognition of and responsiveness to appropriate dimensions of diversity. Chilisa makes four critical points:

1. In Botswana, important dimensions of diversity include the multiethnic nature of the population, with most of the people speaking one of 25 ethnic languages.

2. The highest rate of HIV/AIDS infection is among the most vulnerable populations in Botswana, that is, those who are living in poverty with less privilege and less education.

3. The highest mortality rates are found among industrial class workers (women and girls especially) who earn the lowest wages and have the lowest education in comparison to the more economically privileged classes.

4. The meaning of HIV/AIDS (revealed in focus groups conducted by Chilisa and her African colleagues) differs from First World definitions. Botswana people have three meanings for what Westerner's call HIV/AIDS that vary, depending on the age at which one is infected and the mode of transmission.

Thus, the needs assessment data that were collected did not accurately reflect the indigenous realities of HIV/AIDS; nor was it responsive to the cultural complexity of the stakeholders. However, it was used as a basis for a prevention program that looked at the Africans as a homogenous universal mass where context-specific differences such as occupation, education, and social class were ignored. The program people, based on the evaluation data, made the assumption that everyone was middle-class and could therefore read English. An educational campaign was developed that used billboards with text such as "Don't be stupid, condomise" and "Are you careless, ignorant, and stupid?" "The lack of representation of appropriate stakeholders in the determination of communication strategies resulted in messages that were offensive, degrading and written from the perspective of a superior who casts the recipients of the message as ignorant" (p. 673). The consequence of this is to delay progress in combating HIV/AIDS for the most vulnerable populations.

Chilisa recommends that the point of reference for legitimating evaluation results should be on the basis of an accumulated body of knowledge that is created by the people impacted by the program. It is incumbent upon the evaluator to interact with all stakeholder groups, including the less powerful stakeholders, to determine the local meanings attached to experiences. She recommends that evaluators work from an ethics protocol that insists that the evaluation be carried out in the local language and that findings be written in the local language, especially where the less powerful stakeholders are not familiar with English. In addition, theories, models, and practices should be embedded in the indigenous knowledge systems and worldviews. Knowledge of the diverse ways of processing and producing knowledge in Botswana is situated in the proverbs, folklore, songs, and myths of that society. As Chilisa notes in the excerpt that appears at the beginning of this chapter, the consequences of ignoring the multiple realities, especially those realities as they are perceived by the less powerful, can be death. This example from Botswana illustrates the importance of cultural competency in evaluation work in order to accurately reflect the needs of stakeholders in culturally complex communities.

CULTURAL COMPETENCY

Cultural competency is a critical disposition that is related to the evaluator's ability to accurately represent reality in culturally complex communities. Symonette (2004) makes explicit the implication that the culturally competent evaluator must understand him- or herself in relation to the community in question. Cultural competence is not a static state. It is a journey in which the evaluator develops increased understanding of differential access to power and privilege through self-reflection and interaction with members of the community (Symonette, 2004; Sue & Sue, 2003). Cultural competence in evaluation can be broadly defined as a systematic, responsive mode of inquiry that is actively cognizant, understanding, and appreciative of the cultural context in which the evaluation takes place; that frames and articulates the epistemology of the evaluative endeavor; that employs culturally and contextually appropriate methodology; and that uses stakeholder-generated interpretive means to arrive at the results and further use of the findings (SenGupta, Hopson, & Thompson-Robinson, 2004). The benefits of cultural competency and culturally responsive evaluation approaches include, but are not limited to, the ability to transform interventions so that they are perceived as legitimate by the community (Guzman, 2003). (The reader may want to imagine what kind of HIV/AIDS prevention program might have been developed in the Botswana example if the evaluators had provided needs assessment data that were reflective of culturally competent practice.) The American Psychological Association (APA) recommends that the evaluator serve as an agent of prosocial change to combat racism, prejudice, bias, and oppression in all their forms (American Psychological Association, 2002). To this end, the culturally competent evaluator is able to build rapport across differences, gain the trust of community members, and self-reflect and recognize one's own biases (Edno, Joh, & Yu, 2003).

A similar sentiment is expressed in the AEA's (2005) Guiding Principles. Both the first and second editions included the same five categories: systematic inquiry, competence, integrity/honesty, respect for people, and responsibilities for general and public welfare. However, the second edition contains a shift in language that is focused on principles of cultural competency. For example, in the competency category, the second edition includes this language that was not present in the first edition:

> To ensure recognition, accurate interpretation and respect for diversity, evaluators should ensure that the members of the evaluation team collectively demonstrate cultural competence. Cultural competence would be reflected in evaluators seeking awareness of their own culturally based assumptions, their understanding of the worldviews of culturally different participants and stakeholders in the evaluation, and the use of appropriate evaluation strategies and skills in working with culturally different groups. Diversity may be in terms of race, ethnicity, gender, religion, socioeconomics, or other factors pertinent to the evaluation context. (Accessed October 14, 2005, from *www.eval.org/Guiding%20Principles.htm*)

The notion of transforming society through evaluation was the theme of my presidential address to the AEA (Mertens, 1999). My major point in that address was that the transformative paradigm provides a useful framework for addressing the role that evaluators and the profession have to play when addressing issues related to oppression, discrimination, and power differences—a role that is also consistent with evaluators as advocates for democracy and democratic pluralism (Greene, 1997; House & Howe, 1999).

DIMENSIONS OF DIVERSITY

Because the transformative paradigm is rooted in issues of diversity, privilege, and power, the recognition of the intersection of relevant dimensions of diversity is a central focus. Thus, program evaluators can raise questions to program personnel to consider the relevant dimensions of diversity, especially with regard to traditionally underserved groups, whether based on race/ethnicity, gender, economic class, religion, disabilities, or other characteristics associated with less privilege, and ways to structure program activities and measure appropriate outcomes, based on those dimensions. For example, if the central focus of a program is on race and ethnicity, what other dimensions need to be considered? The answer to that question is clearly context-dependent and could include gender, disability, socioeconomic status, reading level, or home language other than English; length of time with the HIV/AIDS infection; role in the family; access to medications and/or a supportive community; and participation in various political parties that have a history of adversarial relationships. By raising such questions, the evaluator's role is that of a provocateur, unsettling the comfortable realities of those traditionally in power for the purpose of guiding both evaluation choices and use of evaluation data for programmatic purposes. An equally important implication of transformative evaluation work is to influence decisions about society's development and the funding of programs that will explicitly address issues of inequities based on the complex dimensions of cultural diversity found in stakeholder groups.

Cultural competency is a necessary disposition when working within the transformative paradigm in order to uncover and respond to the relevant dimensions of diversity. Some semblance of cultural competence is required to identify those dimensions that are important to the specific context. Who needs to be included? How should they be included? How can they be invited in a way that they feel truly welcome and able to represent their own concerns accurately? What kinds of support are necessary to provide an appropriate venue for people with less privilege to share their experiences, with the goal of improving teaching and learning? or health care? or participation in governance? or reduction of poverty? What is the meaning of interacting in a culturally competent way with people from diverse backgrounds?

How can relevant dimensions of diversity be identified and integrated into programs designed to serve populations characterized by diversity? Understanding the critical dimensions of diversity that require representation for a transformative evaluation to contribute to social change is dependent on the realization that relevant characteristics are context-dependent.

Race/Ethnicity

In the United States, race and ethnicity are commonly viewed as salient dimensions of diversity that require focused attention. The APA's *Guidelines on Multicultural Education, Training, Research, Practice, and Organizational Change for Psychologists* (2002) focused primarily on four racial/ethnic groups because of the unique salience of race/ethnicity for diversity-related issues in the United States. The organization developed guidelines for research (and evaluation) for inquiries conducted with Asian American/Pacific Islander populations, persons of African descent, Hispanics, and American Indians. The APA used race/ethnicity as the organizing framework; however, it also recognized the need to be aware of other dimensions of diversity. This is illustrated in the following guiding principle:

> Recognition of the ways in which the intersection of racial and ethnic group membership with other dimensions of identity (e.g., gender, age, sexual orientation, disability, religion/spiritual orientation, educational attainment/experiences, and socioeconomic status) enhances the understanding and treatment of all people. (p. 19)

The evaluation of the Talent Development Model of School Reform provides an example of an evaluation conducted from a transformative stance with specific attention to dimensions of race/ethnicity, because it is designed to enhance the educational experiences of students in urban schools, the majority of whom are from racial/ethnic minority groups (Boykin, 2000). This model was developed by the Center for Research on Education of Students Placed at Risk (CRESPAR), a collaborative effort between Howard University and Johns Hopkins University, as an alternative to educational reform approaches that ignore contextual and cultural issues. With an overtly transformative agenda, the evaluation of Talent Development interventions incorporates both scientific methodological and political activist criteria (Thomas, 2004). The transformative evaluation was designed to provide information to enlighten and empower those who have been oppressed by or marginalized in school systems. A key element in the quality of the evaluation is the engagement of stakeholders who may have had negative or even traumatic occurrences with the school system in their youth. Evaluators demonstrate respect for the stakeholders and create opportunities for those who have traditionally had less powerful roles in discussions of urban school reform to have their voices heard. The evaluators facilitate authentic engagement by holding multiple meetings, along with the field implementers and key stakeholder groups, with the intention of obtaining genuine buy-in by these groups. To the extent possible, stakeholder suggestions are incorporated into the Talent Development activities and the evaluation.

The Talent Development (TD) evaluators also place a premium on cultural competence in the context of the urban school. To that end, they seek evaluators of color or from underrepresented groups. When this is not possible, evaluators are required to obtain a fundamental understanding of the cultural norms and experiences of the stakeholders by means of building relationships with key informants, interpreters, or critical friends to the evaluation. TD evaluators are encouraged to engage in ongoing self-reflection and to immerse themselves in the life stream of the urban school through attendance at meetings, informal discussions, and attendance at school functions such as fund-raisers or parent information nights. These are strategies that increase stakeholders' access to the evaluators and program implementers, with the goal being improved school performance for those who are placed at risk.

Evaluation of the Promoting Reflective Inquiry in Mathematics Education Project (PRIME) provides another example of the importance of stakeholder involvement in a project focused on Native American students (Sayler, Apaza, & Austin, 2005). Disaggregated results from multiple measures confirmed the gap between Native Americans and non-Native Americans in terms of achievement in mathematics. While 70% of white students in the school system achieved proficiency at grade level, only 40% of Native American students did so. In addition, the proficiency rate for Native Americans was reported to be inflated because well over half of the Native Americans entering high school dropped out before graduation

Course-taking patterns revealed Native Americans were nearly absent in upper-level math courses: of the 140 Native Americans who started as an elementary grade-level cohort, 15 succeeded in algebra in 2003–3004 and only 3 passed the advanced-placement calculus course.

The evaluators scheduled frequent meetings with project directors to review their findings. The evaluators felt frustrated because the tribal representatives did not come to the meetings to discuss the evaluation findings, even with repeated invitations.

A transformative lens focused on this evaluation, which revealed differential experiences in math in a comparison of white and Native American students, elicits such questions as the following: What is the importance of involving members of the Native American community in the early stages of this project? How can members of the Native American community be involved? Who in the Native American community needs to be involved? What are the political ramifications of demonstrating the gap in achievement and access to advanced math and science courses between white and Native American students? How can evidence of an achievement gap be obtained and be viewed as information of value to the Native American community rather than solely as a negative reflection on their community? How can the evaluator encourage program developers to identify those contextual variables that are of a causal nature in determining learning? Once the gaps have been identified, how can the interventions be structured so that they are responsive to the context in which the people live? How can evaluators encourage responsiveness to the multiple dimensions of diversity? LaFrance (2004) provides many insights into the conduct of culturally competent evaluation in Native American settings, starting with recognition of the need to follow traditional lines of authority in contacting members of a tribal nation.

Intersection of Disability, Race, and Gender

Race/ethnicity is not always the critically defining dimension of diversity that needs to be recognized in a program for social change. Seelman (2000) reported that there is great diversity within the 20% of the U.S. population with disabilities. For example, women have higher rates of severe disabilities than men (9.7% vs. 7.7%), while men have slightly higher rates of nonsevere disabilities. Considering both sex and race, black women have the highest rate of severe disability (14.3%), followed by black men (12.6%). Rates of severe disability for men and women who are American Indian, Eskimo, or Aleut are nearly as high; persons who are American Indian have the highest rates of nonsevere disability. Evaluators who are aware of the diversity within the disability community can use this information to avoid errors based on assumptions of homogeneity and strengthen the potential for their work to address marginalized populations by inclusion of appropriate subgroups.

Rousso and Wehmeyer (2001) examined the intersection of gender and disability in their book *Double Jeopardy*. They conclude that disparities on such indicators as educational and employment-related outcomes support the idea that girls and women with disabilities are in a state of double jeopardy. The combination of stereotypes about women and stereotypes about people with disabilities leads to double discrimination that is reflected in the home, school, workplace, and society as a whole.

However, not all indicators support the position that males with disabilities are favored over females. The U.S. Department of Education (2004) reports that males, especially those from minority ethnic and racial groups, are diagnosed as having disabilities in much greater numbers—roughly by a ratio of 2:1, versus females. According to the Civil Rights Project at Harvard University, black children constitute 17% of the total school enrollment of those labeled mentally retarded, with only marginal improvement over a 30-year period (Losen & Orfield, 2002). During this same period, disproportionality in the areas of emotional disturbance and specific learning disabilities grew significantly for blacks. Between 1987 and 2001, students from homes whose first language was not English (primarily Spanish-speaking families) exhibited a fourfold increase in the proportion of students identified with a disability (U.S. Department of Education, 2002). Evaluators need to be aware of these complexities, because people with disabilities are likely present in almost all stakeholder groups (Gill, 1999; Mertens, Wilson, & Mounty, 2007). To some, this level of awareness of diversity and inclusion of diverse stakeholders may seem to be hallmarks of good practice or just plain common sense. However, voices of members of marginalized communities suggest that this is not always or often the case (Chilisa, 2005; Mertens, 2005; Mertens & McLaughlin, 2004). Thus, the transformative paradigm provides the framework for explicitly raising these issues related to cultural diversity and evaluation theory and practice. Awareness of issues related to differential access and outcomes at the intersection of race, disability, and gender are particularly relevant for evaluators whose work relates to the "No Child Left Behind" agenda.

Meadow-Orlans, Mertens, and Sass-Lehrer (2003) provide an example of working within a culturally complex community where the primary focus was on the hearing status of children. They used a mixed-methods design to evaluate parent satisfaction with services offered to parents with deaf and hard-of-hearing children. A national-level survey of parents of young deaf and hard-of-hearing children revealed different levels of satisfaction with services when the data were disaggregated by race/ethnicity, parental hearing status, child's hearing level (deaf or hard-of-hearing), presence of additional disabilities beyond deafness, and parents' choice of communication mode for their child. In order to gain a more thorough understanding of the reasons for differences in reported levels of satisfaction based on these dimensions of diversity, the national survey was followed by individual interviews with the specific goal of determining the supportive and challenging factors associated with each group's experiences.

As the individual interviews proceeded, it became clear that racial/ethnic minority parents were not appearing in adequate numbers in the follow-up data collection. The investigators conferred with the leaders of programs that served parents and children primarily from racial and ethnic minority groups. They recommended the use of focus groups held at the school site, with the invitation issued by the school staff who normally worked with the parents and the provision of food, transportation, and child care. Under these circumstances, it was possible to gain insights from the less-represented stakeholders with regard to program satisfaction.

The need for accommodations to authentically include people with different communication choices was critical to obtaining accurate data. Parents who were deaf were interviewed through the use of an on-site interpreter who voiced for the parent's signs and signed what the interviewer said to the parent. By being culturally aware and responsive to the demands of this culturally complex community, the evaluation team was able to identify both supports and challenges that were common across groups and those that were unique to specific groups. Information of this type is important for programs that serve diverse clients as well as for the parents themselves. The use of a transformative paradigm in this evaluation of services for parents of young deaf and hard-of-hearing children provided the guidance necessary to realize what dimensions of diversity were relevant in this situation as well as what type of invitation and support was necessary in order to obtain an accurate reflection of parents' experiences. Such information is used to prepare new professionals in the field and to modify existing service systems.

More elaborate accommodations may be necessary depending on the context and the dimensions of diversity that are salient in that context. For example, in a study of court access for deaf and hard-of-hearing people across the United States, Mertens (2000) worked with an advisory board to identify the dimensions of diversity that would be important and to devise ways to accommodate the communication needs of the individuals who were invited to focus groups to share their experiences in the courts. The advisory board recognized the complexity in the deaf community in terms of communication modes. Thus, individuals who were well educated and sophisticated in the use of American Sign

Language (ASL) were accommodated by having deaf and hearing co-moderators, along with an interpreter who could sign for the hearing moderator and voice for the signing participants. In addition, individuals skilled in real-time captioning were in the room and produced text of the verbal comments that appeared on television screens visible to the group members. When deaf people who were less well educated and had secondary disabilities were invited to share their experiences, additional accommodations were necessary. For example, a deaf blind participant required an interpreter who signed into her hands so that she could follow the discussion. One individual did not use ASL as a language but, rather, communicated using some signs and gestures. For this individual, the evaluators provided a deaf interpreter who could watch the signs of others and "act out" the communications occurring in the group. One focus group included users of Mexican Sign Language, which required the use of a Mexican Sign Language interpreter, who then translated the participants' comments into American Sign Language, and those were translated by a third interpreter, who voiced in English.

In addition to the communication accommodations and diversity associated with hearing levels and communication modes, the focus groups were also designed to incorporate other dimensions of diversity, such as gender, race/ethnicity, and role in the court proceedings (e.g., victim, perpetrator, witness, and jurist). Through this carefully constructed evaluation, based on the principles of the transformative paradigm, it was possible to accurately reflect the views of the deaf and hard-of-hearing community for judges, court staff, and advocates for social justice for deaf and hard-of-hearing people in the U.S. court system.

Political Parties as Dimensions of Diversity

Irwin (2005) provides an example in which adversarial political parties constitute the key dimension of diversity. He wrestled with the representation of stakeholders in the politically charged atmosphere of Northern Ireland in his use of public opinion polls. His preliminary work suggested that innovations that might lead to peace in that region were supported by a majority of the people; however, they were being blocked by religious and political elites who were benefiting from maintaining social divisions and the status quo. Irwin contacted recently elected politicians from 10 different political parties and asked them to nominate a member of their team to work with him and his colleagues to write questions and run polls on any matters of concern to them. Thus, parties from across the political spectrum representing loyalist and republican paramilitary groups, mainstream democratic parties, and cross-community parties all agreed on the questions to be asked, the methods to be used, and the timing and mode of publication. The group conducted nine different polls, progressively identifying more specifically the choices for government that would be acceptable to the majority of the people.

Irwin experienced several challenges. Early in the process, the British and Irish governments were opposed to the use of an independent needs-sensing activity. Not only did they not want to participate in the writing of any of the questions, design of the study, or funding of the effort, but also they objected to Irwin's presence in the building where he met with the politicians. However, the stakeholders overruled the government officials and went forward with the process, making public the results of each poll. The results of the ninth poll indicated a majority of the electorate would say yes to a referendum that would bring peace through a power-sharing agreement between the British and Irish governments. By insisting on having longtime adversaries represented in the planning and implementation of the polling, Irwin was able to contribute significantly to the Belfast Agreement being brought before the people and the passage of that referendum. The building of a political consensus, while time-consuming and difficult, was necessary to reaching an agreement that can help to build peace in the world.

Irwin notes a number of critical areas of conflict that exist in the world, some of which are decades and even centuries old (e.g., Greek and Turkish Cypriots, Israelis and Palestinians, Serbs and Albanians in the former Yugoslav Republic of Macedonia, and the Britons, Americans, and Iraqis). In order for public polling to be successful as a means of contributing to world change, evaluators must identify the appropriate dimensions of diversity that need to be represented at the table. This might include both moderate and extremist groups as well as liberal and conservative politicians, grassroots community organizations, and religious groups. If the appropriate stakeholders are not identified or involved in a meaningful way, then the results of the evaluation will not be linked to the desired social action.

CAUTIONS AND CHALLENGES

Accurate and appropriate representation of stakeholders is not without its challenges, some of which have been explored in this chapter. Inclusion of multivocal constituencies may be accompanied by disagreements among the stakeholders that may slow or derail the evaluation. Different cultural groups, by definition, hold different values and expectations. Thus, the search for common ground is a challenge. Exposure of incompetence or resistance to implementation of a program raises tensions between competing directives found in the Joint Committee on Standards for Educational Evaluation (1994). How can an evaluator present a balanced report (identifying strengths and weaknesses) and treat stakeholders with respect and avoid harming them?

King, Nielsen, and Colby (2004) wrestled with several of these ethical dilemmas in their evaluation of a multicultural education program that foregrounded social justice issues. As is typical in many programs, they found a continuum in the implementation of the intervention. They expressed their dilemmas thusly: How can they report on the differences in implementation without attacking individuals? From a social justice perspective, what do they do with the anger that is expressed by some of the participants because they see some of their colleagues as choosing not to reform their instructional practices to incorporate the multicultural principles? What do they do with the demands of some of the stakeholders that names be named and made public in the interest of exposing "their colleagues with the hope of bringing them into alignment with the initiative's goals" (p. 74)? What do you do when the lead decision maker rejects your carefully crafted, inclusive stakeholder representative data and asks for a one-page checklist that principals can use to "check off . . . ideas they should think about to raise the visibility of multicultural issues in the building. Something really short that won't make anyone mad" (p. 76)?

King et al. (2004) provide the following advice: "Multicultural competence in evaluation necessarily involves explicit attention to articulation of stakeholder values, especially when they have the potential to conflict, and to the likely tensions and necessary trade-offs among propriety, utility, and feasibility, and social action concerns" (p. 78). They hypothesize that evaluators may be more successful if they give explicit attention to value differences and necessary trade-offs in the steering committee, coupled with purposeful conflict resolution or mediation.

CONCLUSION

As the field of evaluation evolves, the importance of involving stakeholders in culturally appropriate ways is reflected in many ways, including the ethical guidelines, standards, theory, philosophy, and methods. The AEA's Guiding Principles and Evaluation Standards reflect this shift in the evaluation community. These changes are accompanied by increasing attention to the concept of cultural competency within the evaluation literature. Cultural competence is not viewed as a static state that is good in all contexts but rather as a growing state of awareness of the important dimensions of diversity and their associated cultural implications. Evaluators may be from indigenous groups and have a sufficient connection from the community to have tacit knowledge of what is of cultural relevance. However, even indigenous evaluators need the level of self-reflection that Symonette (2004) recommends, because there are many dimensions of diversity that can be relevant in each context. Evaluators need to have sufficient contact with the community in a respectful way to learn what is important, as did Chilisa (2005) in her study of HIV/AIDS interventions in Botswana, Thomas (2004) in the Talent Development Model of School Reform, and Mertens (2000) in the evaluation of court access for deaf and hard-of-hearing people. Appropriate invitations need to be extended and circumstances must be provided so that all stakeholders have an opportunity to contribute their ideas.

The Transformative Paradigm is based on philosophical assumptions that explicitly address issues of power and privilege in the definition of what is accepted as being real, involvement with the community in a respectful way, and use of data collection methods that are appropriate to the accurate reflection of stakeholders in recognition of the important dimensions of diversity. In addition, the axiological assumption situates ethics in terms of the promotion of human rights and an increase in social justice. To this end, the evaluator's role in a transformative context is to raise such questions as: What are the relevant dimensions of diversity in this context? What are the relative positions of power? How can those stakeholders with traditionally less power be identified, invited, and supported in a way that their voices can be heard? What are the dangers of involving stakeholders with less power in the program evaluation? What are the consequences of not involving them? How can stakeholders be involved in appropriate ways and, if necessary, protected from those with more power? How can stakeholder groups be involved in the evaluation, even if they have a long history of animosity? Partial answers to some of these questions are presented in this chapter; however, the evaluation community has a long road ahead in dealing appropriately with the representation of stakeholders in culturally complex communities.

REFERENCES

Alkin, M. C. (2004). *Evaluation roots*. Thousand Oaks, CA: Sage.

American Evaluation Association (2005). *American Evaluation Association's Guiding Principles*. Accessed June 11, 2007, from *www.eval.org/Guiding%20Principles.htm*.

American Psychological Association. (2002). *Guidelines on multicultural education, training, research, practice, and organizational change for psychologists*. Washington, DC: Author.

Boykin, A. W. (2000). The Talent Development Model of Schooling: Placing students at promise for academic success. *Journal of Education for Students Placed at Risk, 5*(1–2; special issue), 1–211.

Chilisa, B. (2005). Educational research within postcolonial Africa: A critique of HIV/AIDS research in Botswana. *International Journal of Qualitative Studies in Education. 18*(6), 659–684.

Edno, T., Joh, T., & Yu, H. C. (2003). *Voices from the field: Health and evaluation leaders on multicultural evaluation.* Oakland, CA: Social Policy Research Associates.

Gill, C. (1999). Invisible ubiquity: The surprising relevance of disability issues in evaluation. *American Journal of Evaluation, 29*(2), 279–287.

Greene, J. C. (1997). Evaluation as advocacy. *Evaluation Practice, 18*(1), 25–35.

Guba, E. G., & Lincoln, Y. S. (2005). Paradigmatic controversies, contradictions, and emerging confluences. In N. K. Denzin & Y. S. Lincoln (Eds.), *The Sage handbook of qualitative research* (3rd ed., pp. 191–216). Thousand Oaks, CA: Sage.

Guzman, B. L. (2003). Examining the role of cultural competency in program evaluation: Visions for new millennium evaluators. In S. I. Donaldson & M. Scriven (Eds.), *Evaluating social programs and problems: Visions for the new millennium* (pp. 167–182). Mahwah, NJ: Erlbaum.

Hood, S., Hopson, R., & Frierson, H. (2005). *The role of culture and cultural context in evaluation: A mandate for inclusion, the discovery of truth and understanding.* Greenwich, CT: Information Age.

House, E. R., & Howe, K. R. (1999). *Values in evaluation and social research.* Thousand Oaks, CA: Sage.

Irwin, C. (2005, September 15–17). Public opinion and the politics of peace research: Northern Ireland, Balkans, Israel, Palestine, Cyprus, Muslim World and the "War on Terror." Paper presented at the World Association for Public Opinion Research 58th annual conference, Cannes, France.

Joint Committee on Standards for Educational Evaluation. (1994). *The program evaluation standards: How to assess evaluations of educational programs.* Thousand Oaks, CA: Sage.

King, J. A., Nielsen, J. E., & Colby, J. (2004). Lessons for culturally competent evaluation from the study of a multicultural initiative. In M. Thompson-Robinson, R. Hopson, & S. SenGupta (Eds.), *In search of cultural competence in evaluation* (New Directions for Evaluation no. 102, pp. 67–79). San Francisco: Jossey-Bass.

LaFrance, J. (2004). Culturally competent evaluation in Indian country. In M. Thompson-Robinson, R. Hopson, & S. SenGupta (Eds.), *In search of cultural competence in evaluation* (New Directions for Evaluation no. 102, pp. 39–50). San Francisco: Jossey-Bass.

Losen, D. J., & Orfield, G. (Eds.). (2002). *Racial inequity in special education.* Boston: Harvard Education Press.

Meadow-Orlans, K., Mertens, D. M., & Sass-Lehrer, M. (2003). *Parents and their deaf children: The early years.* Washington, DC: Gallaudet Press.

Mertens, D. M. (1999). Inclusive evaluation: Implications of transformative theory for evaluation. *American Journal of Evaluation, 20*, 1–14.

Mertens, D. M. (2000). Deaf and hard of hearing people in court: Using an emancipatory perspective to determine their needs. In C. Truman, D. M. Mertens, & B. Humphries (Eds.), *Research and inequality*. London: Taylor & Francis.

Mertens, D. M. (2005). *Research and evaluation in education and psychology: Integrating diversity with quantitative, qualitative and mixed methods* (2nd ed.). Thousand Oaks, CA: Sage.

Mertens, D. M. (in press). *Transformative research and evaluation*. New York: Guilford Press.

Mertens, D. M., & McLaughlin, J. (2004). *Research and evaluation methods in special education*. Thousand Oaks, CA: Corwin Press.

Mertens, D. M., Wilson, A., & Mounty, J. (2007). Gender equity for people with disabilities. In S. Klein (Eds.), *Handbook for achieving gender equity through education* (pp. 583–604). Mahwah, NJ: Erlbaum.

Rousso, H., & Wehmeyer, M. L. (2001). *Double jeopardy*. Albany, NY: State University of New York Press.

Sayler, B., Apaza, J., & Austin, M. (2005, September). *Using data to "make a case" for mathematics reform within a K–12 district*. Paper presented at the National Science Foundation Evaluation Summit, Minneapolis, MN.

Seelman, K. D. (2000). *The new paradigm on disability: Research issues and approaches*. Washington, DC: National Institute for Disability and Rehabilitative Research.

SenGupta, S., Hopson, R., & Thompson-Robinson, M. (2004). Cultural competence in evaluation: An overview. In M. Thompson-Robinson, R. Hopson, & S. SenGupta (Eds.), *In search of cultural competence in evaluation* (New Directions for Evaluation no. 102, pp. 5–20). San Francisco: Jossey-Bass.

Stufflebeam, D. L. (2001). *Evaluation models* (New Directions for Evaluation no. 89). San Francisco: Jossey-Bass.

Stufflebeam, D. L. (2004). The 21st centrury CIPP model: Origins, development, and use. In M. Alkin (Ed.), *Evaluation roots* (pp. 245–266). Thousand Oaks, CA: Sage.

Sue, D. W., & Sue, D. (2003). *Counseling the culturally diverse: Theory and practice* (4th ed.). New York: Wiley.

Symonette, H. (2004).Walking pathways toward becoming a culturally competent evaluator: Boundaries, borderlands, and border crossings. In M. Thompson-Robinson, R. Hopson, & S. SenGupta (Eds.), *In search of cultural competence in evaluation* (New Directions for Evaluation no. 102, pp. 95–110). San Francisco: Jossey-Bass.

Thomas, V. G. (2004). Building a contextually responsive evaluation framework: Lessons from working with urban school interventions. In V. G. Thomas & F. I. Stevens (Eds.), *Co-constructing a contextually responsive evaluation framework* (New Directions in Evaluation no. 101, pp. 3–24). San Francisco: Jossey-Bass and American Evaluation Association.

U.S. Department of Education. (2002). *Twenty-fourth annual report to Congress on the Implementation of the Individuals with Disabilities Education Act*. Accessed December 19, 2005, from *www.ed.gov/about/reports/annual/osep/2002/index.html*.

U.S. Department of Education. (2004). The facts about . . . investing in what works. Retrieved October 25, 2004, from *www.ed.gov/nclb/methods/whatworks/whatworks.html*.

Whitmore, E., Guijt, I., Mertens, D. M., Imm, P. S., Chinman, M., & Wandersman, A. (2006). Embedding improvements, lived experience, and social justice in evaluation practices. In I. F. Shaw, J. C. Greene, & M. M. Mark (Eds.), *The Sage handbook of evaluation* (pp. 340–359). Thousand Oaks, CA: Sage.

PART II

ISSUES OF METHOD

Methods are the tools and procedures with which evaluators practice their trade and attempt to achieve their goals. Indeed, methods are such a dominant aspect of evaluation that they are often seen as its defining characteristic. There are innumerable examples.

- Lay audiences often understand evaluation in terms of its methods for collecting and analyzing data.
- Ask an evaluator to describe a recent study, and a description of the method is likely to be a prominent part of the response.
- Many evaluators see themselves as having strong methodological skills, if not as actually being methodologists.
- One way to differentiate evaluation from research is through contrasting their methods (e.g., see Mathison's discussion in Chapter 9).

Further, the focus of most graduate training in evaluation is on the classroom development of methodological skills of study design, data collection and analysis, and reporting, and on field training in planning, resource management, and interpersonal skills.

Training in new method skills is the primary focus, and a source of considerable revenue, of professional development sessions held during annual conferences and at regional workshops. Methods are a primary topic of textbooks and professional references.

Much of the evaluation literature deals with evaluation methods—proposals of new methods and arguments about old methods. For example, the now classic debates of the superiority of qualitative versus quantitative methods consumed a great many journal pages and considerable professional meeting time. Of course, disagreements about methods continue; see, for example, Smith's discussion of the debate about randomized controlled trials in Chapter 1.

Methods are closely related to the other aspects of evaluation. Methods are needed to operationalize evaluation theories, and, in turn, theories are used to justify the use of particular methods—a theme evident throughout this volume. It is methods that practitioners learn in graduate programs and professional development sessions and employ to perform evaluations; the quality of a method is sometimes judged in terms of how well it performs in actual practice; and professional presentations by practitioners are often of the form "what methods I used in my evaluation and how well they worked (or didn't)." Finally, as noted above, the evaluation profession itself is often defined in terms of what tools evaluators use.

Given this pervasive preoccupation with issues of evaluation method, it is not surprising that Thomas A. Schwandt warns against ignoring the role of practical knowledge in evaluation and of characterizing evaluation expertise solely as knowledge of what techniques to use in what situations (see Chapter 2). Tom's cautions not withstanding, in Part II: Issues of Method we include three chapters that examine fundamental issues of evaluation method.

The recent redirection of a proportion of evaluation funds at the U.S. Department of Education toward studies of evaluation effects, with a preference for randomized designs, resulted in considerable, often rancorous, discussion among evaluators about such long-recurring fundamental evaluation issues as: What is the appropriate use of experimental designs in program evaluation? and, How can experimental studies best be designed for practical use in the field? This second issue is addressed by Judith A. Droitcour and Mary Grace Kovar in Chapter 4, "Multiple Threats to the Validity of Randomized Studies."

Going beyond the usual discussion about the lack of generalizability of randomized trials, Droitcour and Kovar focus instead on two threats to validity when using experiments: differential reactivity and biasing social interactions. Differential reactivity is error due to study subjects' self-reports that occur differently in the treatment group than in the control group. Biasing social interactions are interactions between treatment group members and control group members that violate the stable unit treatment value assumption (that is, the assumption that the effects of treatment in one group are not influenced by the treatment or lack thereof in another group). Droitcour and Kovar summarize what is known about each of these two validity threats, with numerous examples; suggest using checklists for prospectively anticipating the threats or retrospectively identifying the threats; suggest building ancillary studies into experiments for the purpose of recognizing the existence and magnitude of the threats; and describe methods for minimizing the threats. This chapter presents a clear, succinct summary of the literature on the threats, with the valuable addition of suggesting prospective identification of the two forms of bias.

In her chapter, "Research Synthesis: Toward Broad-Based Evidence" (Chapter 5), Susan N. Labin continues the discussion of experimental designs but within a consideration of the broader fundamental issue of: What is the proper way to synthesize evaluation and social science research findings?

Labin presents an overview of types of research syntheses; she describes their advantages and disadvantages, with particular emphasis on the criteria for including studies in syntheses. Her discussion covers traditional reviews, including traditional literature reviews, qualitative reviews, and broad-based research syntheses; meta-analyses; evaluation syntheses and retrospective evaluation syntheses; and the synthesis method presented in the *Guide to Community Preventive Services*, as well as others. She describes the narrow inclusion criteria of meta-analyses and presents an argument against limiting synthesis analyses to randomized trials. Further, she summarizes the limitations of randomized trials and presents other designs that deal with some of these limitations.

This chapter addresses several fundamental issues about design that take into consideration context, knowledge accumulation, and knowledge use: How do we identify, collect, and use prior knowledge when we do an evaluation? What type of synthesis is appropriate for what type of evaluation purpose? What constitutes credible, valid, useful, and relevant evidence in an evaluation? To what extent and in what circumstances should evaluators rely on strongly warranted evidence or on weaker evidence? The chapter provides a comprehensive look at some of the considerations that go into addressing these issues.

The third chapter in Part II shifts attention from methods for designing experimental studies and for synthesizing research findings to methods for studying evaluation itself. Although evaluators have long drawn on their own personal experiences to shape their work, a fundamental concern has been: How can evaluators systematically study evaluation practice in order to better inform evaluation theory, method, and future practice?

In Chapter 6, "Building a Better Evidence Base for Evaluation Theory: Beyond General Calls to a Framework of Types of Research on Evaluation," Melvin M. Mark goes beyond the general call for more research on evaluation, which has been made repeatedly over the years, by providing a taxonomy of types of studies for researching evaluation, including descriptive studies, classification studies, causal analyses, and values inquiries. The taxonomy includes categories of evaluation context, evaluation activities, evaluation consequences, and professional issues, and is intended as a guide for the design, classification, and interpretation of research on evaluation. Borrowing from previous work, Mark provides case examples of studies addressing the categories and concludes with caveats about the limitations of the taxonomy.

As Mark points out, a stronger empirical understanding of prior evaluation work can contribute to better responses to other fundamental issues, such as: What are the possible and proper stakeholder roles in evaluation? What are the best approaches and methods for a given evaluation, how have those choices been manifested in previous studies, and what have been the consequences of those choices? Effective research on evaluation could have a strong positive impact on improvement of the field.

The chapters in Part II demonstrate the accumulating knowledge and increasing sophistication with which three long-term fundamental issues in evaluation are being addressed: How do we effectively use experimental designs in evaluation? Which type of research synthesis is best for which use? And what are the best ways to conduct research on evaluation itself? All three chapters provide theoretical arguments concerning which methods will most improve evaluation practice. Collectively, they portray the profession of evaluation as an empirically based, inquiry-focused enterprise. Although the underlying intent may be the improvement of society, the focus of these chapters is on the technical issues of evaluation method.

CHAPTER 4

Multiple Threats to the Validity
of Randomized Studies

JUDITH A. DROITCOUR and MARY GRACE KOVAR

The basic premise of evaluation can be stated as follows: "In order that society can learn how to improve its efforts to mount effective [educational and social] programs, rigorous evaluations of innovations must . . . be conducted" (National Research Council, 2002, p. 12). The issue of what constitutes rigorous evaluation design, in relation to a specific evaluation question, is therefore crucial. And the effort to identify multiple threats to validity or sources of bias—indeed, the range of strengths and weaknesses associated with various design alternatives—is fundamental to the evaluation field. This is evidenced by numerous evaluation texts, reports, and articles that are specifically devoted to examining a range of threats to validity or to recognizing the value of multimethod approaches in combating such threats. (See, e.g., Campbell & Stanley, 1963, 1966; Cook & Campbell, 1979; Datta, 1997; Droitcour, 1997; Fetterman, 1982; Greene, Caracelli, & Graham, 1989; Shadish, 1993; Shadish, Cook, & Campbell, 2002; Webb, Campbell, Schwartz, & Sechrest, 2000.)

Studies that randomly assign subjects to alternative conditions (classically, to treatment versus control) have recently been championed as the best design for assessing program impact in areas such as education, health education, and delinquency prevention (see, e.g., Boruch, de Moya, & Snyder, 2002). Random assignment has long been deemed a crucial ingredient in impact evaluations, chiefly because randomization rules out the possibility of selection bias, a key threat to internal validity.

Evaluators generally agree that randomized studies may be weak with respect to *external* validity—that is, results from randomized studies may lack generalizability because of limited population coverage or atypical treatment implementation. But there has been little consideration of threats to valid comparison of outcomes across treatment and control groups, which may apply to randomized studies. We believe that such threats deserve fuller consideration and wider discussion in the evaluation community. The aim is to encourage and improve assessments of bias in randomized studies—and, as a result, to foster more realistic expectations, where needed, or to stimulate wider use of strategies to combat bias. This chapter takes a first step in that direction by examining two relatively neglected but potentially major bias-source categories: (1) differential reactivity and (2) biasing social interactions.[1]

BACKGROUND

Randomized studies have been used to assess the impact of interventions in a wide variety of social policy areas. For example, Powers and Witmer (1951) report an early randomized test of whether friendly adult mentors and counselors might help prevent teenage delinquency; Botvin, Baker, Dusenbury, Botvin, and Diaz (1995) report a randomized test of whether teaching "life skills" (such as resisting peer pressure) to seventh-, eighth-, and ninth-grade students would result in lower rates of tobacco, alcohol, and marijuana use; and Moffitt (2004) analyzes numerous randomized studies assessing the impact of social welfare rules on individuals' and families' economic behavior and benefit use.

Assignment based on a chance or statistical method (most informally, a coin flip) ensures that subjects receiving an intervention are statistically equivalent to subjects in the comparison group. That is, randomization essentially rules out the possibility of between-group differences (that are larger than expected based on chance alone) attributable to selection bias. Random assignment is thus viewed as the sine qua non for ensuring valid comparison of subsequent outcomes in the alternative groups.

But random assignment is not, in and of itself, a sufficient condition to ensure valid comparison of outcomes across treatment and control groups—not, at least, in the social policy area. The reason is that biases deriving from a variety of sources *not countered by randomization* may threaten a significant number of studies. Two general bias-source categories that we believe are potentially significant are (1) differential reactivity and (2) biasing social interactions.

Reactivity has been defined, most basically, as error stemming from a survey respondent (Webb et al., 2000) or, analogously, from a study subject (or other person) who is asked to provide a self-report or a judgment. For example, subjects in a prevention study may be asked to self-report whether they have engaged in (or avoided) certain risky behaviors; such self-reports may be skewed by subjects' perceptions of the social desirability associated with the behaviors in question. *Differential reactivity* has been defined as reactivity that differentially affects outcomes in treatment and control groups, thus biasing results and, more specifically, affecting internal validity (Webb et al., 2000).[2] To illustrate how *differential* reactivity may occur, treatment providers may emphasize the negative impacts that risky behaviors can have—and thus heighten treatment subjects' (but not controls') perceptions of the social *un*desirability of these risky behaviors.

Social interaction that involves treatment or control subjects (or both) can, directly or indirectly, violate the "stable unit treatment value assumption" (SUTVA), thus biasing treatment-control comparisons.[3] The SUTVA assumption is that "the value of Y [an outcome variable] for unit *u* when exposed to treatment *t* will be the same . . . no matter what treatment the other units receive" (Rubin, 1986, p. 961). *Biasing social interactions* are defined here as interactions that violate SUTVA. For example, if treatment subjects interact with control subjects, there may be a potential for the treatment being, intentionally or unintentionally, "passed on"; in other words, the control subjects may be affected by fact that other subjects—with whom they are in contact—are receiving a particular treatment.

Differential reactivity and biasing social interactions are general bias-source categories. Each encompasses more specific sources of bias that can be described in terms of

- Process: How the bias source affects comparisons across treatment groups.
- Support: The evidence or logic that underlies our belief that a biasing effect can occur (extensive discussion in the literature, one or more empirical studies, or persuasive logic).
- Direction of bias: The likely impact of the bias on results (inflation versus understatement of the intervention's true effect).

As summarized in the first row of Table 4.1, unblinded studies—especially unblinded studies that rely on reactive measures—may be vulnerable to differential reactivity. Most social policy studies are unblinded (McCall & Green, 2004; Shadish et al., 2002). And unblinded studies in some social program areas—for example, studies assessing prevention programs for teenagers—often rely fairly heavily on self-reports or other reactive measures, such as records that involve judgments of unblinded "outsiders" (authors' judgment based on informal review).

TABLE 4.1. Potential Vulnerability to Two Sources of Bias[a], by Key Study Characteristics

Design, measures	Social networks split	Social networks not split
Unblinded, reactive[b]	Potentially vulnerable to differential reactivity and biasing social interaction	Potentially vulnerable to differential reactivity
Unblinded, nonreactive	Potentially vulnerable to differential reactivity (lessened) and biasing social interaction	Potentially vulnerable to differential reactivity (lessened)
Double-blind, nonreactive	Potentially vulnerable to biasing social interaction	Not vulnerable to either source of bias

[a]Differential reactivity and biasing social interaction.
[b]Reactive measures include, for example, subjects' self-reports, treatment providers' judgments, and, in some cases, records based on reactive outsider reports or judgments.

The middle column of Table 4.1 shows studies that split social networks—typically through randomization that assigns some friends assigned to treatment, others to control. These types of studies may be vulnerable to biasing social interactions. This appears to be common in social policy studies—for example, the units of allocation are individuals (as opposed to larger clusters) in virtually all methodological studies that compare results for randomized and nonrandomized trials (Boruch, 2005). Thus, it appears that—at least in some social policy areas—many randomized studies are potentially vulnerable to differential reactivity or biasing social interactions or both; few fall into the clearly "not vulnerable" category (Table 4.1, lower right).

OBJECTIVES, SCOPE, AND METHODOLOGY

Our objectives in this chapter are to (1) summarize information on specific sources of differential reactivity and potential indicators of vulnerability, (2) summarize analogous information with respect to biasing social interactions, and (3) suggest strategies for assessing and minimizing vulnerability to both differential reactivity and biasing social interactions.

The scope of this chapter is limited to biases in randomized studies. We do not attempt to cover nonrandomized designs or to compare randomized to nonrandomized studies. Additionally we do not

- Address potential sources of bias other than differential reactivity and biasing social interaction.[4]
- Consider issues or problems other than bias (for example, ethical issues or implementation problems).
- Discuss conceptualizations of bias other than the bias-source categories specified above.[5]

Methods we used to address our study objectives included reviewing selected literature, applying logic to issues and concepts and discussing them with colleagues, and subjecting initial results to review.[6] In some cases, we based our literature selections on our judgment of likely potential to elucidate bias issues or on suggestions from colleagues. Because this initial paper is intended to be exploratory and suggestive, we did not attempt a comprehensive literature review.

With respect to categorization, we found that, in some cases, conceptually distinct categories or subcategories overlapped to some degree. Where this occurred, we selected the category that seemed primary or most relevant to the case at hand.

RESULTS

Differential Reactivity: Preexisting Beliefs or Preferences and During-Study Changes in Attitudes

Conceptualizing differential reactivity as a general bias-source category, we identified two key subcategories or more specific sources of bias: preexisting beliefs or preferences regarding treatments, and during-study changes in attitudes toward outcomes. This section examines each of these subcategories in terms of (1) key descriptors (such as how bias is created) and (2) indicators of unblinded studies' vulnerability. Key descriptors of the first subcategory—subjects' or treatment providers' *preexisting beliefs or preferences* with respect to the treatment—are summarized in the top half of Table 4.2.

As has been discussed extensively in the literature, preexisting beliefs that a treatment is likely to be effective can result in a "self-fulfilling prophecy" (item 1 of Table 4.2), generally inflating estimates of the treatment effect. Similarly, various discussions in the literature (see Corrigan & Salzer, 2003) as well as specific studies point to preexisting preferences that lead to a disappointment process when subjects do not receive their preferred assignment (item 2).[7] If the treatment group is preferred, then subjects assigned to the control group (or standard treatment) may suffer decreased motivation—and some intended change pro-

TABLE 4.2. Differential Reactivity: Specific Sources and Key Descriptors

	Key descriptor		
Specific source	Process: how bias can be created	Support: what underlies our belief that bias can occur	Bias: likely direction

Preexisting attitudes, beliefs, preferences re: treatment

1. Expectation that a treatment is more effective than the alternative treatment or the control condition	Treatment providers or subjects who expect an intervention to provide better results than the control condition may create a "self-fulfilling prophecy," especially if outcomes are based on reactive measures, such as the treatment provider's judgment or subjects' self-reports.	Extensive literature: Shadish et al. (2002, p. 73)	Inflation of the true effect
2. Preference for a treatment and disappointment if assigned to the alternative treatment or the control condition	Disappointment may cause subjects to (a) become less engaged in pursuing the outcome, if in the control group, or (b) report lower levels of satisfaction with the treatment and higher levels of depression or other negative psychological states, after treatment.	Studies and literature: (a) Fetterman (1982); (b) Fallowfield, Hall, Maguire, & Baum (1990)	Varies by whether disappointed subjects are concentrated in treatment or control group and by type of reaction

During-study changes in attitudes, beliefs re: outcome behaviors

3. Raised consciousness among treatment subjects	Subjects whose consciousness of outcome behaviors is raised (e.g., by the treatment or treatment providers) may be more likely to note occurrences of those behaviors. Self-reports may be differentially affected—treatment versus control—independent of behavior changes.	Logic: Orpinas et al. (2000)	Under- or overstatement of the true effect
4. Heightened perception of social desirability among treatment subjects	The intervention group's tendency to underreport a socially undesirable outcome behavior (such as unprotected sex) may be increased by an intervention that heightens awareness of the behavior's socially undesirably status. Self-reports may be differentially affected—treatment versus control—independent of behavior changes.	Logic: National Research Council (1991); studies: survey research	Inflation of the true effect

cesses are vulnerable to lack of motivation (see Hoza, 2001). Disappointed subjects may also report lessened satisfaction or increased negative psychological outcomes, such as depression or anxiety—because of disappointment in assignment rather than as a result of the treatment itself.

The bottom half of Table 4.2 displays the second differential-reactivity subcategory: *during-study changes in subjects' perceptions of key outcomes*. Differential changes can occur for treatment and control groups if the treatment itself sensitizes subjects to aspects of the outcome. As Table 4.2, item 3, illustrates, some interventions may have a consciousness-raising effect such that treatment subjects become more likely than controls to recognize and remember—and, thus, report—more instances of an outcome behavior on a posttest. For example, schoolchildren receiving a violence-reduction intervention may become more likely to notice—and report—aggressive behaviors like bullying on the posttest. But controls would not. (This possibility is suggested by Orpinas et al., 2000.) To the extent that this occurs with respect to negative outcomes like bullying, study results would understate the actual impact of the intervention. Conversely, if the sensitization process were to occur with regard to a *positive* outcome behavior—that is, a behavior that the treatment seeks to increase—increased reporting on the part of treatment subjects would inflate the estimated impact of the intervention.

As illustrated in Table 4.2, item 4, a somewhat similar source of during-study attitude change consists of sensitization to social desirability issues. As the literature on survey research has documented, when respondents are asked "threatening questions" about socially undesirable behaviors, those behaviors tend to be underreported, whereas desirable behaviors or attitudes may be overreported (Sudman & Bradburn, 1974; and Harrell, 1985, citing Hyman, 1944, Cahalan, 1968, and Weiss, 1968). When socially undesirable behaviors (such as risky sex, early pregnancy, drug use, or delinquency) represent key outcomes that the treatment seeks to reduce, a side effect of the treatment may be to heighten social desirability issues in treatment subjects' minds (but not in those of the control group). Under this scenario, if the study relies on self-reported outcome measures, there is a potential for lessened reporting of risky behaviors by subjects in the intervention group, as suggested by the National Research Council (1991) when considering evaluation issues for AIDS prevention programs. Logically, this would inflate the treatment effect. Overall, the far right column of Table 4.2 suggests that differential reactivity has diverse effects—it may tend to either inflate estimates of a social intervention's beneficial effect or understate the intervention's impact, depending on the circumstances.

Turning to indicators of unblinded studies' vulnerability to differential reactivity, a preliminary list, based on the items in Table 4.2, would include the following:

- Relatively strong preexisting beliefs about treatment effectiveness on the part of subjects (or their significant others) or treatment providers, if they are randomly assigned.
- Strong preferences for certain treatments on the part of subjects or treatment providers; reliance on reactive outcome measures.
- Outcomes that reflect satisfaction or psychological states.
- Treatments that require of subjects a high level of motivation.
- Processes that link treatments to outcomes, in which motivation is key.
- A combination of self-report outcomes and a treatment that—in contrast to the control condition—heightens either (1) treatment subjects' awareness or recognition of outcome behaviors or (2) their perceptions of the social desirability associated with outcome behaviors.

Biasing Social Interactions: Between Subjects or between Subjects and Outsiders

In Table 4.3, we distinguish two subcategories of biasing social interactions involving study subjects. The first, in the top half of the table, consists of *interactions between treatment and control subjects* that result in "contamination" across groups. An example might be a preteenage subject who is randomly assigned to the control group of a study assessing the impact of a smoking prevention program but whose attitudes and behavior are affected, directly or indirectly, by his best friend, who is assigned to the treatment condition.

The potential for contamination based on interaction between treatment and control subjects has received considerable attention in the literature (see, for example, Shadish et al., 2002). As is often pointed out, in a randomly formed intervention group, subjects or treatment providers may intentionally "pass on" the intervention to (and thus "contaminate") members of the control group (Table 4.3, item 1), especially if treatment subjects are in the same social network as controls. (This is least likely when large clusters are randomly assigned. In some cases, however, social networks may span clusters, or subjects may cross over from a treatment to a control cluster partway through the study.[8]) To the extent that this bias process occurs, dilution or underestimation of the treatment impact is the likely result.

TABLE 4.3. Biasing Social Interactions: Specific Sources and Key Descriptors

Specific source	Key descriptor		
	Process: how bias can occur	Support: what underlies our belief that bias can occur	Bias: likely direction

Interaction among subjects

1. Treatment subjects "pass on" an intervention to controls (diffusion, contamination)	In one example, randomly selected students were warned about plagiarism while others were not; the warning's apparent lack of impact may have resulted from students' communicating with one another.	Extensive literature: for example, Weinstein & Dobkin (2002, citing Braumoeller & Gaines, 2001)	Dilution or understatement of effect
2. Two or more persons engage in the outcome behavior jointly—at least one in treatment and one in control	If a friendship network includes members of the intervention and control groups, treatment and control subjects may engage in joint (multiperson) activities or influence one another by example.	Studies: show that some outcomes involve joint actions (e.g., Shaw & McKay, 1931)	Dilution or understatement of effect[a]
3. A control's behavior may be influenced by treatment group friends' modeling a behavior change, and a treatment subject's behavior change (or lack of change) may be influenced by control group friends' reactions	Where subcultures denigrate school achievement or glorify violence, nonintervention peers (e.g., random controls not exposed to the treatment) may ridicule intervention subjects who improve behavior.	Logic: Weiss (2002)	Dilution or understatement of effect

Interaction between study participants and outsiders

4. Negative labeling of intervention group subjects	In the Cambridge–Somerville Youth Study, some adults labeled boys receiving the treatment predelinquent. For example, a school nurse asked a teen subject, "What's wrong with you?"	Studies: one or more show outsider labeling occurs (e.g., Powers & Witmer, 1951).	Understatement of effect
5. Positive labeling of intervention group subjects	Teen boys may label teen girls participating in a sex abstinence program "chaste," and may "chase after" other girls.	Logic: Metcalf (1997)	Inflation of effect

[a]For example, skipping school decreased as a result of mentoring in a study that randomized same-school sixth-grade classrooms (Rogers & Taylor, 1997), but the positive impact of the intervention may have been understated. The logic is that two or more students may decide together to skip school (or not to skip school).

In a somewhat similar form of contamination, less emphasized in the literature, members of intervention and control groups pursue outcome behaviors jointly. For example, if one teenager is randomly assigned to an intervention designed to prevent delinquency, while his close friend is assigned to the control condition, they may subsequently make "co-mingled decisions" to jointly engage in delinquent outcome behaviors. Again, the result is dilution or understatement of the treatment effect. How likely are joint behaviors? The answer may depend on the outcomes in question. As first documented by Shaw and McKay (1931), teen delinquents appearing in court typically have peer accomplices; more recently, Haynie (2001) reports that various surveys have pointed to the often social, nonsolitary nature of youthful delinquent behaviors.

A related version of biasing interaction between subjects involves the process of behavior change—and the potential for undermining it when "best friends" are randomly assigned to treatment versus control. Suppose that an intervention subject begins to change his or her attitudes and behavior in response to a treatment program—for example, begins to reject violence or pursue school achievement. (See Table 4.3, item 3, citing Weiss, 2002.) Suppose further that the subject is an opinion leader who, by example, influences friends in the control group. Additionally, a control group member could logically be affected by even "second-hand" learning about the behavior changes of one or more intervention subjects in his or her social network—particularly if some of the intervention subjects changing their behaviors happen to be "opinion leaders." The potential for this sort of interpersonal influence is suggested by a study documenting similar study habits of randomly assigned college roommates (Sacerdote, 2001).

Although the literature has more often discussed the potential for a treatment group to influence controls, the reverse may occur. For example, suppose that a treatment subject who changes behavior is, as a result, negatively labeled by a "best friend" in the control group. The likely outcome would be to dilute subsequent treatment–control comparisons on study outcomes.[9]

Turning to *interaction between study participants and study outsiders* in their environment (bottom half of Table 4.3), we see that bias can occur if outsiders differentially label treatment and control subjects. In one version of this, outsiders may negatively label subjects in the intervention group relative to controls (possibly lumping controls together with other persons who are not in the study). For example, study outsiders may perceive boys who are receiving a delinquency prevention intervention as predelinquents—a situation that can affect treatment group boys in terms of their interactions with the labelers and, ultimately, their own self-image. In the Cambridge–Somerville Youth Study, a boy in the intervention group told investigators, "I began to wonder if there was something wrong with me," after a school nurse, questioning why he was in the study, asked him, "Well, what's wrong with you?" (Powers & Witmer, 1951, p. 31). The likely differential impact on treatment and controls in this example is based on the fact that it was easy for study outsiders to identify boys in the treatment group, because of the treatment activities; such boys were negatively labeled. By contrast, participation by boys in the control group appears to have been generally "invisible."

A number of variations are possible, depending on the circumstances. Positive labeling of an intervention group can occur. Differential labeling can occur when outsiders are aware of *both* treatment and control group membership, as suggested in Table 4.3, item 5.

This discussion suggests that, more often than not, social interaction biases probably tend to dilute or understate an intervention's benefit—although the reverse is possible in some circumstances.

Turning to indicators of study vulnerability to biasing social interactions, a preliminary list of candidate indicators, based on items in Table 4.3, would include the following:

- Randomization splits a social group or social network, especially if it splits best friends or family members or if some subjects are opinion leaders.
- The treatment is easily passed on from one person to another (e.g., by word of mouth); outcome behaviors are often engaged in jointly.
- Subjects are vulnerable to peer influence (as in teenage years) and may imitate friends' behaviors.
- Treatment activities signal (to others) treatment subjects' participation in the study.
- There is public openness regarding assignments to treatment and control (outsiders not "blinded").
- Outsiders may react to knowledge of subjects' study participation or to their categorization in treatment versus control groups.

Assessing and Countering Study Vulnerability

One strategy for enhancing assessments of bias vulnerability is to develop and use a reference *checklist* or provisional set of *starter questions* about a study. Such a tool could be based on the candidate indicators of study vulnerability listed in the previous sections of this chapter.

Readers or reviewers could use a provisional checklist either retrospectively, when striving to evaluate a completed study or set of studies, or prospectively, when making a thorough effort to anticipate possible pitfalls so as to improve the design of a randomized social policy study. (We would caution, however, that relying on a reference checklist or set of starter questions as more than helper tools—that is, as more than adjuncts to a larger understanding of bias vulnerability within the conditions of an individual study—could represent less than the highest standard of assessment. We also note that many of the tools described in this section could potentially be used with quasi-experimental studies as well with the randomized studies that are the focus of this chapter.)

Additionally, study investigators, having prospectively determined that some vulnerability most likely exists, might decide to pursue an ancillary strategy of *concurrent bias assessment*. These two assessment strategies—checklists and concurrent bias assessment—are discussed below.

Various checklists have been used to rate study quality (e.g., Chalmers et al., 1981). The strategy suggested here is somewhat analogous, but the goal is not to achieve a rating score. The goal is to raise the consciousness of investigators or readers and reviewers—to help them think more thoroughly about and to better understand the nature of bias vulnerability. Thus, we anticipate that some questions on a bias assessment checklist might stimulate further questions, new questions not on the initial checklist, or a set of starter questions. Further, some answers to the starter questions might point to the need for further investigation, consultation with experts, or data collection.

After prospectively determining that it is likely that vulnerability exists in one or more of the two general bias source categories, a randomized study investigator might decide to pursue an ancillary strategy of assessing bias concurrently with the main activity. The two major alternatives for implementing concurrent bias assessment are (1) bias assessment questions for study participants and, in some cases, their significant others or study outsiders, to be implemented as checks throughout the randomized study and (2) a qualitative, possibly ethnographic, side study to assess randomized study biases.[10]

With respect to the first concurrent assessment strategy, a bias assessment flow chart analogous to a program logic model could be constructed. The difference is that, while program logic models are often based on program managers' views about how a program works (see McLaughlin & Jordan, 1999), bias assessment would be based on an evaluator's understanding of bias vulnerability and methodological risks.

The second concurrent assessment strategy would incorporate qualitative research such as ethnography or qualitative interviews. The specific strategy of building separate ethnographic efforts into each "arm" of a randomized study has been put forward (Sherman & Strang, 2004). Within the context of this paper, using this strategy would have as its goal bias assessment—uncovering and elucidating potential study biases based on the attitudes, preferences, and social relationships of subjects and treatment providers. Ethnography is suitable because it focuses on understanding the perspectives of study participants (Harrell et al., 2002).

A somewhat similar but less time-consuming approach would be to add qualitative tape-recorded interviews to obtain subjects' perspectives, as at the conclusion of a study. A qualitative-interview add-on approach was implemented in a randomized study examining treatment for back pain and using structured questionnaire self-reports as the main outcome measures (Evans, Maiers, & Bronfort, 2003). The qualitative interviews elucidated patients' interpretations of "satisfaction" with treatment and "improvement"—that is, the meaning and importance of these terms to the patients.

Limited reports of add-on bias assessment strategies are available, but the idea is not new. For example, some Hawthorne studies supplemented workplace experiments with extensive interviewing and observation (Tashakkori & Teddlie, 2003, citing Roethlisberger & Dickson, 1939). More recently, combining quantitative and qualitative work (Greene & Caracelli, 1997; Tashakkori & Teddlie, 2003) appears to have been steadily gaining recognition as a way of obtaining information additional to that provided by traditional approaches.

Specific design approaches may help counter or even potentially eliminate biases in each of the two bias source areas discussed in this chapter. As described below, these design approaches are intended to control or minimize reactive biases and minimize social interaction effects.

MINIMIZING DIFFERENTIAL REACTIVITY

As previously discussed, reactive biases may be based in either (1) randomized subjects' (and in some cases treatment providers') preexisting differential perceptions about the effectiveness of the intervention as compared with the control condition, for example, or (2) during-study sensitization to outcomes in the intervention but not in the control group. Either way, an effective countermeasure would be to substitute blinded coders for more reactive and thus more vulnerable measures. For example, a violence prevention study used playground observers to code children's aggressive behaviors; the coders did not know which schools received the intervention and which were controls (Stoolmiller, Eddy, & Reid, 2000).

When it is not feasible to use blinded coders or observers, as may happen in many social policy studies, investigators may draw on a variety of alternative data collection strategies to minimize or mitigate reactive biases. A variety of unobtrusive or nonreactive outcome measures may be feasible (Webb et al., 2000). Adding such a measure—which should either represent or be correlated with an outcome of interest— avoids exclusive reliance on subjects' self-reports or an investigator's judgments. Nonreactive measures include

1. Administrative records pertaining to study participants (an example was individual students' school attendance records supplementing self-reports of problem behaviors in a randomized study in which elderly volunteers mentored sixth-grade students (LoSciuto, Rajala, Townsend, & Taylor, 1996; Rogers & Taylor, 1997).

2. Physical or biological tests, such as breath samples, that may be taken together with self-reports concerning tobacco use (Botvin et al., 1995).

3. Psychological tests that indirectly measure subjects' attitudes or orientations, such as the Implicit Association Test (Nosek, Greenwald, & Banaji, 2005).

Other more creative approaches (perhaps to be used on a sample of subjects) can test the validity of self-reports. One example was that, following a self-report survey of college students' delinquent behavior, Clark and Tifft (1966) paid students $8 for a follow-up interview, at which time the usual questionnaire approach was tested by offering subjects the chance to change their answers and then conducting a polygraph test on the same questions.[11]

The successful use of these strategies for collecting data on outcomes has potential barriers. For example:

1. Reasonably complete and reliable records may not exist, and other nonreactive measures (such as breath samples or psychological tests) may not be relevant or available.

2. Some administrative records may be vulnerable to biasing influence by study outsiders who become aware of subjects' study participation or assignment.[12]

3. Use of the relevant records or special tests may be sensitive or deemed intrusive, which may either rule out their use altogether or at least require subjects' permission. Requiring their permission may create two further problems. If permission is not obtained in a substantial num-

ber of cases, the results may be suspect, and if permission is obtained in advance, the "unobtrusive" measure may become a reactive one. For example, a subject who prospectively gives permission to access certain sources of medical records may, under certain circumstances, avoid seeking medical help from those sources. (However, if whole organizations are randomized to alternative conditions, it might be possible to use summary statistics based on records for whole schools, for example, rather than individuals and avoid the need to obtain permission from individuals. Additionally, special techniques for masked data sharing may be useful in some randomized studies [see Government Accountability Office, 2001, citing Boruch & Cecil, 1979, and Spruill & Gastwirth, 1982].)

4. In some cases, these approaches may be prohibited by cost, complexity, controversy, or overall difficulty of implementation.

Seemingly easier but potentially less effective data collection strategies that might, to some extent, help address self-report bias include self-reporting outcomes anonymously, using diaries, and staff corroborating subjects' self-reports. For example:

1. Anonymous self-reporting means no names on questionnaires—simply identification of whether each subject-respondent is treatment or control. Investigators may limit anonymity to only some measures or only some subjects. For example, a randomized study aimed at reducing violence among middle school students (Orpinas et al., 2000) used self-report surveys that were anonymous for just eighth graders. For those students, a cross-sectional evaluation was conducted; responses from most other students were not anonymous, and these allowed evaluation of the intervention, based on repeated measures for individuals. (Logically, anonymity might help address the social desirability issue but would not address the issue of consciousness raising and heightened awareness and recall.)

2. Diaries may encourage the accuracy of self-reports. For example, a randomized study in which the intervention encouraged sedentary expectant mothers to increase physical activity asked subjects to (a) use a pedometer to count steps taken and (b) observe the step-counts and record them accurately in a daily diary questionnaire (N. L. Fahrenwald, personal communication with Judith A. Droitcour, 2004; Fahrenwald, Atwood, Walker, Johnson, & Berg, 2004).

3. Some value staff corroboration of subjects' reports. For example, in a randomized study assessing an intervention aimed at reducing teens' risky sex practices (Philliber, Kaye, Herrling, & West, 2002), staff mem-

bers who had developed rapport with the teens in the intervention group corroborated their self-reports.

Nevertheless, if a randomized study relies on self-reports—without blinding, without adding nonreactive measures, and without other corroboration on at least a sample of responses—then there is a potential risk that the results may not reflect the true impact of the intervention.

For randomized studies that are vulnerable to preference biases and a resultant lack of motivation, lack of satisfaction, and so forth, a randomized three-group preference design (Long, Little, & Lin, 2004) provides a strategy for unbiased assessment. This three-group design, which is relevant when substantial numbers of subjects prefer each of the alternative treatments, randomizes subjects to Group 1: treatment A; Group 2: alternative treatment or control B; and Group 3: a preference arm in which subjects choose between A and B.

All subjects are also asked which treatment condition they prefer. The difference is that for Group 3 subjects' answers will determine their treatment. For Groups 1 and 2, the information is for research purposes only. The comparisons facilitated by this design allow the assessment of preference effects.[13]

MINIMIZING SOCIAL INTERACTION BIASES

As indicated above, social interaction sources of bias in randomized studies can be categorized as involving primarily interactions between study participants or interactions between study participants and study outsiders. For biases deriving from interaction between study participants, an effective remedy is random assignment of clusters—at an appropriate level of clustering and, where needed, with adequate geographic dispersion. Cluster assignment involves units of allocation larger than a single individual—whole families, classrooms, schools, communities (Boruch & Foley, 2000). Entire clusters are randomly assigned to alternative treatments. When the goals of a cluster assignment design include isolating the intervention and control groups—in order to prevent interaction between them—the clusters should be defined and selected so that relevant social networks are fully contained within clusters and do not reach across them. This means that the investigator must (1) define an appropriate level of clustering and, in some cases, also (2) select geographically dispersed clusters.

To illustrate a level of clustering that appears to be *inadequate* to isolate intervention and control groups in some studies, we can look at a study evaluating a mentoring approach (aimed at preventing problem behaviors) that selected three sixth-grade classrooms within each of several participating schools (Rogers & Taylor, 1997). Within each school, the three classes were randomized to three alternative treatments. Logically, it seems possible that sixth-grade children's social networks cross classes in the same school, as, for example, when children who live next door to one another are in different classrooms. For example, two sixth graders in different classrooms deciding to skip school together potentially dilute the estimated effect of the intervention.[14]

In some cases, defining units of allocation as relatively large clusters, such as schools, may not ensure isolation of intervention and control subjects or treatment providers. In such cases, it may be necessary to select geographically diverse clusters. For example, a previously mentioned study aimed at violence reduction randomized eight schools to alternative treatments (Orpinas et al., 2000), but all eight schools were in the same school district. At the four intervention schools, violence reduction strategies included, among others, training students to be peer mediators and peer helpers, training teachers in conflict resolution, and sending newsletters to parents. During the course of the 3-year study, 36% of students transferred out of participating schools, and teacher turnover was also high (more than 50% at one of the four intervention schools). The investigators questioned whether some teachers and students from intervention schools may have moved to control schools; unfortunately, the investigators were not able to track actual crossovers (because of budget problems). To the extent that students and teachers who left intervention schools crossed over to control schools, the study is vulnerable to cross-contamination through social interaction.

Another alternative would be to define very large clusters—whole communities—as units of allocation. This has been done, for example, in studies of the effectiveness of media campaigns designed to prevent teens' cigarette use (Boruch & Foley, 2000, citing LaPrelle, Bauman, & Koch, 1992). In sum, the larger or more widely dispersed the clusters, the less likely it is that members of intervention and control groups will interact. Of course, whether very large or widely dispersed clusters are actually needed will depend on features of the study participants' social networks and their mobility patterns.

Using random cluster assignment may carry certain disadvantages. Some have pointed to issues of statistical power (Boruch & Foley, 2000). Others have suggested that investigators *avoid* randomizing whole-school clusters in order to address some schools' concerns that their students not be denied a promising intervention. For example, a participant in a 2004 National Academy of Sciences workshop said that the Power4Kids study partially addressed this concern through a design that ensured that "in each participating school, some students will receive the tutorials, while a control group will continue to receive conventional instruction" (National Research Council, 2004, p. 14). But in fielding some studies, it may be necessary to weigh school recruitment concerns against the potential for contamination from interaction between intervention and control study participants.

For social interaction effects involving *contacts between study participants and study outsiders*, the concern is that outsiders may label participants—whether positively or negatively. Labeling seems to follow from a situation in which only some persons within a natural group are assigned to a treatment. In other words, labeling might occur whenever a substantial number of persons in a cluster do not participate in the intervention.

Combining random assignment of relatively large clusters with broad or "universal" recruiting would address this problem, provided that the recruiting is effective. The disadvantages would be likely to be the same as those that pertain to cluster assignment, discussed above.

CONCLUSIONS

The exploratory work reported here suggests three conclusions, with caveats based on the limited scope of our work. The first conclusion is that randomized studies of social policy alternatives—particularly those assessing teen prevention programs—may be vulnerable to differential reactivity or biasing social interactions or both. An important caveat to this conclusion is that we have not systematically examined the importance of these biases overall or for specific social policy areas. However, systematic studies may be justified.

The second conclusion is that, at least in some areas of study, rigorous evaluation requires special efforts to assess and counter differential reactivity and biasing social interactions. Without such efforts, a strong emphasis on randomized social policy studies could fall short of the promise of knowledge improvement and evidence-based policy suggested by those who have championed randomized studies—at least in some policy areas. This also argues for systematic efforts to assess the importance of biases other than selection bias in social policy studies.

The third conclusion is that investigators, readers, and reviewers can

- Assess randomized studies' vulnerability to differential reactivity and bias social interactions, with help of a checklist, or explicate studies' vulnerability through multimethod designs for bias assessment.
- Minimize their vulnerability with randomized study designs that target specific biases.

We are optimistic, but cautiously so, because the biases listed in this chapter may not represent a comprehensive list, and we have not assessed the capacity of the evaluation field—or various social science disciplines—to undertake high-quality randomized designs that target specific biases.

ACKOWLEDGMENT

In expressing their views in this chapter, the authors have not necessarily represented the views of the U.S. Government Accountability Office, the National Opinion Research Center, or the University of Chicago.

NOTES

1. While this chapter focuses on the issue of biases additional to selection bias, other evaluators have responded to the new emphasis on randomized studies by highlighting (a) the need to balance the focus on program impact (implied by a strong call for more randomized studies) against the pursuit of a wider variety of evaluation questions and (b) the need to consider the varied conditions under which fielding randomized studies may not be appropriate (e.g., where clear evidence of a benefit already exists—or could be successfully demonstrated—without a randomized study).

2. That is, "If the reactive effect is plausibly differential, then it may generate a pseudodifference" in outcomes, which threatens a conclusion regarding the impact of an intervention "quite apart from external validity" concerns (Webb et al., 2000, pp. 14–15, citing French, 1955).

3. Such interpersonal interactions involve, but are not necessarily limited to, study participants.

4. Other, less well established, bias-source categories, not covered here, may also be relevant—for example, in some interventions, randomization may interfere with an intended process empowerment through choice (see Ford & Regoli, 1993).

5. For a conceptual framework categorizing biases according to impacts on various types of validity (rather than categorizing according to the bias source), see Shadish et al. (2002). Logically, an advantage of considering bias in terms of its *source* is that this may facilitate (a) assessing studies for vulnerability and (b) identifying targeted strategies for minimizing bias.

6. This included methodological texts and articles, reports of randomized social policy studies, reviews of randomized studies, and studies of social behaviors that may be used as outcomes in social policy studies.

7. Potentially, disappointed subjects (or their significant others) may also try to compensate for a perceived disadvantage relative to treatment subjects—a process termed "compensatory equalization" (Shadish et al., 2002). For

example, the parents of preschoolers randomly assigned to *not* receive a special program might seek a substitute program elsewhere. From a social program perspective, this result could be instructive. From a scientific perspective, however, the study would not provide information on outcomes resulting from the presence or absence of a general type of treatment.

8. In one study, investigators found that a treatment-school principal was married to a control-school teacher (Cook & Payne, 2002). In another study, some students trained to be peer advisers in a violence prevention program moved from their intervention school to a control school, raising the potential for at least some level of contamination (Orpinas et al., 2000).

9. A somewhat related effect may occur during the treatment, as, for example, when friends are assigned to the same "guided group interaction" program—versus not (see Valente, Hoffman, Ritt-Olson, Lichtman, & Johnson, 2003).

10. Ethnographic studies emphasize the perspectives of the people in the research setting (LeCompte & Schensul, 1999). Ethnographic research is inductive, involves face-to-face interaction with participants to establish researcher–participant trust, and may combine several data collection approaches, such as participant observation, open-ended questioning, quantitative data collection, and, if appropriate, collection of relevant artifacts.

11. The original answers had been previously recorded.

12. As previously mentioned, for example, adults may deal with an apparent incident of delinquent behavior by reporting youngsters to police or by handling it informally. Such decisions may be influenced by adults' knowledge about a young person's study participation. Study participation may be more obvious for subjects in the intervention group than for those in the control group.

13. Obviously, there is a cost in terms of the sample size requirement for a given level of precision.

14. The exception would be for outcomes measured before class was dismissed—for example, short-term attitude change or comprehension of a lesson.

REFERENCES

Boruch, R. F. (2005). Preface: Better evaluation for evidence-based policy: Place randomized trials in education, criminology, welfare, and health. *Annals of the American Academy of Political and Social Science, 599,* 6–18.

Boruch, R. F., & Cecil, J. S. (1979). *Assuring the confidentiality of social research data.* Philadelphia: University of Pennsylvania Press.

Boruch, R. F., & Foley, E. (2000). The honestly experimental society: Sites and other entities as the units of allocation and analysis in randomized trials. In L. Bickman (Ed.), *Validity and experimentation: Donald Campbell's legacy* (pp. 193–238). Thousand Oaks, CA: Sage.

Boruch, R. F., de Moya, D., & Snyder, B. (2002). The importance of randomized field trials in education and related areas. In F. Mosteller & R. F. Boruch (Eds.), *Evidence matters: Randomized trials in education research* (pp. 50–79). Washington, DC: Brookings Institution Press.

Botvin, G. J., Baker, E., Dusenbury, L., Botvin, E. M., & Diaz, T. (1995). Long-term follow-up results of a randomized drug abuse prevention trial in a white middle-class population. *Journal of the American Medical Association, 273*(14), 1106–1112.

Braumoeller, B. F., & Gaines, B. J. (2001). Actions do speak louder than words: Deterring plagiarism with the use of plagiarism-detecting software. *PS: Political Science and Politics, 34,* 835–839.

Cahalan, D. (1968). Correlates of respondent accuracy in the Denver validity survey. *Public Opinion Quarterly, 32,* 607–621.

Campbell, D. T., & Stanley, J. C. (1963). Experimental and quasi-experimental designs for research on teaching. In N. L. Gage (Ed.), *Handbook of research on teaching* (pp. 171–246). Chicago: Rand McNally.

Campbell, D. T., & Stanley, J. C. (1966). *Experimental and quasi-experimental designs f J. C. or research.* Chicago: Rand McNally.

Chalmers, T. C., Smith, H., Jr., Blackburn, B., Silverman, B., Schroeder, B., et al. (1981). A method for assessing the quality of a randomized control trial. *Controlled Clinical Trials, 2*(1), 31–49.

Clark, J. P., & Tifft, L. L. (1966). Polygraph and interview validation of self-reported delinquent behavior. *American Sociological Review, 31,* 516–523.

Cook, T. D., & Campbell, D. T. (1979). *Quasi-experimentation: Design and analysis for field settings.* Chicago: Rand McNally.

Cook, T. D., & Payne, M. R. (2002). Objecting to the objections to using random assignment in educational research. In F. Mosteller & R. F. Boruch (Eds.), *Evidence matters: Randomized trials in education research* (pp. 150–178). Washington, DC: Brookings Institution Press.

Corrigan, P. W., & Salzer, M. S. (2003). The conflict between random assignment and treatment preference: Implications for internal validity. *Evaluation and Program Planning, 26,* 109–121.

Datta, L. (1997). Multimethod evaluations: Using case studies together with other methods. In E. Chelimsky & W. R. Shadish (Eds.), *Evaluation for the 21st century: A handbook* (pp. 344–359). Thousand Oaks, CA: Sage.

Droitcour, J. (1997). Cross-design synthesis: Concept and application. In E. Chelimsky & W. R. Shadish (Eds.), *Evaluation for the 21st century: A handbook* (pp. 360–372). Thousand Oaks, CA: Sage.

Evans, R. L., Maiers, M. J., & Bronfort, G. (2003). What do patients think?: Results of a mixed methods pilot study assessing sciatica patients' interpretations of satisfaction and improvement. *Journal of Manipulative and Physiological Therapeutics, 26,* 502–509.

Fahrenwald, N. L., Atwood, J. R., Walker, S. N., Johnson, D. R., & Berg, K. (2004). A randomized pilot test of "Moms on the Move": A physical activity intervention for WIC mothers. *Annals of Behavioral Medicine, 27*(2), 82–90.

Fallowfield, L. J., Hall, A., Maguire, G. P., & Baum, M. (1990). Psychological outcomes of different treatment policies in women with early breast cancer outside a clinical trial. *British Medical Journal, 301*(6752), 575–580.

Fetterman, D. M. (1982). Ibsen's baths: Reactivity and insensitivity (a misapplication of the treatment-control design in a national evaluation). *Educational Evaluation and Policy Analysis, 4*, 261–279.

Ford, D. A., & Regoli, M. J. (1993). The criminal prosecution of wife assaulters: Process, problems, and effects. In N. Z. Hilton (Ed.), *Legal responses to wife assault: Current trends and evaluation* (pp. 151–157). Thousand Oaks, CA: Sage.

French, E. G. (1955). Some characteristics of achievement motivation. *Journal of Experimental Psychology, 50*, 232–236.

Government Accountability Office. (2001). *Record linkage and privacy: Issues in creating new federal research and statistical information* (GAO-01-126SP). Washington, DC: Author.

Greene, J. C., & Caracelli, V. J. (Eds.). (1997). *Advances in mixed-method evaluation: The challenges and benefits of integrating diverse paradigms* (New Directions for Evaluation no. 74). San Francisco: Jossey-Bass.

Greene, J. C., Caracelli, V. J., & Graham, W. F. (1989). Toward a conceptual framework for multimethod evaluation designs. *Educational Evaluation and Policy Analysis, 11*, 255–274.

Harrell, A. V. (1985). Validation of self-report: The research record. In B. A. Rouse, N. J. Kozel, & L. G. Richards (Eds.), *Self-report methods of estimating drug use: Meeting current challenges to validity* (pp. 12–21). Rockville, MD: National Institute on Drug Abuse.

Harrell, A. V., Burt, M., Hatry, H., Rossman, S., Roth, J., & Sabol, W. (2002). Evaluation strategies for human service programs: A guide for policymakers and providers. In J. Buck & J. Butts. *National youth court center evaluation and grant writing training seminar: Evaluation session* (app. B). Washington, DC: Urban Institute. Available at *www.bja.evaluationwebsite. org/html/documents/evaluation_strategies.html.*

Haynie, D. L. (2001). Delinquent peers revisited: Does network structure matter? *American Journal of Sociology, 106*, 1013–1058.

Hoza, B. (2001). Psychosocial treatment issues in the MTA: A reply to Greene and Ablon. *Journal of Clinical Child Psychology, 30*, 126–130.

Hyman, H. (1944). Do they tell the truth? *Public Opinion Quarterly, 8*, 557–559.

LaPrelle, J., Bauman, K. E., & Koch, G. G. (1992). High intercommunity variation in adolescent cigarette smoking in a 10-community field experiment. *Education Review, 16*, 115–130.

LeCompte, M. D., & Schensul, J. (1999). *The ethnographer's toolkit: Book 1. Designing and conducting ethnographic research.* Littlefield, NJ: AltaMira Press.

Long, Q., Little, R., & Lin, X. (2004). *Causal inference in hybrid intervention trials involving treatment choice* (University of Michigan Department of Biostatistics working paper series, paper 34). Available at *www.bepress. com/umichbiostat/paper34.*

LoSciuto, L., Rajala, A. K., Townsend, T. N., & Taylor, A. S. (1996). An outcome evaluation of across ages: An intergenerational mentoring approach to drug prevention. *Journal of Adolescent Research, 11,* 116–129.

McCall, R. B., & Green, B. L. (2004). Beyond the methodological gold standards of behavioral research: Considerations for practice and policy. *Social Policy Report, 18,* 3–19.

McLaughlin, J. A., & Jordan, G. B. (1999). Logic models: A tool for telling your program's performance story. *Evaluation and Program Planning, 22,* 65–72.

Metcalf, C. E. (1997). The advantages of experimental designs for evaluating sex education programs. *Children and Youth Services Review, 19,* 507–523.

Moffitt, R. A. (2004). The role of randomized field trials in social science research: A perspective from evaluations of reforms of social welfare programs. *American Behavioral Scientist, 47,* 506–540.

National Research Council. (1991). *Evaluating AIDS prevention programs: Expanded edition.* Washington, DC: National Academy Press.

National Research Council. (2002). *Scientific research in education.* Washington, DC: National Academy Press.

National Research Council. (2004). *Implementing randomized field trials in education: Report of a workshop.* Washington, DC: National Academy Press.

Nosek, B. A., Greenwald, A. G., & Banaji, M. R. (2005). Understanding and using the Implicit Association Test: II. Method variables and construct validity. *Personality and Social Psychology Bulletin, 31*(2), 166–180.

Orpinas, P., Kelder, S., Frankowski, R., Murray, N., Zhang, Q., & McAlister, A. (2000). Outcome evaluation of a multi-component violence-prevention program for middle schools: The Students for Peace project. *Health Education Research, 15*(1), 45–58.

Philliber, S., Kaye, J. W., Herrling, S., & West, E. (2002). Preventing pregnancy and improving health care access among teenagers: An evaluation of the Children's Aid Society–Carrera program. *Perspectives on Sexual and Reproductive Health, 34,* 244–251.

Powers, E., & Witmer, H. (1951). *An experiment in the prevention of delinquency: The Cambridge–Somerville youth study.* New York: Columbia University Press.

Roethlisberger, F. J., & Dickson, W. J. (1939). *Management and the worker.* Cambridge, MA: Harvard University Press.

Rogers, A. M., & Taylor, A. S. (1997). Intergenerational mentoring: A viable strategy for meeting the needs of vulnerable youth. *Journal of Gerontological Social Work, 28,* 125–140.

Rubin, D. B. (1986). Comment: Which ifs have causal answers. *Journal of the American Statistical Association, 81,* 961–962.

Sacerdote, B. (2001). Peer effects with random assignment: Results for Dartmouth roommates. *Quarterly Journal of Economics, 116,* 681–704.

Shadish, W. R. (1993). Critical multiplism: A research strategy and its attendant tactics. *New Directions in Evaluation, 60,* 1–57.

Shadish, W. R., Cook, T. D., & Campbell, D. T. (2002). *Experimental and quasi-*

experimental designs for generalized causal inference. New York: Houghton Mifflin.

Shaw, C. R., & McKay, H. D. (1931). *Report on the causes of crime: Vol. 2. Social factors in delinquency.* Washington, DC: Government Printing Office.

Sherman, L. W., & Strang, H. (2004). Experimental ethnography: The marriage of qualitative and quantitative research. *Annals of the American Academy of Political and Social Science, 595*(1), 204–222.

Spruill, N. L., & Gastwirth, J. L. (1982). On the estimation of the correlation coefficient from grouped data. *Journal of the American Statistical Association, 77,* 614–620.

Stoolmiller, M., Eddy, J. M., & Reid, J. B. (2000). Detecting and describing preventive intervention effects in a universal school-based randomized trial targeting delinquent and violent behavior. *Journal of Consulting and Clinical Psychology, 68,* 296–306.

Sudman, S., & Bradburn, N. M. (1974). *Response effects in surveys: A review and synthesis.* Chicago: Aldine.

Tashakkori, A., & Teddlie, C. (Eds.). (2003). *Handbook of mixed methods in social and behavioral research.* Thousand Oaks, CA: Sage.

Valente, T., Hoffman, B. R., Ritt-Olson, A., Lichtman, K., & Johnson, C. A. (2003). Effects of a social-network method for group assignment strategies on peer-led tobacco prevention programs in schools. *American Journal of Public Health, 93*(11), 1837–1843.

Webb, E., Campbell, D. T., Schwartz, R. D., & Sechrest, L. (2000). *Unobtrusive measures* (rev. ed.). Thousand Oaks, CA: Sage.

Weinstein, J. W., & Dobkin, C. E. (2002). *Plagiarism in U.S. higher education: Estimating internet plagiarism rates and testing a means of deterrence.* Paper prepared under graduate student grant, Center for Studies in Higher Education, University of California, Berkeley, CA. Available at *scholar. google.com/scholar?hl=en&lr=&q=cache:ZVi8Aly_5_UJ:webdisk.berkeley. edu/~Weinstein/Weinstein-JobMarketPaper.PDF+author:%22Weinstein%22 +intitle:%22Plagiarism+in+US+Higher+Education:+Estimating+Internet+... %22+.*

Weiss, C. H. (1968). Validity of welfare mothers' interview responses. *Public Opinion Quarterly, 32,* 622–633.

Weiss, C. H. (2002). What to do until the random assigner comes. In F. Mosteller & R. Boruch (Eds.), *Evidence matters: Randomized trials in education research* (pp. 198–224). Washington, DC: Brookings Institution Press.

CHAPTER 5

Research Synthesis
Toward Broad-Based Evidence

SUSAN N. LABIN

Research synthesis is a type of secondary data analysis that aggregates findings from primary research. It establishes a base of current knowledge and illuminates directions for future policies, programs, and research. This chapter presents various types of research syntheses. It also demonstrates the precedent for and presents advantages of research syntheses with broad inclusion criteria. Such broadly defined research syntheses include data from a variety of different kinds of data sources and research designs. Examples of such syntheses include the Cross-Design Synthesis developed at the General Accountability Office (GAO) (General Accounting Office, 1992a; Droitcour, 1997), and the *Guide to Community Preventive Services* (Briss, Brownson, Fielding, Zaza, 2004; Briss et al., 2000) developed by the Centers for Disease Control and used by them as well as a number of other agencies in the U.S. Department of Health and Human Services (DHHS), some separate federal agencies, and myriad independent organizations and associations.

In contrast to these broadly defined inclusive research syntheses, some syntheses have more restrictive inclusion criteria. For example, currently meta-analysis usually includes only data from the randomized control trial (RCT) design. Since meta-analysis is the best known and most widely used type of research synthesis, its tendency to use only data from RCTs has significant implications not only for synthesizing existing research but also for funding, methods, and practices of new primary research. Because of these far-reaching implications of inclusion criteria of research syntheses, I consider it a fundamental issue for evaluation.

This chapter begins by briefly describing the background and history of methods for primary research and their relevance for research synthesis. A typology describes and contrasts major features of various types of reviews. The research synthesis differs from traditional reviews in its emphasis on systematic decision rules. Research syntheses are further described by delineating their purposes and common methodological steps. Meta-analysis and broadly defined inclusive syntheses are then further specified and contrasted.

The most controversial of the inclusion criteria is the restriction in current meta-analysis to select only data from RCTs. Therefore, the limitations of RCTs and methods to address some of these limitations are explored, as well as some empirical differences between the findings from RCTs and quasi-experimental designs. The conclusions and recommendations are directed toward further development and usage of broad-based research synthesis methods.

BACKGROUND AND HISTORY
OF RESEARCH METHODOLOGIES

Brief History of Primary Evaluation Methods

The RCT derives from laboratory and field methods from the physical and biological sciences and is most often assumed to be the "gold standard" for assessing causal effects in social research. This was manifested during the 1960s, when the RCT methodology was utilized for evaluating the War on Poverty and other Johnson-era social interventions (Rossi, Freeman, & Lipsey, 1999).

The primacy of RCTs for evaluating social programs continued unchallenged through the 1970s (Labin, 1980). However, during the 1980s, the inability of rigorous designs and methods such as the RCT to document positive program results when social program staff and clients attested to the effectiveness of a program, led to the flourishing of alternative approaches. Some funders and practitioners turned away from scientific "research" exemplified by the RCT, rejected its model of external "arms-length, unbiased objectivity," and sought insider knowledge through collaborative methods (Green, 2004; Minkler, 2004).

Collaborative methods include participatory and empowerment approaches. They reflect phenomenological philosophy and epistemological perspectives that stress the importance of experience (Heidegger, 1962). They also manifest an underlying sociological perspective that stresses the importance of the social meanings of the actors or "members" (Becker, 1963; Blumer, 1969; Garfinkel, 1967; Mead & Blumer, 1980). Thus, collaborative approaches bring a plurality of perspectives and experiences to program planning, evaluation, and research methodology (Fetterman, Kaftarian, & Wandersman, 1996; Fetterman & Wandersman, 2005; Green et al., 1995; Minkler, 2004; Rapkin & Trickett, 2005).

Brief History of Meta-Analysis and the Central Role of RCTs

Contemporaneous with the above-mentioned developments in conducting primary research during the 1970s and 1980s, social policy researchers and statisticians accelerated the development of synthesis methods, including meta-analysis, the best known and most widely used type of research synthesis.

One impetus to develop research syntheses was to enhance the credibility of the social sciences. Social science research was being criticized by influential policymakers in the 1980s for spawning more controversies than it provided answers. Synthesis offers the opportunity to assess and reconcile findings from individual studies.

The development of meta-analysis derives from its ability to increase the power of clinical trials, which typically have small samples, in order to improve external validity or generalizability (Volmink, Siegrid, Robertson, & Gulmezoglu, 2004). Since the RCT was considered the first choice for primary research (Campbell & Stanley 1963), it is understandable that meta-analysis would increasingly focus on methods for combining RCTs.

Inclusion Criteria of Research Syntheses

Research syntheses are used to aggregate existing primary data. They are important in summarizing the state of current knowledge in an area. They define what we learn from past research, and thus, what will be used for developing policies and programs, and for funding and designing future evaluations.

Because synthesis inclusion criteria define what types of primary research will be selected, they set the standards of evidence. Broadly defined syntheses include data from a variety of different kinds of data sources and designs, whereas currently meta-analysis usually includes data only RCTs, in which treatment and controls are randomly assigned.

While attention to design for primary research has consistently been the topic of discussion for a wide research and evaluation audience, outside of statistical discussions, less attention has been paid to the inclusion criteria of research syntheses. However, a greater awareness of the issue resulted from the What Works Clearinghouse (WWC), funded by the U.S. Department of Education in 2002 (What Works Clearinghouse, 2006a;). The WWC was designed by experienced and exemplary meta-analysts and initially defined the standard of evidence for the WWC to be limited to data only from RCTs. This restrictive inclusion criteria for the WWC sparked significant controversy (American Evaluation Association, 2003), and the inclusion criteria were subsequently broadened to include regression discontinuity and some quasi-experimental designs (What Works Clearinghouse, 2006b).

TYPES OF RESEARCH REVIEWS
Typology of Reviews

The two most commonly known and widely used types of methods to summarize previous research are the traditional literature review and the meta-analysis. Both are used for the same general purposes: to summarize a set of research findings and to guide future programs and research. They can be seen as two ends of the spectrum of possible types of reviews, with broad-based research syntheses falling in the middle and incorporating features from both the traditional review and meta-analysis (see Table 5.1). However, it is good to keep in mind that the distinctions made here apply in general but have some variability in particular instances and over time.

Reviews vary on a number of dimensions including such key issues as (1) the extent to which they are systematic, (2) whether the analysis is qualitative or quantitative, and (3) what kinds of data sources and designs are included.

A literature review (1) is characterized by a lack of systemization, (2) is qualitative in the sense that it does not use quantitative means to summarize findings, and (3) generally bases its conclusions on qualitative and quantitative data from a variety of data sources and designs.

A precursor to meta-analysis was the "qualitative" or "traditional review" (Beaman, 1991; Cook & Leviton, 1980, Pillemer, 1984). It (1) had some systematic inclusion rules, (2) was quantitative in the sense that it often used some basic quantitative means to summarize findings—generally "vote counting" or "box counting" of statistically significant results (Cook & Leviton, 1980, Cook et. al, 1992), and (3) usually based its conclusions on qualitative as well as quantitative data from a variety of data sources and designs.

A less well known type, the *broad-based research synthesis* (Labin, Goplerud, Myerson, & Woodside, 1992; Labin, 1996) is explicitly systematic as is meta-analysis, yet it retains certain characteristics of the earlier "qualitative review." It (1) emphasizes systematic decision rules, (2) generally uses qualitative and quantitative means to summarize findings, and (3) usually includes or integrates qualitative and quantitative information from various data sources and designs and thus is not limited to data from RCTs.

TABLE 5.1. Typology of Research Reviews

Types	Traditional reviews
	Inclusive or broad-based
Literature	Not systematic, qualitative analysis, variety of data sources and designs
Qualitative	Somewhat systematic, qualitative and quantitative analyses, variety of data sources and designs
	Research syntheses
	Inclusive or broad-based
Evaluation and prospective evaluation syntheses	Moderately systematic, qualitative and quantitative analyses, variety of data sources and designs, somewhat consensus building, evaluation frameworks, may have visual models
Guide to community and preventive services	Moderately systematic, qualitative and quantitative analyses, variety of data sources and designs, very consensus building
Cross-design synthesis	Very systematic, quantitative analysis, stratifies and integrates results by data sources and designs such as administrative databases and RCTs
	More restrictive
Meta-analysis	Very systematic, quantitative pooling of effect sizes, usually only RCTs

Note. The distinctions in this typology apply in general but have some variability in particular instances and over time. For example, meta-analysis's restriction of data only from RCT designs has varied mostly over time, but also in specific instances.

A meta-analysis is a research synthesis that also uses systematic decision rules for each step in the methodological process. It (1) is characterized by statistical pooling of quantitative results to summarize findings (usually standardized effect sizes) and (2) usually includes data results only from RCTs.

The research syntheses discussed in this chapter focus on summarizing outcomes and impacts from social research. While many of the principles elaborated here may apply to the synthesis of other types of information or knowledge, the exploration of wider applications is beyond the scope of this chapter.

Systematic Decision Rules:
The Defining Feature of Research Syntheses

Systemization is the most important distinction between traditional reviews and research syntheses. An alternative term for a research synthesis is a "systematic review" (Chalmers, Hedges, & Cooper, 2002; Moncrieff, 1998; Oakley, 2003). This systematic nature is a valuable contribution derived from meta-analysis (Bullock & Svyantek, 1985). At each stage in the synthesis (see "Methodological Steps" below), the documentation of decision rules is essential. The stress on documentation addresses such questions as: What databases were searched? What key words were used? What design or quality features were used as selection criteria for inclusion? What coding criteria were used for selection of outcomes or effect sizes? What level of reliability was obtained by coders of results?

FURTHER SPECIFICATION OF RESEARCH SYNTHESES

Purposes

There are two major complementary purposes of research syntheses: (1) retrospective summarizing of existing knowledge and (2) prospective planning of future policies, programs, and evaluations. Syntheses with retrospective purposes help answer such questions as "What do we know?" or "What works?" Syntheses can be used to identify patterns in data or a preponderance of evidence. They can help identify conflicting evidence, gaps in information, and methodological strengths and weaknesses of primary research studies. They can also be used to clarify the relationships between methodology (study design and measurement), program issues (setting, population, and implementation), and treatment effects (Lipsey & Wilson, 2001).

Generally, the results of retrospectively focused syntheses will be used in planning future policies, programs, and research. However, a synthesis can be explicitly designed for prospective purposes and thus tailored to address questions for future decisions. Two such examples are the Prospective Evaluation Synthesis (General Accounting Office, 1989) and the prospective use of the Cross-Design Synthesis (Boruch & Terhanian, 1998; General Accounting Office, 1992a). Both integrate data from a variety of designs and sources (see "Broad-Based Synthesis Methodologies from the Government Accountability Office" below).

Methodological Steps

Conducting a synthesis, whether for retrospective or explicitly prospective purposes, involves a series of methodological steps similar to those in primary studies:

1. Define the research question.
2. Collect information sources.

3. Select information sources based on inclusion criteria.
4. Extract and code data.
5. Analyze data.
6. Present findings.

These are steps conducted in all syntheses, including meta-analyses. However, there is some minor variation in how these steps are enumerated. For example, some collapse steps one and two, the collecting and selecting of sources, into one step (Cooper & Hedges, 1994). Each synthesis or meta-analysis must explicitly address decision rules about how comprehensive to be in the collection of sources (Rubin, 1990), how inclusive in terms of research design, how to select and code effects sizes or other results, and what formulas and models to use (Wachter & Straf, 1990).

Meta-Analysis

EARLY DEVELOPMENT

The earliest reference to combining research results is cited from the 17th century in astronomy (Volmink et al., 2004). Over a 100 years ago, Karl Pearson (1904) used quantitative statistics to combine results from medical studies and published what is considered to be the first modern-day meta-analysis (Cooper & Lindsay, 1998; Mullen & Ramirez, 1987). Fisher in his study of agricultural research used statistical methods in the 1930s (Volmink et al., 2004).

Meta-analysis drew on these existing methods for aggregating data that included physical and biological outcomes. Gene Glass is credited with first using the term "meta-analysis" in 1976 to refer to the statistical analysis of aggregated or pooled data results from numerous sources (Glass, 1976).

STATISTICAL POOLING OF RESULTS

Statistical pooling increases power by combining results from individual studies. Effect sizes are currently the common type of statistical results that are pooled. Usually the standardized effect sizes, the difference between the means of treatment and control groups, are used in the statistical analyses (Valentine & Cooper, 2003).

INCLUSION RESTRICTED TO RCTS

Another major distinguishing feature of current meta-analyses is inclusion criteria that restrict studies to the RCT. As mentioned earlier, it is this restriction that has given rise to the most controversy. Yet some consider the inclusion rules to "control for bias," which is the intent of limiting studies to the RCT design, to be the core distinguishing feature of meta-analyses, more important than the "optional element" of "quantitative statistical procedures" (Chalmers et al., 2002, p. 16).

Because meta-analysis is the type of research synthesis that is most widely known and used, its restriction to only RCTs has significant ramifications. The justification for broadening inclusion criteria to include designs other than the RCT derives mainly from concerns about the limitations of any given research design and, in particular, those of the RCT. Some of the latter limitations are explored in recent work by Rapkin and Trickett (2005) as well as that of Droitcour and Kovar (2004, 2005a, 2005b), Greenhouse and Kelleher (2005), and Green and Glasgow (2006). Some of these limitations of RCTs will be summarized after a brief description of broad-based research syntheses.

CONTINUING CHALLENGES

Meta-analysis has systematized the synthesis methodology and continues to bring new advances and positive attention to the need for aggregating primary research. There is now an extensive literature on meta-analysis and its myriad methodological and statistical issues (Cooper & Hedges, 1994; Rosenthal & DiMatteo, 2001). While it is beyond the scope of this chapter to delve into those issues and advances, a few macro-level challenges that were identified early on in the development of meta-analysis remain relevant today.

First is the challenge to maintain the "wisdom" that occurs when creating an "alliance" between qualitative and quantitative information (Light & Pillemer, 1984). This limitation is addressed in the broad-based synthesis methods that are discussed below.

Second, while meta-analysis is systematic as compared with traditional reviews, there are still a considerable number of "judgment calls" (Wanous, Sullivan, & Malinak, 1989; Wortman, 1994). These judgment calls inherently result in more subjectivity in the results than the formality and statistical precision of meta-analysis implies. Cook and Leviton (1980) concluded: "While qualitative reviews may be equally prone to bias, the descriptive accuracy of a point estimate in meta-analysis can have mischievous consequences because of its apparent 'objectivity,' 'precision,' and 'scientism.' " (p. 455)

Broad-Based Synthesis Methodologies from the Government Accountability Office

Meta-analysts influenced the development of synthesis methods at the United States Government Accountability Office (formerly the General

Accounting Office) in the 1980s and 1990s. For example, the systematic decision-rules included in the syntheses at the GAO reflect this influence. However, perhaps because of the pragmatic necessity to answer a range of policy questions with existing data, the synthesis methods developed at the GAO were broader-based and included quasi-experimental, qualitative, and administrative data sources (General Accounting Office, 1992b; Labin, 2001).

EVALUATION SYNTHESIS

The Evaluation Synthesis was developed at the GAO in 1983 (updated in 1992; General Accounting Office, 1992b). Chelimsky and Morra (1984) brought the method to a wider policy audience. They also drew on Ward and Reed's (1983) work, which defined synthesis as a "consensus-building" endeavor.

Explicit features of the evaluation synthesis include that it: (1) starts with a policy question, (2) is moderately systematic, (3) integrates qualitative and quantitative analyses (4) includes data from a variety of sources and designs, and (5) uses a consensus-building process (General Accounting Office, 1986, 1987a). It is systematic in its use of an evaluation framework to structure the questions, its clarity of decision rules for the various steps, and its use of quality criteria for selecting studies. The results are based on patterns of results or an "alliance of evidence" (General Accounting Office, 1992b).

PROSPECTIVE EVALUATION SYNTHESIS

The Prospective Evaluation Synthesis (General Accounting Office, 1989) derived its methodology from the evaluation synthesis (General Accounting Office, 1987b; 1988, 1989). However, it expands and enhances the evaluation synthesis with the following changes: (1) an explicit focus on future decision making, (2) more substantive selectivity in what is included, and (3) the inclusion of conceptual and operational models to visually display the causal or operational logic of the program. These models are precursors to today's widely used logic models.

While the purpose of the evaluation synthesis is to eventually shed light on future decisions, the prospective evaluation synthesis makes this explicit and is often more narrowly defined by the substantive policy options being assessed. These principles were applied in developing an evaluation framework based on the various features of legislation for catastrophic health insurance that were being considered by Congress (General Accounting Office, 1987b; Labin, 1988) and in developing an evaluation framework to make future decisions on children's programs (General Accounting Office, 1988).

The prospective evaluation synthesis method described and utilized several types of quality judgment models: (1) single criteria, (2) multiple equally weighted criteria; (3) multiple unequally weighted criteria, and (4) threshold or fatal flaw. The fatal flaw method appears to have the advantage of ensuring overall quality. In this method, a study must meet multiple criteria, but if one of the essential features is sufficiently below acceptable quality standards, that weakness can override other positive features (General Accounting Office, 1989; Labin et al., 1992).

CROSS-DESIGN SYNTHESIS

The Cross-Design Synthesis developed by Judith Droitcour at the General Accounting Office (General Accounting Office, 1992a; Droitcour, 1997) can be seen as the bridge between meta-analysis and the evaluation and prospective synthesis methodologies from the GAO. It is an innovative and integrative methodology that can be used for both retrospective and prospective purposes.

The cross-design synthesis makes the explicit assumption that data from any given type of method or design have their own inherent strengths and biases and are potentially complementary rather than competing. This is the same rationale for usage of the broad-based synthesis methods discussed in this chapter. The cross-design synthesis stratifies and integrates data from RCTs and administrative databases and assesses the direction and degree of biases of these two data sources in order to maximize the strengths of each design and to minimize the impact of design weaknesses.

While the original usage of cross-design synthesis by Droitcour aggregated RCTs and administrative data, the principles of cross-design synthesis have broader application. Results from experimental studies, quasi-experimental studies, epidemiological studies, and administrative databases can be pooled within separate design strata, that is, groups with data from similar designs (Sutton, Abrams, Jones, Sheldon & Song, 2000). These results can then be compared and adjusted for bias in order to gain a broad perspective on the implications of existing data (Greenhouse & Kelleher, 2005).

Boruch and Terhanian (1998) took Droitcour's retrospectively oriented cross-design synthesis and proposed to use the same assumptions and principles for prospective planning of research strategies.

A Broad-Based Synthesis Method from the U.S. Department of Health and Human Services

It is not only the GAO synthesis methodologies that demonstrate the precedent for a broad vision of development of knowledge and strategies for the future but also the Task Force and its *Guide to Community Preventive Services*. The Task Force is an independent decision-making body appointed by the Director of the Centers for Disease Control and Prevention (CDC) that was first convened in 1996 by U.S. Department of Health and Human Services (DHHS). About 10 agencies within DHHS participate as well as 5 separate federal agencies and approximately 20 independent organizations and associations (*Guide to Community Preventive Services*, 2004b).

The principles and many of the specific methods of the Guide are similar to and consistent with those of the various research syntheses developed at the GAO. Critical features of the *Guide to Community Preventive Services* include: (1) moderate systematization, (2) qualitative and quantitative analysis, (3) a variety of data sources and designs, and (4) consensus building between academics and practitioners.

The Guide systematically uses quality ratings of design appropriateness and of fidelity of implementation. It quantitatively assesses the number of studies and the number and magnitude of effect sizes. Regarding the issue of quality and the role of RCTs, it concludes that: "a well-conducted case control or prospective cohort study [is] to receive greater weight than a poorly-conducted randomized trial." (Briss et al., 2000, p. 41).

The Guide makes recommendations based on a "preponderance of evidence," concluding that "systematic and participatory processes will reduce errors" (Briss et al., 2000, p. 42).

Other Broad-Based Synthesis Methods

Other examples of research syntheses with broad inclusion criteria are found in Lipsey and Wilson's work (Lipsey & Wilson, 2001). They coded over 300 meta-analyses encompassing over 16,000 individual studies of various designs. They empirically assessed results by design strata as well as other methodological and intervention characteristics (see "Comparing Results from Experimental versus Quasi-Experimental Designs" below).

Rutledge, DePalma, and Cunningham (2004) developed and implemented the "Triad Model of Research Synthesis." Similar to the Guide, the model allows for evidence from a variety of research designs and specifies a collaborative process between practitioners, educators who understand advanced practice, and researchers, to "appraise studies and synthesize findings" (p. 543).

Greenhouse and Kelleher (2005) in their work regarding pharmacological anti-depressants and suicidality build on Droitcour's cross-design synthesis and suggest conducting research syntheses that include "randomized and nonrandomized studies. Examples of the latter include administrative databases (such as claims data), epidemiologic studies, and health-survey data" (p. 232). They also use Bayesian statistical methods (Kaizar, Greenhouse, Seltman, & Kelleher, 2005) and cite other developments and usages of such statistical methods to combine data from various designs (Eddy, Hasselblad, & Shachter, 1992; Spieghelhalter, Abrahms, & Myles, 2004).

Sutton and associates also build on the cross-design synthesis method and analyze and combine results from different design strata of primary studies (Sutton et al., 2000).

Shadish and associates stratified findings and analyzed the effects of design, measurement, program, and other factors (Shadish & Ragsdale, 1996, Shadish, Matt, Navarro, & Phillips, 2000).

As these examples indicate, there is a rich synthesis practice that supports the precedent of including data from a variety of types of designs (Oakley, 2003). As Glass (1978) advised, rather than restricting the inclusion by types of designs, we should let the data demonstrate empirically whether different methods give rise to different results. These broad-based methods support Green and Glasgow's (2006) recent recommendation that research syntheses should "weigh the wider range of relevant evidence."

IMPLICATIONS OF EXISTING
PRIMARY RESEARCH FOR SYNTHESIS

Nature and Value of Existing Primary Research

It is important to consider the significant amount of evaluation and research that we would lose by not being inclusive in the types of designs of primary research that are aggregated in syntheses. For example, we have seen the evaluation discipline enriched, especially over the past 15 years, by insights from collaborative approaches. The influence is so extensive and pervasive that many, if not most, traditional evaluators and auditors incorporate some degree of collaborative methods in their approaches and designs. Even if we could assume that there is nothing mutually exclusive about RCTs and collaborative evaluation models, for a combination of historical, social, and political reasons, one could estimate that the current set of evaluations demonstrating the highest degree of collaborative principles is likely to have a limited number with RCT designs. Thus, inclusion criteria that limit designs to only RCTs would disproportionately exclude an important type of existing evaluations.

Some Limitations of RCTs

While many might agree that broad inclusion criteria are warranted when aggregating data from *existing* research designs and approaches, some are likely to see the need to reexamine this conclusion when considering what types of *future* research and evaluations should be planned for and funded. The controversy over the Department of Education's policies regarding the WWC was not only about synthesis inclusion criteria for existing research but also about priorities for funding future primary research. A fundamental issue is whether the RCT is always the "gold standard" when addressing issues of causality in social research.

One of frequently cited limitations of the RCT is its emphasis on "black box" results because typically little is revealed about the mechanism by which results are incurred. However, RCTs can and sometimes do include theory of change, logic models, and other techniques that indicate the "causal mediating processes" and avoid the "black box" tendency (Cook, 2005; Labin, 1980).

Other frequently cited limitations of the RCT that theoretically can be addressed include the: (1) significant amount of resources required; (2) ethics of withholding "treatment" or services; (3) difficulty of maintaining the separateness of the treatment and control groups to meet the stable unit treatment value assumption (SUTVA) that one's unit assignment does not influence another unit's outcome; and (4) the related issue of focusing on effects for individuals (Droitcour & Kovar, 2005a, 2005b) when group processes may be an inextricable part of the treatment.

There also has been an examination of limitations that are less frequently cited, considered, or addressed that involve some basic characteristics of the RCT. Rapkin and Trickett (2005) have delineated some such limitations, which are summarized as follows:

1. A hierarchical and "disengaged investigator–subject relationship."
2. Ignoring the potential importance of individual choice.
3. Assumptions about the replicability of the protocol or intervention.
4. Emphasis on a primary outcome that is "equally applicable to all."
5. Incomparability of treatment and control groups in terms of variables that influence outcomes.
6. Response shifts or reactivity that differentially occur in treatment and control group participants.

Rapkin and Trickett (2005) examine these limitations in some depth. However, a few with the most relevance for this chapter are commented on here. The hierarchical disengaged investigator–subject relationship (number 1 above) is the same quality that was described earlier as the external "expert" model and was contrasted with collaborative models. This characteristic can lead to insensitivity to participants' experience with negative consequences for the efficacy of the intervention and the validity of measures. It also, in conjunction with a lack of individual choice inherent in random assignment (number 2 above), may render the RCT less applicable in social interventions where motivation and self-responsibility for one's actions are fundamental to the intervention and intended outcomes. Additionally, the assumption of an RCT that the intervention should be implemented with fidelity to its original plan prevents the adaptation of the intervention to individual needs and local conditions.

Further, Rapkin and Trickett question assumptions about replicating all the critical features of the intervention (number 3 above). They enumerate about a dozen features that are inconsistently changed or preserved in the replication of interventions, for example, curriculum, leadership, format, dosage, timing, population, recruitment, setting, incentives (Rapkin & Trickett, 2005). This examination of the assumptions and complexity in replicating an intervention is consistent with current thinking, as articulated by Green (2001), that an intervention is as much a process as it is a packaged discrete entity.

Droitcour and Kovar (2004) have been exploring the differences between RCTs in the physical and biological sciences versus those in the social and behavioral sciences. They identify several differences. The former (1) apply to an individual, (2) ideally and often use double blinding (Schultz, Chalmers, Hayes, & Altman, 1995), and (3) involve a chemical or physical change process with a biological outcome. In contrast, evaluations of social interventions (1) often apply to groups, (2) blinding and double blinding are generally not possible, and (3) the change process and outcomes are social or cognitive rendering motivation and personal choice crucial considerations (Droitcour & Kovar, 2004, 2005a, 2005b).

Some Recent Developments in Addressing Limitations of RCTs

GROUP RANDOMIZED TRIALS

Given that results of many social interventions are inextricably linked with reinforcing social interactions or culture (Cook, 2005), the practice of randomly assigning *groups,* rather than individuals, to treatment or control conditions is becoming more widely used (Boruch, 2005). This is intended to address two of the earlier mentioned limitations of RCTs, their assumption that one unit's assignment does not influence another unit's outcome, and the focus on individual level change.

Other terms for the "group randomized trial" are "place randomized trial," "cluster randomized trial," and "saturation trial" (Boruch, 2005). The concept is to randomly select by the "group" or "place"—school, community, hospital—to either receive the intervention or to be the control condition.

COMPREHENSIVE DYNAMIC TRIAL DESIGNS

Rapkin and Trickett (2005) propose several types of Comprehensive Dynamic Trial Designs to address the limitations of the RCT design. For example, the Collaborative Consultation and Empowerment Model is designed to improve outcomes for everyone and use growth curve analysis to model "how differential use of resources shapes trajectories for different people" (p. 265).

THREE-GROUP RANDOM-PREFERENCE DESIGN

In order to partition out the effects of preference, Droitcour and Kovar (2005) suggest a "three-group random-preference design" that would compare two groups that are randomly assigned to either treatment A or B and a third group that *chooses* either A or B (Long, Little, & Lin, 2004).

Comparing Results from Experimental versus Quasi-Experimental Designs

One of the most common reasons offered against broader inclusion criteria is that results from experimental designs (RCTs) are different from those from quasi-experimental designs. However the consistency of the direction of that difference—whether RCTs result in stronger or weaker effects—has a long history of contradictory empirical results (Light & Pillemer, 1984).

In assessing differences in results between experimental designs with random assignment and quasi-experimental designs with comparison groups, Lipsey and Wilson did not find a major difference in mean effect sizes (Lipsey & Wilson, 1993, 2001). However, they did find that the one-group pre–post design "generally overestimates treatment effects relative to comparison designs" (Wilson & Lipsey, 2001, p. 421).

Among their noteworthy findings is that the method for measuring constructs contributed nearly twice the proportion of variance (.07) as did design type—random or nonrandom assignment (.04) (Lipsey & Wilson, 2001; Wilson & Lipsey, 2001).

As the work of Shadish and colleagues demonstrates (Shadish & Ragsdale, 1996; Heinsman & Shadish, 1996; Shadish et al., 2000), the comparison of results from experimental and quasi-experimental studies is a complex area warranting careful consideration of numerous confounding factors. In some cases they found that quasi-experimental studies may underestimate treatment effects. Their work offers helpful techniques for comparing results from experimental and quasi-experimental designs, including scatterplots that visually and succinctly convey the distribution of results by factors such as type of design (Shadish et al., 2000).

Others have made comparisons of results from quasi-experimental and experimental designs and concluded that "[a quasi experimental study with the] same labor market . . . same questionnaire [measurement] and weighting . . . produces estimates of program impacts that are fairly close to those produced from an experimental evaluation [RCT]" (Heckman, Ichimura, & Todd, 1997, p. 646).

CONCLUSIONS AND RECOMMENDATIONS

The purpose of this chapter has been to clarify that there are precedents, rationales, methodologies, and technologies that support synthesis methods that include a variety of types of data and research designs. Starting with the assumption that each type of data and design has inherent strengths and weaknesses, a broad base of evidence is the recommended method for balancing these differences. Given the importance of synthesis for aggregating existing data and planning future policies, programs, and evaluations, a specific major conclusion of this chapter is that we need to develop and utilize synthesis methodologies that include data from nonexperimental designs and not restrict evidence to RCTs.

We can enhance our current synthesis methodologies by drawing both from current meta-analytic methodological practices, with their emphasis on systematic decision rules and statistical techniques, and from the broader-based synthesis methods such as those from the GAO and the Task Force's *Guide to Community Preventive Services*. Experienced RCT researchers at MDRC have concluded: "Implicit in these new directions is a view that random assignment cannot stand alone, and that researchers and policymakers must look beyond the 'experimental versus non-experimental' debate toward productive ways of combining both approaches" (Riccio & Bloom, 2001, p. 4).

More usage of participatory processes, as utilized by the Task Force and its *Guide to Community Preventive Services*, would encourage reconciling anomalies in data from different types of sources and designs. The development and use of common measures across various designs, interventions, populations, and settings would build on our knowledge that measurement is a more important contributor to variation in results than is type of comparison group (random or nonrandom). Common measurement would also allow for greater use of naturally occurring comparison groups. Further exploration of the differences between social field evaluations and those in the physical and biological sciences would have useful implications for our primary and synthesis methodologies.

Fortunately, technology can play an instrumental role in implementing syntheses with broader inclusion criteria. As Lipsey and Wilson (1993, 2001) have demonstrated, it is possible to analyze a large quantity of studies with numerous characteristics and compare results using multiple regression. There are also comprehensive evaluation and information systems that could be adapted to facilitate large-scale categorization, access, and analysis of studies (Zhang, 2005).

A further advancement could involve the application of geographic information systems (GIS) in the mapping of synthesis findings. Instead of geographical physical locations, conceptual outcomes or relationships could be the background (perhaps drawing on Trochim's [2006] concept mapping), and synthesis findings from various designs, interventions, populations, and measures could be mapped in order to identify patterns and facilitate interpretation of findings.

In sum, researchers and funders alike can build on a broad base of current information, maximize our resources, and accelerate achieving our common goals of developing and utilizing knowledge to achieve outcomes by developing and supporting the following:

1. Systematic synthesis methodologies for aggregating data from a variety of different kinds of data sources and designs in addition to the RCT.

2. Participatory and transparent processes for decision rules and quality criteria.

3. Common measures for use across designs and interventions.

4. Technologies for categorizing various features of studies and depicting patterns of results.

REFERENCES

American Evaluation Association. (2003). *Scientifically based evaluation methods*. Retrieved June 20, 2005, from *www.eval.org/doestatement.htm*.

Beaman, A. L. (1991). An empirical comparison of meta-analytic and traditional reviews. *Personality and Social Psychology Bulletin, 17,* 253–257.

Becker, H. (1963). *The outsiders*. New York: Free Press.

Blumer, H. (1969). *Symbolic interactionism: Perspective and method*. Englewood Cliffs, NJ: Prentice Hall.

Boruch, R. F. (2005). Preface—Better evaluation for evidence-based policy: Place randomized trials in education, criminology, welfare, and health. *Annals of the American Academy of Political and Social Science, 599,* 6–18.

Boruch, R. F., & Terhanian, G. (1998). Cross-design synthesis. In H. Walberg & A. Reynolds (Eds.), *Advances in educational productivity* (pp. 59–86). Greenwich, CT: JAI Press.

Briss, P. A., Brownson, R. C., Fielding, J. A., & Zaza, S. (2004). Developing and using the Guide to Preventive Health Services: Lessons learned about evidence-based public health. *Annual Review of Public Health, 25,* 281–302.

Briss, P. A., Zaza, S., Pappaioanou, M., Fielding, J., Wright-de-Aguero, L., Truman, B. I., et al. (2000). Developing an evidence-based guide to community preventive services—methods. *American Journal of Preventive Medicine, 18,* 35–43.

Bullock, R. J., & Svyantek, D. J. (1985). Analyzing meta-analysis: Potential problems, an unsuccessful replication, and evaluation criteria. *Journal of Applied Psychology, 70,* 108–115.

Campbell, D., & Stanley, J. (1963). *Experimental and quasi-experimental designs for research*. Chicago: Rand McNally.

Chalmers, I., Hedges, L. V., & Cooper, H. (2002). A brief history of research synthesis. *Evaluation and the Health Professions, 25,* 12–37.

Chelimsky, E., & Morra, L. G. (1984). Evaluation synthesis for the legislative user. In W. H. Yeaton & R. M. Wortman (Eds.), *Issues in data synthesis* (New Directions for Program Evaluation no. 24, pp. 75–89). New York: Wiley.

Cook, T. D. (2005). Emergent principles for the design, implementation, and analysis of cluster-based experiments in social science. *Annals of the American Academy of Political and Social Science, 599,* 176–198.

Cook, T. D., Cooper, H., Cordray, D. S., Hartmann, H., Hedges, L. V., Light, R. J., et al. (1992). *Meta-analysis for explanation*. New York: Russell Sage.

Cook, T. D., & Leviton, L. C. (1980). Reviewing the literature: A comparison of traditional methods with meta-analysis. *Journal of Personality, 48,* 449–472.

Cooper, H., & Hedges, L. V. (1994). *The handbook of research synthesis*. New York: Russell Sage.

Cooper, H. M., & Lindsay, J. J. (1998). Research synthesis and meta-analysis. In L. Bickman & D. Rog (Eds.), *Handbook of applied social research methods* (pp. 315–337). Thousand Oaks, CA: Sage.

Droitcour, J. A. (1997). Cross-design synthesis: Concept and application. In E.

Chelimsky & W. Shadish (Eds.), *Evaluation for the 21st century: A handbook* (pp. 360–372). Thousand Oaks, CA: Sage.

Droitcour, J. A., & Kovar, M. G. (2004, November). *Exploring ways to compensate for RFT weaknesses.* Paper presented at the American Evaluation Association annual meeting, Atlanta.

Droitcour, J. A., & Kovar, M. G. (2005a). *Randomized field trials: The "gold-standard" for policy research?* Paper presented at the Washington, DC, Sociological Society Meeting, Washington, DC.

Droitcour, J. A., & Kovar, M. G. (2005b). *Should the RCT gold standard apply for social policy impact evaluations?* Paper presented at the Washington DC, Sociological Society and Washington Evaluators Joint Session, Washington, DC.

Eddy, D. M., Hasselblad, V., & Shachter, R. (1992). *Meta-analysis by the confidence profile method: The statistical synthesis of evidence.* New York: Academic Press.

Fetterman, D., Kaftarian, S., & Wandersman, A. (Eds.). (1996). *Empowerment evaluation.* Thousand Oaks, CA: Sage.

Fetterman, D., & Wandersman, A. (Eds.). (2005). *Empowerment evaluation principles in practice.* New York: Guilford Press.

Garfinkel, H. (1967). *Studies in ethnomethodology.* Englewood Cliffs, NJ: Prentice Hall.

General Accounting Office. (1986). *Teenage pregnancy: 500,000 births a year but few tested programs* (GAO/PEMD-86-16BR). Washington, DC: Author.

General Accounting Office. (1987a). *Drinking-age laws: An evaluation synthesis of their impact on highway safety* (GAO/PEMD-87-10). Washington, DC: Author.

General Accounting Office. (1987b). *Medicare: Catastrophic illness insurance* (GAO/PEMD-87-21BR). Washington, DC: Author.

General Accounting Office (1988). *Children's programs: A comparative evaluation framework and five illustrations* (GAO/PEMD-88-28BR). Washington, DC: Author.

General Accounting Office (1989). *Prospective evaluation methods: The prospective evaluation synthesis* (GAO/PEMD-10.1.10). Washington, DC: Author.

General Accounting Office. (1992a). *Cross-design synthesis* (GAO/PEMD-92-18). Washington, DC: Author.

General Accounting Office. (1992b). *The evaluation synthesis* (GAO/PEMD-10.1.2). Washington, DC: Author.

Glass, G. V. (1976). Primary, secondary, and meta-analysis of research. *Educational Researcher, 5,* 3–8.

Glass, G. V. (1978). Integrating findings: The meta-analysis of research. *Review of Research in Education, 5,* 351–379.

Green, L. W., (2001). From research to "best practices" in other settings and populations. *American Journal of Health Behavior, 25,* 165–178.

Green, L. W. (2004). Ethics and community-based participatory research: Commentary on Minkler. *Health Education and Behavior, 31,* 698–701.

Green, L. W., George, M. A., Daniel, M., Frankish, C. J., Herbert, C., & Bowie,

W. (1995). *Study of participatory research in health promotion.* Ottawa: The Royal Society of Canada.

Green, L. W., & Glasgow, R. (2006). Evaluating the relevance, generalization, and applicability of research: Issues in external validation and translation methodology. *Evaluation and the Health Professions, 29,* 126–153.

Greenhouse, J., & Kelleher, K. J. (2005). Thinking outside the (black) box: Antidepressants, suicidality, and research synthesis, *Pediatrics, 116,* 231–233.

Guide to Community Preventive Services. (2004a). *Data abstraction form.* Retrieved October 15, 2004, from *www.thecommunityguide.org/methods/htm.*

Guide to Community Preventive Services. (2004b). *Participating organizations.* Retrieved October 15, 2004 from *www.thecommunityguide.org/about/participating-organizations.htm.*

Heckman, J., Ichimura, H., & Todd, P. (1997). Matching as an econometric evaluation estimator: Evidence from evaluating a job training program. *Review of Economic Studies, 64,* 646.

Heidegger, M. (1962). *Being and time.* (J. Macquarrie & E. Robinson, Trans.). San Francisco: HarperSanFrancisco.

Heinsman, D. T., & Shadish, W. R. (1996). Assignment methods in experimentation: When do nonrandomized experiments approximate answers from randomized experiments? *Psychological Methods, 1,* 154–169.

Kaizar, E., Greenhouse, J., Seltman, H., & Kelleher, K. (2005). *Do antidepressants cause suicidality in children? A Bayesian meta-analysis.* Paper presented at the Society for Clinical Trials annual meeting, Portland, OR.

Labin, S. N. (1980). *A labeling process in the juvenile justice system.* Paper presented at the Society for the Study of Social Problems annual meeting, New York.

Labin, S. N. (1988). *Synthesis informing policy: Experiences from state catastrophic illness programs.* Paper presented at the American Evaluation Association annual meeting, Boston.

Labin, S. N. (1996). *Data syntheses: Specific tools and underpinnings for broader strategies.* Atlanta: American Evaluation Association.

Labin, S. N. (2001). *Evaluation synthesis: Theory to practice.* Ottawa: International Methodology Conference—Evaluation and Data Development, Human Resources Development Canada.

Labin, S. N., Goplerud, E., Myerson, S., & Woodside, C. (1992, November). *Preliminary observations of alcohol and other drug prevention programs and evaluations.* Paper presented at the American Evaluation Association annual meeting, Seattle, WA.

Light, R. J., & Pillemer, D. B. (1984). *Summing up: The science of reviewing research.* Cambridge, MA: Harvard University Press.

Lipsey, M. W., & Wilson, D. B. (1993). The efficacy of psychological, educational, and behavioral treatment. *American Psychologist, 48,* 1181–1209.

Lipsey, M. W., & Wilson, D. B. (2001). The way in which intervention studies have "personality" and why it is important to meta-analysis. *Evaluation and the Health Professions, 24,* 236–254.

Long, Q., Little, R., & Lin, X. (2004, March). Causal inference in hybrid intervention trials involving treatment choice. *The University of Michigan Department of Biostatistics Working Paper Series,* paper 34. Available at *www.bepress.com/umichbiostat/paper34.*

Mead, G. H., & Blumer, H. (1980). The convergent methodological perspectives of social behaviorism and symbolic interactionism. *American Sociological Review, 45,* 4.

Minkler, M. (2004). Ethical challenges for the "outside" researcher in community-based participatory research. *Health Education and Behavior, 31,* 684–697.

Moncrieff, J. (1998). Research synthesis: Systematic reviews and meta-analyses. *International Review of Psychiatry, 10,* 304–311.

Mullen, P., & Ramirez, G. (1987). Information synthesis and meta-analysis. *Advances in Health Education and Promotion, 2,* 201–239.

Oakley, A. (2003). Research evidence, knowledge management and educational practice: Early lessons from a systematic approach. *London Review of Education, 1*(1), 21–33.

Pearson, K. (1904). Report on certain enteric fever inoculation statistics. *British Medical Journal, 3,* 1243–1246.

Pillemer, D. B. (1984). Conceptual issues in research synthesis. *Journal of Special Education, 18,* 27–40.

Rapkin, B. D., & Trickett, E. J. (2005). Comprehensive dynamic trial designs for behavioral prevention research with communities: Overcoming inadequacies of the randomized controlled trial paradigm. In E. Trickett & W. Pequenaut (Eds.). *Increasing the community impact of HIV prevention interventions* (pp. 249–277). New York: Oxford University Press.

Riccio, J. A., & Bloom, H. S. (2001). *Extending the reach of randomized social experiments: New directions in evaluations of American welfare-to-work and employment initiatives.* New York: MDRC. Retrieved October 15, 2004, from *www.mdrc.org/publications_research_methodology.html.*

Rosenthal, R., & DiMatteo, M. R. (2001). Meta-analysis: Recent developments in quantitative methods for literature reviews. *Annual Review Psychology, 52,* 59–82.

Rossi, P. H., Freeman, H., & Lipsey, M. (1999) *Evaluation: A systematic approach* (6th ed.). Thousand Oaks, CA: Sage.

Rubin, D. B. (1990). A new perspective. In K. W. Wachter & M. L. Straf (Eds.), *The future of meta-analysis* (pp. 155–167). New York: Russell Sage.

Rutledge, D. N., DePalma, J. A., & Cunningham, M. (2004). A process model for evidence-based literature syntheses. *Oncology Nursing Forum, 31,* 543–550.

Schulz, K. F., Chalmers, I., Hayes, R. J., & Altman, D. G. (1995). Empirical evidence of bias: Dimensions of methodological quality associated with estimates of treatment effects in controlled trials. *Journal of the American Medical Association, 273,* 408–412.

Shadish, W. R., Matt, G. E., Navarro, A. M., & Phillips, G. (2000). The effects of psychological therapies under clinically representative conditions: A meta-analysis. *Psychological Bulletin, 136,* 512–529.

Shadish, W. R., & Ragsdale, K. (1996). Random versus nonrandom assignment in controlled experiments: Do you get the same answer? *Journal of Consulting and Clinical Psychology, 64,* 1290–1305.

Shojania, K. G, McDonald, K. M., Wachter, R. M., & Owens, D. K. (2004, August). *Closing the quality gap: A critical analysis of quality improvement strategies: Vol. 1. Series overview and methodology* (AHRQ Publication No. 04-0051, Appendix C: Article Review Triage Forms). Rockville, MD: Agency for Healthcare Research and Quality.

Spieghelhalter, D., Abrahms, K. R., & Myles, J. P. (2004). *Bayesian approaches to clinical trials and health-care evaluation.* Chichester, UK: Wiley.

Sutton, A. J., Abrams, K. R., Jones, D. R., Sheldon, T. A., & Song, F. (2000). *Methods for meta-analysis in medical research,* Wiley Series in Probability and Statistics, pp. 239–255). West Sussex, UK: Wiley.

Trochim, W. (2006). *Concept mapping.* Retrieved March 1, 2006, from *www.social research methods.net.*

Valentine, J. C., & Cooper, H. (2003). *Effect size substantive interpretation guidelines: Issues in the interpretation of effect sizes.* Washington, DC: What Works Clearinghouse. Retrieved March 1, 2006, from *www.whatworks.ed.gov/reviewprocess/essig.pdf.*

Volmink, J., Siegried, N., Robertson, K., & Gulmezoglu, A. M. (2004). Research synthesis and dissemination as a bridge to knowledge management: The Cochrane collaboration. *Bulletin of the World Health Organization, 82,* 778–783.

Wachter, K. W., & Straf, M. L. (1990). *The future of meta-analysis.* New York: Russell Sage.

Wanous, J. P., Sullivan, S. E., & Malinak, J. (1989). The role of judgment calls in meta-analysis. *Journal of Applied Psychology, 74,* 259–264.

Ward, S. A., & Reed, L. J. (1983). *Knowledge structure and use: Implications for synthesis and interpretation.* Philadelphia: Temple University.

What Works Clearinghouse (2006a). *Overview.* Retrieved March 1, 2006, from *www.whatworks.ed.gov/whoweare/overview.html.*

What Works Clearinghouse (2006b). *Study design classification.* Retrieved March 1, 2006, from *www.whatworks.ed.gov/reviewprocess/study_standards_final.pdf.*

Wilson, D. B., & Lipsey, M. W. (2001). The role of method in treatment effectiveness research: Evidence from meta-analysis. *Psychological Methods, 6,* 413–429.

Wortman, P. M. (1994). Judging research quality. In H. Cooper & L. Hedges (Eds.), *The handbook of research synthesis.* New York: Russell Sage.

Zhang, X. (2005). *Prevention service.* Retrieved February 27, 2006, from *www.kitsolutions.net/company.*

CHAPTER 6

Building a Better Evidence Base for Evaluation Theory
Beyond General Calls to a Framework of Types of Research on Evaluation

Melvin M. Mark

There appear to be an increasing number of calls for more and better research on evaluation. After noting the benefits of having an increased evidence base about evaluation, I argue that there is also some merit in developing a *framework of different types of studies of evaluation*. I then present a framework of alternative types of research and illustrate it with various examples. The framework offered here includes (1) a classification of different "subjects of study" in research on evaluation and (2) a set of four functional types of studies. Expanding on the framework, tentative suggestions are given about the expected benefits of engaging in different types of research on evaluation.

RESEARCH ON EVALUATION: A FUNDAMENTAL ISSUE?

Why include a chapter about research on evaluation in a book addressing fundamental issues in evaluation? In Chapter 1, Smith indicates that fundamental issues recur over time, are interpreted in light of the current context, and are a topic of discussion and debate. From this vantage point, consider how research on evaluation can be seen as constituting a fundamental issue.

Research on evaluation has been a topic of interest for some time. For example, in a volume published in 1975, Bernstein and Freeman assessed the quality of a set of 236 federally funded evaluations on a number of aspects of methodology. Major studies of evaluation use took place roughly 30 years ago (e.g., Patton et al., 1977; Weiss, 1977). Studies of evaluation have continued to appear since then (e.g., Lipsey, Crosse, Dunkle, Pollard, & Stobart, 1985; Torres, Preskill, & Piontek, 1997; Christie, 2003), albeit sporadically and with limited cumulativity. Calls for more research on evaluation have occurred both earlier (e.g., Bernstein & Freeman, 1975) and more recently in the field's history (e.g., Alkin, 2003). Interest in research on evaluation ebbs and flows, but it seems inevitably to resurface.

Turning to another characteristic of fundamental issues, views about research on evaluation can vary in light of the current context. Take one noteworthy example. Carol Weiss, through her important studies of evaluation influence (e.g., Weiss, 1977), is one of if not the most notable practitioner of research on evaluation. Nevertheless, she recently wrote:

> I'll admit that it is fun to talk to each other about evaluation theory, and having more research about evaluation (Henry & Mark, 2003b; King, 2003) can no doubt contribute to our knowledge and skills. But I think it is time we spent more time *doing* evaluation, teaching people how to do evaluation, advising on evaluations, reviewing and critiquing evaluations, meta-analyzing evaluations, and in general, advancing the *practice* of evaluation." (Weiss, 2004, p. 166)

Weiss's recent expression of concern about research on evaluation appears to have been stimulated by recurring requests from graduate students for her to participate in dissertations using survey methods to study evaluation. But perhaps her diminished interest in research on evaluation was also influenced by more general concerns about possible limits of the evidence-based practice movement as practiced (cf. Weiss, Murphy-Graham, & Birkeland, 2005). Views about research on evaluation may well depend on the context within which the idea is considered.

Moreover, research on evaluation is subject to sharp debate among evaluators. Contrast Weiss's recent comment, above, with the view of Marv Alkin (e.g., 2003), who, among others, has been calling recently for more research on evaluation. Alkin says "We *must* make a start" (p. 88) toward an empirical theory of evaluation based on systematic research. Yet another position has been voiced recently by Donaldson and Lipsey (2006). They suggest that research on evaluation in principle would be useful but that there will never be enough research to be helpful as a guide to evaluation practice. Again reflecting Smith's analysis of fundamental issues, evaluators debate the value of research on evaluation.

The idea of research on evaluation is not minor. Rather, the potential consequences are considerable. For example, early research on use led to the concept of conceptual use or enlightenment, which remains influential today (Weiss, 1977). Early research on use also led to the notion of the "personal factor," which became the foundation of Patton's (1997) utilization-focused evaluation. For several other examples of the impact of research on evaluation, see Shadish, Cook, and Leviton (1991) and Smith (1993). Contemporary and future research on evaluation likewise should have important implications.

In short, research on evaluation has long been of interest. Research on evaluation, and discussion of it, recurs and resurfaces in different forms. Views seem to vary at different times and in different contexts. And research on evaluation has potentially important consequences, as illustrated historically by the impact of early research on use on evaluation theory and practice. In short, research on evaluation can be seen as a fundamental issue akin to the others addressed in this book. In another sense, research on evaluation can contribute to our understanding of several other fundamental issues that exist in evaluation (e.g., what are the consequences of alternative evaluation approaches?). Research on evaluation might even help to provide an answer to perhaps our most fundamental practice issue: How should one choose from among the multitude of options available for evaluation?

RESEARCH ON EVALUATION: PREVIOUS CALLS

A key premise of this chapter is that value exists in moving beyond general calls for more and better research on evaluation to a taxonomy of types of research on evaluation. Put differently, this chapter is an attempt to contribute to a conversation about (1) the different categories of research on evaluation that can be conducted and (2) the relative benefits of different kinds of research on evaluation.

The idea that it would be helpful to increase the evidence base about evaluation practices and their consequences is not new. Consider, for example, Shadish et al. (1991), who reviewed a select set of major evaluation theorists. They concluded that the best way to improve advice for evaluation practice would be by moving "Toward More Data-Oriented Evaluation Theory" (p. 477). Shadish et al. indicate that "one of the most important but least frequent ways that evaluation theory has improved over the years is by increasing its empirical content" (p. 478).

And they conclude that evaluation "need[s] empirical study to answer the unanswered questions" that remain (p. 480). Similarly, Smith (1993) noted that "Empirical knowledge about the practice of evaluation is essential for the development of relevant and useful evaluation theories" (p. 237). These and other advocates of research on evaluation suggest that such research can help answer a range of questions. For example, how do we know whether a particular approach to evaluation meets its promises? What evidence, if any, exists for assessing whether a specific evaluation left clients better off? Indeed, do we have good answers to simple descriptive questions, such as what evaluation practice looks like in various areas of application?

Despite the hopes of Shadish et al., Smith, and others, many past and current debates about evaluation appear not to be based on careful and shared empirical evidence. Instead, debates are usually based on untested beliefs, testimonials by advocates, and anecdotes (Smith, 1993). It is probably more accurate to say that today we have an expert-based or evaluation-model-advocate-based evaluation practice rather than an evidence-based evaluation practice.[1]

Against this backdrop, it appears that the number of voices calling for systematic research on evaluation may be increasing in recent years. For instance, Marv Alkin has in several publications advanced the argument Smith (1993), Shadish et al. (1991), and others have made for a "descriptive theory" of evaluation. Roughly, descriptive theory refers to an empirically based assessment of what evaluation looks like, under different conditions, and what kinds of consequences result from various approaches to evaluation (e.g., Alkin, 2003; Smith, 1993). As another example, several contributors to a 2001 special issue of the *American Journal of Evaluation* on the past, present, and future of evaluation issued a call for increased research on evaluation (see Mark's 2001 summary).

These and other recent calls for more research on evaluation (e.g., Henry & Mark, 2003a) have an important cousin. That is, several studies of various kinds of evaluation (e.g., Christie, 2003; Campbell & Mark, 2006; Agodini & Dynarski, 2004; Petrosino, 2003; Weiss et al., 2005) have appeared in recent years. It is not possible to say whether this represents either a long-term trend or a response to the calls for more research from Shadish et al., Smith, Alkin, and others. Still, it seems a favorable sign, with potentially important benefits.

Possible Benefits of More Research on Evaluation

Calls for more and better evidence to guide evaluation theory and practice appear to make great sense. Shouldn't evaluation itself be open to systematic inquiry, just as the policies, programs, and practices that we evaluate are (Dahler-Larsen, 2006)? Viewed from this perspective, a growing evidence base about evaluation should help answer questions such as: Which approaches to evaluation, implemented how and under what conditions, actually lead to what sort of improvements? A growing evidence base can also answer simpler questions, such as whether particular evaluative methods are used more in one program or policy area than another (see, e.g., Petrosino, 2003, who assessed the relative frequency of randomized trials in six different areas of interventions targeted at children).

In addition to providing better advice for evaluation practitioners (Shadish et al., 1991), a larger evidence base about evaluation might have several other benefits (Smith, 1993). For instance, increasing the evidence base of evaluation might:

- Improve the terms of debate among evaluators by helping to substitute some degree of empirical evidence for rhetorical style.
- Allow us to document and understand evaluation's current and past contributions.
- Facilitate appropriate claims about what evaluation can do, *perhaps* most often by moving evaluators in the direction of modesty.[2]
- Stimulate efforts to improve evaluation practice, in part by identifying circumstances in which evaluation demonstrably fails to meet its promise.
- Increase a sense of professionalism among evaluators by making it clear that evaluation itself is worthy of systematic study.
- Help move the field past generic and relatively abstract standards and guiding principles to more empirically supported guidance about the relative benefits of different evaluation practices.[3]

Possible Benefits of a Framework of Types of Research on Evaluation

Despite the arguments for a more evidence-based evaluation practice, a case can be made that a *global call* for more research on evaluation is not sufficient. This chapter expands on past calls for additional research on evaluation by *describing a possible typology that can be used to classify different kinds of research on evaluation.*

Why might such a framework be worth developing? A taxonomy or classification system of alternative kinds of research can be of benefit in several ways:

- It can help us identify gaps in the developing evidence base.
- It can therefore help guide the design of additional research on evaluation. In other words, the classification system can help discussion of research on evaluation move beyond general discussion of the need for research on evaluation to more specific talk about the benefits of particular *kinds* of research on evaluation.
- The mere existence of a classification system might also help stimulate further research on evaluation.
- A taxonomy can guide subsequent efforts to *synthesize* research on evaluation.
- In the preceding ways, a taxonomic system of the kind provided here might be able to help us move toward better answers to the questions about evaluation practice noted by Shadish et al. (1991).
- Thus, a taxonomy may aid in moving debates about evaluation practice away from claims based on rhetoric and perceived expertise rather than sharable evidence.
- Down the road, a taxonomy can serve a knowledge management function that helps guide the use of research on evaluation by others, including prospective evaluation users.
- Efforts to develop and refine a taxonomy of research on evaluation may help us move forward to a better framework of talking about evaluation issues in general.

If we assume, however tentatively, that at least some of these potential benefits would result, then the task of developing a framework of different kinds of research on evaluation seems worthwhile.

FROM GENERAL CALLS TO A FRAMEWORK

In thinking about a taxonomy of research on evaluation, one need is to organize the focus of such research. That is, a taxonomy should help clarify *what* is studied. A second possible part of a taxonomy would address *how* the investigation is done, that is, which kind of methods a particular study of evaluation uses. Consider first the focus of inquiry.

What Is Studied

Table 6.1 offers one way of organizing the various foci that research on evaluation might have. The table suggests that there are (at least) four

TABLE 6.1. Subjects of Inquiry in Research on Evaluation

	Evaluation context	Evaluation activities	Evaluation consequences	Professional issues
Concept	The circumstances within which evaluation occurs	The procedures used in planning, carrying out, and disseminating evaluation	Changes that do (or do not) occur as a result of evaluation	Issues involving the structure, norms, and continuation of the field of evaluation
Subcategories	• Societal • Organizational • Evaluation-specific	• Approaches • Components (within an evaluation model) • Practices	• Use/influence • Participants • Evaluation context, context, activities, and professional issues	• Training • Standards • Etc.
Example	Segerholm (2003) on national context and implications for evaluation	Christie's (2003) mapping of global evaluation approaches as represented by theorists	Classic studies of use; Henry's (2004) study of the consequences of evaluation for client outcomes	Jones & Worthen's (1999) survey about credentializing evaluators

overarching broad categories into which the subjects of research on evaluation will fall: evaluation context, evaluation activities, evaluation consequences, and professional issues. As we shall see, these are not mutually exclusive categories. To the contrary, important studies of evaluation often will examine relationships across these categories.

The categories in Table 6.1 emerged inductively from an attempt to classify real and hypothetical cases of research on evaluation. Interestingly, the categories that emerged resemble, to some degree, other frameworks familiar to evaluators. One correspondence is to logic models, where the current categories of context, activities, and consequences mirror similar categories used in logic models, and with professional issues corresponding to part of the inputs of a logic model. The Table 6.1 categories also correspond in part to the CIPP model of Stufflebeam (2003), with CIPP's context, input, process, and product corresponding, respectively, to Table 6.1's evaluation context, professional issues, activities, and consequences. These correspondences suggest that the current inductively developed categories reflect meaningful distinctions.

Another category could be added to Table 6.1, one capturing *domain-specific* research questions. Domain-specific questions arise within a specific area of evaluation practice. For instance, one might test, meta-analytically, how well various instruments used in evaluations of early childhood interventions relate to subsequent academic performance. Or a researcher might compare across evaluations to try to assess whether a particular health intervention works in both rural and urban settings. Domain-specific research on evaluation can be extremely important. However, the focus here is on the more general categories in Table 6.1. Relative to domain-specific research, research on Table 6.1's more general categories should better contribute to *general* evaluation theory and practice.

The first of the categories in Table 6.1 involves *evaluation context.* Several subcategories fall within, reflecting different levels of context (here, as elsewhere in this model, only a subset of the myriad possible subcategories are described). Segerholm (2003), in her analysis of how evaluation plays out within a specific national context, reminds us that evaluation context can be examined at a *societal* level. For example, cross-national comparisons could be made. Alternatively, many studies of context will emphasize an *organizational* level (within a given society). For example, one might study the suggestions offered by Preskill and Torres (e.g., 1998) about which kinds of organizations are most open to incorporating evaluation in their ongoing routines. Background characteristics of a specific *evaluation* also form part of the context. For example, is the evaluator internal or external, what is the history of evaluation in the local context, what kind of training and experience has the evaluator had, etc.?[4]

The second category in Table 6.1 refers to *evaluation activities.* Several alternatives exist in terms of the way evaluation activities can be examined within research on evaluation. For instance, one might study a *global evaluation approach.* In a sense, Christie (2003) did this when she used multidimensional scaling to map the relative location of a selected set of evaluation theorists. For example, Christie (2003) found that the global evaluation approaches represented by Bob Boruch and Huey Chen differed on a methodology dimension from approaches represented by Ernie House and Michael Patton (see Christie, 2003, Fig. 1.1, p. 17).

As suggested in Table 6.1, an alternative way to study evaluation activities is to take a *given model* of evaluation, break it down into its *component parts,* and study each part. This approach has been used frequently in studies of therapeutic models in psychology; for example, researchers might identify the distinctive parts of, say, cognitive-behavioral therapy for generalized anxiety disorder, and then conduct studies examining the effects of each part in isolation and in conjunction with each other component. The study of a particular model's components will likely be infrequent as research on evaluation grows, but it is an alternative worth keeping in mind. Among its benefits is that the componential approach requires you to do the work of identifying what the distinct parts are of a given evaluation model.

A more likely kind of research focus on evaluation activities will address specific *evaluation practices*. The idea here is to examine some specific aspect (or aspects) of the way evaluation is done in detail. (Unlike the previous option, this does not entail taking a particular evaluation model and decomposing it into its component parts.) As an example, Campbell and Mark (2006) studied the effects of alternative ways of structuring stakeholder involvement. In an "analog experiment," Campbell and Mark examined the consequences of having stakeholder dialogue take place either with each stakeholder feeling accountable only to others who shared his or her beliefs, or alternatively with the stakeholders feeling accountable to a group of people with diverse views on the issue being discussed. In addition, the participants in stakeholder dialogue either did or did not receive instructions drawn from the literature on effective negotiations.

As the Campbell and Mark example suggests, studies of evaluation practices can focus on a wide variety of aspects of the work evaluators do. For example, Torres et al. (1997) focused on how evaluators report on their work. Julian, Reischl, Carrick, and Katrenich (1997) examined the consequences of different levels of participation by stakeholders (though in United Way decision making, rather than evaluation). As another example, a growing number of papers report the consequences of creating a comparison group in one way or another (typically, at random versus through some matching procedure; e.g., Agodini & Dynarsky, 2004). As these examples suggest, an almost limitless number of specific topics could fall under the subcategory of practices.

Third, arguably the most important focus of research on evaluation involves *evaluation's consequences*. This focus is well represented in classic (e.g., Weiss, 1977) and more contemporary (e.g., Simons, Kushner, Jones, & James, 2003) research on evaluation *use*. Research on evaluation use (or influence; Henry & Mark, 2003a; Kirkhart, 2000; Mark & Henry, 2004) has been quite important. Continued research is needed, in part because the world has changed since the seminal research on evaluation use, including new arrangements that can alter the likelihood of use (Weiss et al., 2005).

Despite the potential importance of additional research on evaluation use/influence, it is important to remember that evaluation consequences can include outcomes other than classic forms of use. For instance, the consequences of evaluation may involve *changes in those who actively participate in the evaluation.* Indeed, some approaches to evaluation explicitly express as a key goal the changing of participants in a certain way. For instance, empowerment evaluation has as one of its goals strengthening participants' sense of empowerment. Research on evaluation seems especially warranted for those evaluation models that advertise such effects.

Quite importantly (though to date, infrequently), research on evaluation can study the consequences of evaluation for actual *client outcomes.* Henry (2004) reported an attempt to do so in the context of a longitudinal evaluation of Georgia's pre-K program. Generally speaking, Henry attempted to examine the effects of the evaluation and its use on children's outcomes at a later point in time. More specifically, an early wave of evaluation had identified benefits when pre-K teachers were credentialed. Evaluation use then occurred, in that policies were changed to provide new incentives for pre-K centers to employ credentialed teachers. Henry subsequently attempted to assess whether this policy change itself resulted in improved student outcomes. If similar studies of evaluation's consequences become more commonplace, synthesis of many such studies would go a long way toward answering questions about the influence and impact of evaluation itself, and also about the relative influence and impact of alternative approaches to evaluation.

Another subcategory under evaluation consequences in Table 6.1 also refers to the consequences of evaluation on the *evaluation context,* or on subsequent *evaluation activities,* or on *professional issues.* For instance, does an evaluation itself change some aspect of the evaluation context? This possibility is often implied, for example, by evaluators who suggest that their preferred approach to evaluation will in one way or another strengthen democratic processes (Greene, 2006). Do these approaches have such consequences in practice? As another example, today's evaluation within an organization may lead to changes in the evaluation approach that is used in that organization tomorrow.

Again, the point is that evaluation consequences should not be narrowly construed in terms of traditional forms of use—and not necessarily even in terms of the more important consequences of client outcomes and other participant consequences. Instead, in a given research study, the focus could be on the consequences of evaluation for subsequent evaluation context, or evaluation activities, or views regarding professional issues.

As the preceding discussion suggests, many important studies of evaluation will cross the categories of Table 6.1. Indeed, a persuasive case can be made that the most important studies of evaluation explicitly examine the relationship across two or more categories. For example, Henry (2004) did not simply look alone at evaluation influence. He also focused on a global evaluation approach. That is, he examined the consequences of his pre-K evaluation as a global whole, without parsing out the contribution of various components or specific practices. More importantly, he examined the effect *of* his global evaluation approach *on* evaluation outcomes, particularly children's outcomes. As another example, Petrosino (2003) examined the *relationship* between program area, as a specific aspect of evaluation context, and the frequency of use of a specific evaluation approach, the RCT. One can imagine many more such intersections across the columns of Table 6.1. For example, studies of the societal component of evaluation context could examine the relationship between types of societies and the evaluation approaches that predominate. One could study the consequences of training for the evaluation practices that evaluators adopt. Many more examples are possible. The key point is that the most important questions for researchers on evaluation may involve trying to assess the influence of one category from Table 6.1 on another.

Turning to the fourth and final column of Table 6.1, *professional issues* are another possible subject of inquiry. Professional issues that might be studied include evaluation training, evaluation standards, and the credentialization or certification of training programs or evaluators (see, e.g., the survey of evaluators' opinions about certification by Jones & Worthen, 1999). Other professional issues include the nature and function of evaluation associations, networks of or modes of professional communication (such as listservs; Christie & Azzam, 2004), professional conferences, and the like.

A Case Example of Research on Evaluation

Table 6.1 summarizes the "what" of research on evaluation, in the form of several general options regarding what the focus of such research can be. Before proceeding to discuss the "how"—that is, the ways of doing research on evaluation—consider one case example in some detail—in part because it foreshadows the subsequent discussion.

In an ongoing project, I am attempting to examine the "evaluation portfolio" at a number of organizations. By evaluation portfolio, in general terms I mean the way that evaluation resources are allocated across different kinds of evaluation activities. One way I am looking at evaluation resource allocations is in terms of the "inquiry modes" that Mark, Henry, and Julnes (2000) suggest constitute method families, or clusters of methodological approaches used by evaluators. The four inquiry modes are displayed in the upper half of Table 6.2.

TABLE 6.2. Four Inquiry Modes and a Case of "Portfolio Analysis"

	Description	Classification	Causal analysis	Values inquiry
Focus	Measuring characteristics of clients, services, outcomes	Categorizing (clients, service settings, etc.)	Estimating effects; identifying mechanisms	Identifying value positions of stakeholders and public
Typical methods	Performance measures; observations	Cluster analysis; taxonomies	Experiments; quasi-experiments; case studies	Group deliberation; surveys
Portfolio: % of evaluations	95.5%	—	3.5%	1%
Approx. % of evaluation spending	20%	—	70%	10%

As indicated in that table, *classification* refers to the use of methods to identify categories, such as various types of program clients or different groupings of service delivery settings. *Causal analysis,* in the context of evaluation, refers to the use of methods designed to do such things as estimate the effects of a program and/or identify or test the mechanisms by which a program has its effects. *Description* refers to methods that measure such things as the characteristics of clients, the nature of service delivery, or the standing of clients on important outcome variables, but without identifying new categories or actually investigating causal relations. *Values inquiry* refers to evaluation methods used to probe the values embedded in and related to a program, such as by assessing which of the potential process and outcome variables stakeholders care most about.

Consider a single case from an ongoing research project. The case involves a private U.S. foundation with a regional focus. This foundation makes grants in the area of health and access to health care, distributing roughly $10–$12 million annually. As summarized in the bottom half of Table 6.2, the vast majority of the evaluations funded by this foundation, roughly 95%, are descriptive. Mostly these involve relatively simple performance measurement and account for perhaps 20% of the spending on evaluation. On the other hand, the relatively small proportion of evaluations that involve causal analysis account for a relatively high proportion of spending on evaluation, perhaps 70% (note: data on total spending for evaluation are, to use a "technical" term, rather "iffy").

Describing the evaluation portfolio of even this one foundation can raise several interesting questions, such as: Is the formulaic approach to most evaluation planning in this foundation appropriate? What are the opportunity costs of the many, relatively cheap, descriptive evaluations? Given the general absence of classification and values inquiry, are these the evaluation "best buys," at least for this foundation? How good is the planning that leads to selecting the projects for high-cost causal analyses? As I hope these questions suggest, descriptive analysis of evaluation practice can raise important issues for further consideration.

In addition to demonstrating the potential of research on evaluation for learning and for generating further questions for practice, the portfolio analysis, including its use of the Mark et al. (2000) taxonomy of inquiry modes, is presented here for another reason: in the process of reviewing numerous real and hypothetical cases of research on evaluation, I found that this taxonomy of research methods appeared to capture useful distinctions among various studies of evaluation. Although the taxonomy was initially developed to describe different kinds of methods that can be used in *doing evaluation*, I suggest here that it can also profitably be used to describe different kinds of *research on evaluation*. Table 6.3 gives a brief overview.

TABLE 6.3. Inquiry Modes and Research on Evaluation, with Examples

	Description	Classification	Causal analysis	Values inquiry
Examples (see text for details)	Torres, Preskill, and Piontek (1997); Petrosino (2003); portfolio analysis	Christie (2003) (close, anyway); Cousins and Whitmore (1998)	Henry (2004); Campbell and Mark (2006)	Segerholm (2003); part of Holbrook, Bourke, Owen, McKenzie, and Ainley (2000)
Potential exemplar	Describing what evaluation actually looks like in various settings	Identification of different types of evaluation practice, contexts	Study of the consequences of evaluation practice	Assessing what stakeholders value re: what evaluation might achieve

Inquiry Modes as Part of a Framework

A range of methods are possible for *description* in research on evaluation, including observational, questionnaire, and content analysis methods. For example, a variety of studies that survey evaluation practitioners or evaluation users typically involve description. To take but one
example, Torres et al. (1997) surveyed a random sample of members of
the American Evaluation Association. The survey asked several questions about the communication and reporting of evaluations. For instance, respondents indicate that the most common forms of communication are written final reports. Other surveys have provided descriptive
information about such things as evaluators' views about use (Preskill &
Caracelli, 1997) and the characteristics of collaborative or participatory
evaluation as practiced (Cousins, Donohue, & Bloom, 1996).

Of course, descriptive methods other than surveys are possible for
studying evaluation. For example, Petrosino (2003) recently examined
abstracts from reports of outcome evaluations drawn from a set of electronic bibliographic databases. Petrosino used the abstracts to estimate
the relative frequency of randomized controlled trials (RCTs) in six different areas of interventions designed for children. He found, for example, that almost 70% of the outcome evaluations of childhood interventions in health care appeared to use an RCT, while only perhaps 15% in
education did.[5] The assessment of evaluation portfolios, illustrated in
Table 6.2, is another example of *description*.[6] In scanning the literature,
it appears that descriptive studies may currently be the most common
form of research on evaluation.

Turning to *classification*, the Christie example comes very close to
being an example. Certainly, if Christie had gone beyond her mapping of
evaluation theorists by reporting cluster analysis results that put the various theorists into groups, it would have been classification. Another
example of classification, though for the most part conceptually and not
empirically driven, is the work by Brad Cousins and his colleagues (e.g.,
Cousins & Whitmore, 1998) that attempts to define different types of
participatory evaluation. A paper by Cousins et al. (1996) that reports a
survey of evaluators' views about their collaborative evaluation practices
reminds us that survey data can be put to use in classificatory analyses.

More generally, classification studies of evaluation can seek to identify the different types of evaluation practice, the varying types of contexts in which evaluation takes place, and the categories of evaluation
users, evaluators, uses, and so on. Classification studies of evaluation are
useful in their own right, in helping us better understand the lay of the
land in evaluation practice. Especially given the relative paucity of classification studies, an increase in their use seems desirable. Classification

studies also have considerable potential when combined with other kinds of methods. For example, one could combine a classification study of different kinds of participatory evaluation with a causal analysis, leading to conclusions about the differential consequences of different forms of participatory evaluation.

Moving to *causal analysis*, both the Henry (2004) and the Campbell and Mark (2006) examples fall into this category. The two cases illustrate some (but certainly not all) of the wide variety of methods that can be used for causal analysis. Henry's study used quasi-experimental methods and statistical controls, while Campbell and Mark used experimental methods (in an analog situation). Yet other methods can be employed, including case studies. An argument can be made that causal investigations are likely in general to be among the most important forms of research on evaluation. This is because, just as program outcomes are typically of keen interest in making bottom-line evaluative judgments, the consequences of evaluation (and of alternative forms of evaluation) are vital for assessing the merit and worth of evaluation and its alternative forms. Given the important benefits of causal analysis as applied to evaluation itself, I briefly return in the "Discussion" section to a few issues regarding this form of research on evaluation.

One of the values of using the Mark et al. (2000) taxonomy is that it reminds us that research on evaluation can include *values inquiry*. In general terms, this would typically involve systematic inquiry into such questions as: What is it that stakeholders value (positively or negatively) about evaluation? Do different stakeholder groups generally value different possible consequences of evaluation? For example, in recent years various members of the evaluation community have discussed such possible consequences of evaluation as empowerment, creation of a space for dialogue, and facilitation of some preferred model of democracy. Despite the importance of such debates within the evaluation community, by most standards these debates do not rise to the level of systematic inquiry or research. And systematic research on stakeholder values could be quite informative. For example, we could assess how strongly various stakeholders value empowerment, dialogue, and related consequences, relative to previously emphasized potential evaluation consequences such as getting a better answer to a question that might be relevant to decision making. Values inquiry applied to evaluation itself includes the (in some sense modest but in practice perhaps radical) idea that, rather than having evaluators arguing among ourselves about the various alternative goals of evaluation, we should also consider attempting, at least in the occasional research study, to assess what relevant stakeholders think about these alternatives. Of course, this effort could involve comparing values across different stakeholder groups, different organizations, different circumstances, etc.

Although empirical examples of values inquiry in research on evaluation do not appear to be plenty, there are some near examples. For instance, in a study of educational research in Australia (most of which was descriptive), one phase involved asking several stakeholder groups about what kind of value they sought in educational research (Holbrook, Bourke, Owen, McKenzie, & Ainley, 2000). Segerholm (2003) also offers suggestions about what values inquiry might look like as applied to evaluation itself. Expanding on Segerholm's analyses, one might undertake a comparative study of the values surrounding evaluation in different nations.

This section and the summary in Table 6.3 offer a few examples of descriptive, causal analysis, classification, and values inquiry in research on evaluation. Space precludes going beyond these few examples and systematically illustrating the intersection between inquiry modes and Table 6.1's subjects of inquiry. I invite readers to consider the combination of inquiry modes and subjects of inquiry, ideally to stimulate their own ideas about possible studies of evaluation. If used well, a taxonomy of research on evaluation will not constrain the way we think, but will foster thoughtful consideration of the many research questions about evaluation that are worth studying.

DISCUSSION

Drawing on previous calls for research on evaluation, this chapter is in part premised on the idea that a more evidence-based practice of evaluation can help (1) to *identify* and (2) over time to *strengthen* the contribution that evaluation makes. The call for an evidence-based evaluation practice is not new. However, openness to and opportunities for research on evaluation may be growing. For instance, the broader evidence-based movement should be conducive to research on evaluation itself. As one example, the activities of the Campbell Collaboration, which supports meta-analyses of evaluations of social and educational programs and practices, appear to be stimulating interest in research on evaluation use and related topics (e.g., Davies, Nutley, & Walter, 2005). In addition, the seemingly growing interest in and commissioning of evaluation in many contexts may imply more resources for research on evaluation. Some sources of funding appear to be open to supporting research on evaluation directly, such as the National Science Foundation's program on Research and Evaluation on Education in Science and Engineering (though this program appears narrower than one of its predecessors, on

Evaluative Research and Evaluation Capacity). Funding for research on evaluation is reportedly growing in Canada (J. Love, personal communication, January, 2006). Further, it appears that the evaluation community itself is growing, including drawing in some people who by virtue of their backgrounds may be interested in conducting research on evaluation itself (e.g., Campbell, Christie, Cousins, Henry, Petrosino). Such circumstances suggest that conditions today may be congenial to at least some increase in research on evaluation.

This, I believe, is good. Nevertheless, I suggest it is also worthwhile at this point to move beyond *general calls* for more research on evaluation. Thus, the framework presented in this chapter is offered as a supplement to more general calls for research on evaluation. This typology could have several benefits, including helping to stimulate further contributions to an evidence base for evaluation practice and offering a way of classifying, comparing, and synthesizing the findings that result. Having a taxonomy should also facilitate more thoughtful discussions about the relative value of different types of research on evaluation.

In this regard, one should expect that, to the extent research on evaluation grows, it will do so largely as a consequence of the interest of individual investigators and the joint actions of the community of scholars. The direction of future research on evaluation, as in any area of research, may also be influenced by such factors as funding opportunities, the relative feasibility of doing research in different areas, and the receptivity of journals to different topics (on the issue of options for funding for research on evaluation, see Henry & Mark, 2003b). In other words, arguing for the value of a taxonomy of research on evaluation does not entail replacing or devaluing the ordinary processes that arise in any area of research.

Brief Comments on Causal Analyses in Research on Evaluation

It is beyond the scope of this chapter to have a detailed discussion of the opportunities and challenges in conducting causal analyses as part of research on evaluation. However, a few brief comments seem warranted. First, those interested in the empirical study of evaluation may need to be opportunistic and clever in order to strengthen causal inference. Second, when comparing the consequences of different approaches to evaluation, researchers need to be mindful of the possibility of unfair comparisons. For more general discussion of unfair comparisons (e.g., confounds between stakeholder information needs and the type of evaluator selected), see Cooper and Richardson (1986). And third, openness to a range of causal methods is to be encouraged, with multiple methods an aspiration.

Metaevaluation and the Taxonomy

A question that can arise in terms of the present taxonomy involves whether, and how, metaevaluation (the "evaluation of evaluation") fits. My answer is not a simple one, because there is no single universally agreed-upon methodology for conducting meta-analyses (Cooksy & Caracelli, 2005). If a given metaevaluation consists simply of expert review of the judgments taken in an evaluation, I probably would not label it as research. On the other hand, a meta-analysis might carefully, and with conscious attention to alternative explanations, trace the apparent consequences of an evaluation; like Henry (2004), this would be an example of causal analysis of the consequences of the evaluation approach used in the evaluation. As another example, a comparative meta-analysis might compare across several evaluations and examine the relationship between some aspect of evaluation context and the kinds of evaluation activities that were carried out (akin to Pretrosino, 2003). Again, this would fairly clearly be an example of research on evaluation. As these two examples show, metaevaluation does not intrinsically fit within one cell of the taxonomy, but can include different types of research on evaluation.

Conclusions and Caveats

The taxonomy described here, I believe, is at a different "level of analysis" than past discussions of research on evaluation. To date, discussion about whether and how to develop an evidence base for evaluation practice has either been quite abstract (e.g., general calls for more research on evaluation, or equally general skepticism) or quite specific (e.g., a solitary study of evaluation practice, or a critique of a single study). This chapter has offered a relatively mid-range analysis, with brief attention to comparative case analysis and with the development of a tentative typology of different kinds of research on evaluation. At some point in the evolution of a research-based evaluation practice, we probably need to move beyond abstract arguments for and against research on evaluation, and even to move beyond individual studies of evaluation and their critique. Taxonomies of research on evaluation are one way to move beyond the individual study and the abstract argument. A taxonomy can, for example, help us see where gaps exist in the literature, stimulate research, and aid in the synthesis and use of research on evaluation. A taxonomy can help achieve some of the cumulativity that is missing in evaluation (Mark, 2001, 2003).

   Several caveats need to be added to this endeavor to move toward a taxonomy of types of research on evaluation:

• A single study (and, even more, a line of research) may partake of multiple kinds of research on evaluation. For example, Christie used simple descriptive methods to study whether her sample of evaluators reported subscribing to any evaluation theory, and she used (or at least approached) classification methods in her mapping of evaluation theorists' responses.

• As with almost any classification system, it is likely that some cases will reside at the boundaries between categories and thus will be difficult to classify.

• At best, the current chapter is a start toward a good framework—and I hope it will not be the last word on the subject. At the least, various elaborations and modifications of the framework described here are possible. For example, if the body of research grows and if this taxonomy is used, revisions will be needed, such as finer distinctions.

• In addition, alternatives to the framework described here are possible. Rather than the list of four "inquiry modes," you probably could use the chapter titles from your favorite research methods textbook. Rather than the "subject of inquiry" categories used here, several alternatives are possible. For instance, one might instead use Shadish et al.'s (1991) five components of evaluation theory: social programming (or, more generally, theory of the evaluand), knowledge, valuing, use, and evaluation practice. Perhaps there is even value in there being multiple complementary taxonomies of research on evaluation.

Despite all these (and, doubtless, other) caveats, I hope that we at least have begun a conversation about alternative forms of research on evaluation, that this conversation will help us move forward in terms of the broad project of creating a larger evidence base to guide evaluation practice (including stimulating thoughtful criticism), and that there also is some positive movement in terms of developing one or more frameworks for classifying the research that results.

One more general caveat: even those of us who advocate the development of more research on evaluation should also of course acknowledge the limits of such an endeavor. Research on evaluation will not be a magic bullet. It will not immediately transform the field. It will not replace all judgment about evaluation practice—but instead should *aid* such judgment. Research on evaluation, like evaluation itself, will raise questions about generalizability and applicability to specific situations. Research on evaluation will at least some of the time be ignored—even in cases where it could be useful. In short, the various problems and limits we all know about regarding evaluation (and research) itself and its use will also arise in the context of research on evaluation.

At the same time, I find it difficult to conceive of a truly compelling rationale for supporting the systematic study of policies, programs, and practices as part of our evaluation work while simultaneously arguing against the systematic study of evaluation itself. And the broad project of doing research on evaluation can move ahead and contribute even as we disagree. As we do with the very nature of evaluation itself, we may vigorously debate what research on evaluation should look like, what kinds of conclusions it should be directed toward, and so on. But, just as those debates about evaluation currently do not keep us from doing evaluation, I hope that any debates about research on evaluation do not keep us from doing research on evaluation.

At the very least, I am certainly persuaded that the broad project of developing an evidence base about evaluation itself is an endeavor worth engaging in, with some potential to strengthen the contribution that evaluation makes. The evidence base that results may even help move the discussion ahead on a variety of other fundamental issues in evaluation.

ACKNOWLEDGMENTS

This chapter is based on a paper presented at the 2004 annual meeting of the American Evaluation Association. Thanks go to Paul Brandon, Nick Smith, Tina Christie, and Gary Henry for helpful comments on a previous version. This chapter is supported in part by a grant from the National Science Foundation (No. REC-02311859).

NOTES

1. This admittedly contentious statement ignores, of course, that the experts and model advocates presumably base their preferences on some form of evidence from their practice experiences. However, in general such practice-based evidence (assuming it exists—as Ernie House (2003) points out, evaluation theorists sometimes get ahead of practice) is not readily shared, critiqued, detailed, and exposed to counterevidence in ways that we in general expect for research in general, or for evidence-based practice in particular—or for most professional evaluation, for that matter.

2. For example, the word *transformative* has been bandied about by many evaluators in recent years, and it would be good either to have evidence that evaluation is indeed transformative or instead to embrace the value of more modest consequences of evaluation.

3. Counterarguments can be made against the idea of a more evidence-based evaluation practice, but I do not see these as compelling. A brief listing and rebuttal of several counterarguments is available from the author.

4. Note that, in specifying these different levels of context, I am *not* suggesting that research on context needs to address all of these levels. As with other parts of the taxonomy, which category or subcategory is represented within a study will depend on the specific research question an investigator is motivated to examine.

5. One kind of descriptive study warrants special note. Many of the post hoc case studies that constitute a good part of the recent research literature on evaluation—in which, for example, the evaluator describes selected aspects of evaluation process and use—do not rise beyond the category of description. Many such case studies of evaluation appear to have been done retrospectively, after an evaluator notices some interesting aspect of the evaluation they are doing. It appears that post hoc case studies, because of their after-the-fact nature and attendant data limitations, often do not include the kind of features that would support reasonably strong conclusions about the evaluation's contributions.

6. This is not considered here as an example of classification, because the four-fold grouping of inquiry modes was not developed empirically during this investigation.

REFERENCES

Agodini, R., & Dynarski, M. (2004). Are experiments the only option? A look at dropout prevention programs. *The Review of Economics and Statistics, 86,* 180–194.

Alkin, M. C. (2003). Evaluation theory and practice: Insights and new directions. In C. A. Christie (Ed.), *The practice–theory relationship in evaluation* (pp. 81–89). San Francisco: Jossey-Bass.

Bernstein, I. N., & Freeman, H. E. (1975). *Academic and entrepreneurial research.* New York: Russell Sage.

Campbell, B. C., & Mark, M. M. (2006). Toward more effective stakeholder dialogue: Applying theories of negotiation to policy and program evaluation. *Journal of Applied Social Psychology, 36,* 2834–2863.

Christie, C. A. (2003). What guides evaluation? A study of how evaluation practice maps onto evaluation theory. In C. A. Christie (Ed.), *The practice–theory relationship in evaluation* (New Directions for Evaluation no. 97, pp. 7–35). San Francisco: Jossey-Bass.

Christie, C. A., & Azzam, T. (2004). What's all the talk about? Examining EVALTALK, an evaluation listserv. *American Journal of Evaluation, 25,* 219–234.

Cooksy, L. J., & Caracelli, V. J. (2005). Quality, context, and use: Issues in achieving the goals of metaevaluation. *American Journal of Evaluation, 26,* 31–42.

Cooper, W. H., & Richardson, A. J. (1986). Unfair comparisons. *Journal of Applied Psychology, 71,* 179–184.

Cousins, J. B., Donohue, J. J., & Bloom, G. A. (1996). Collaborative evaluation in North America: Evaluators' self-reported opinions, practices and consequences. *Evaluation Practice, 17,* 207–226.

Cousins, J. B., & Whitmore, E. (1998). Framing participatory evaluation. In E. Whitmore (Ed.), *Understanding and practicing participatory evaluation* (New Directions for Evaluation no. 80, pp. 5–24). San Francisco: Jossey-Bass.

Dahler-Larsen, P. (2006). Evaluation after disenchantment?: Five issues shaping the role of evaluation in society. In I. Shaw, J. C. Greene, & M. M. Mark (Eds.), *The Sage handbook of evaluation* (pp. 141–160). London: Sage.

Davies, H. T. O., Nutley, S. M., & Walter, I. (2005, May 12–13). *Approaches to assessing the nonacademic impact of social science research* (Report of the Economic and Social Research Council Symposium on Assessing the Nonacademic Impact of Research). St. Andrews, Scotland: Research Unit for Research Utilisation, University of St Andrews.

Donaldson, S. I., & Lipsey, M. W. (2006). Roles for theory in contemporary evaluation practice: Developing practical knowledge from evaluation. In I. Shaw, J. C. Greene, & M. M. Mark (Eds.), *The Sage handbook of evaluation* (pp. 56–75). London: Sage.

Greene, J. C. (2006). Evaluation, democracy, and social change. In I. Shaw, J. C. Greene, & M. M. Mark (Eds.), *The Sage handbook of evaluation* (pp. 118–140). London: Sage.

Henry, G. T. (2004). *Coming full circle: Assessing evaluation's influence on program performance.* Paper presented at the annual meeting of the American Evaluation Association, Atlanta.

Henry, G. T., & Mark, M. M. (2003a). Beyond use: Understanding evaluation's influence on attitudes and actions. *American Journal of Evaluation, 24,* 293–314.

Henry, G. T., & Mark, M. M. (2003b). Toward an agenda for research on evaluation. In C. A. Christie (Ed.), *The practice–theory relationship in evaluation* (pp. 69–80). San Francisco: Jossey-Bass.

Holbrook, A., Bourke, S., Owen, J. M., McKenzie, P., & Ainley, J. (2000). *Mapping educational research and exploring research impact: A holistic, multimethod approach.* Paper presented at the annual conference of the American Educational Research Association, New Orleans.

House, E. R. (2003). Evaluation theory. In T. Kellaghan & D. L. Stufflebeam (Eds.), *International handbook of educational evaluation* (pp. 9–13). Boston: Kluwer Academic Press.

Jones, S. C., & Worthen, B. R. (1999). AEA members' opinions concerning evaluator certification. *American Journal of Evaluation, 20,* 495–506.

Julian, D. A., Reischl, T. M., Carrick, R. V. & Katrenich, C. (1997). Citizen participation: Lessons from a local United Way planning process. *Journal of the American Planning Association, 63,* 345–355.

King, J. (2003). The challenge of studying evaluation theory. In C. A. Christie (Ed.), *The practice–theory relationship in evaluation* (New Directions for Evaluation no. 97, pp. 57–67). San Francisco: Jossey-Bass.

Kirkhart, K. (2000). Reconceptualizing evaluation use: An integrated theory of influence. In V. Caracelli & H. Preskill (Eds.), *The expanding scope of evaluation use* (New Directions for Evaluation no. 88, pp. 5–24). San Francisco: Jossey-Bass.

Lipsey, M. W., Crosse, S., Dunkle, J., Pollard, J., & Stobart, G. (1985). Evaluation: The state of the art and the sorry state of the science. In D. S. Cordray (Ed.), *Utilizing prior research in evaluation planning* (New Directions for Evaluation no. 27, pp. 7–28). San Francisco: Jossey-Bass.

Mark, M. M. (2001). Evaluation's future: Furor, futile, or fertile? *American Journal of Evaluation, 22,* 457–479.

Mark, M. M. (2003). Toward a comprehensive view of the theory and practice of program and policy evaluation. In S. I. Donaldson & M. Scriven (Eds.), *Evaluating social programs and problems: Visions for the new millennium* (pp. 183–204). Hillsdale, NJ: Erlbaum.

Mark, M. M., & Henry, G. T. (2004). The mechanisms and outcomes of evaluation influence. *Evaluation, 10,* 35–57.

Mark, M. M., Henry, G. T., & Julnes, G. (2000). *Evaluation: An integrated framework for understanding, guiding, and improving policies and programs.* San Francisco: Jossey-Bass.

Patton, M. Q. (1997). *Utilization-focused evaluation: The new century text.* Thousand Oaks, CA: Sage.

Patton, M. Q., Grimes, P. S., Guthrie, K. M., Brennan, N. J., French, B. D., et al. (1977). In search of impact: An analysis of the utilization of federal health evaluation research. In C. H. Weiss (Ed.), *Using social research in public policy making.* Lexington, MA: Lexington Books.

Petrosino, A. (2003). Estimates of randomized controlled trials across six areas of childhood intervention: A bibliometric analysis. *Annals of the American Academy of Political and Social Science, 589,* 190–202.

Preskill, H., & Caracelli, V. J. (1997). Current and developing conceptions of use: Evaluation use TIG survey results. *Evaluation Practice, 18*(3), 209–225.

Preskill, H. S., & Torres, R. T. (1998). *Evaluative inquiry for learning in organizations.* Thousand Oaks, CA: Sage.

Segerholm, C. (2003). Researching evaluation in national (state) politics and administration: A critical approach. *American Journal of Evaluation, 24,* 353–372.

Shadish, W. R., Cook, T. D., & Leviton, L. C. (1991). *Foundations of program evaluation: Theories of practice.* Newbury Park, CA: Sage.

Simons, H., Kushner, S., Jones, K., & James, D. (2003). From evidence-based practice to practice-based evidence: The idea of situated generalization. *Research Papers in Education, 18*(4), 347–364.

Smith, N. L. (1993). Improving evaluation theory through the empirical study of evaluation practice. *Evaluation Practice, 14,* 237–242.

Stufflebeam, D. L. (2003). The CIPP model for evaluation. In T. Kelleghan & D. L. Stufflebeam (Eds.), *The international handbook of educational evaluation.* Boston: Kluwer.

Torres, R. T., Preskill, H., & Piontek, M. (1997). Communicating and reporting practices and concerns for internal and external evaluators. *Evaluation Practice, 18*(2), 105–126.

Weiss, C. H. (Ed.). (1977). *Using social research in public policy making.* Lexington, MA: Lexington Books.

Weiss, C. H. (2004). Routine for evaluation: A Cliff's Notes version of my work. In M. C. Alkin (Ed.), *Evaluation roots* (pp. 153–168). Thousand Oaks, CA: Sage.

Weiss, C., Murphy-Graham, E., & Birkeland, S. (2005). An alternate route to policy influence: Evidence from a study of the Drug Abuse Resistance Education (D.A.R.E.) program. *American Journal of Evaluation, 26,* 12–31.

PART III

ISSUES OF PRACTICE

Practice is the actual doing of evaluation. It involves the hard work of daily professional performance, often under difficult conditions and limited resources. Practice consists of implementing work plans, dealing with diverse political interests, responding to changing field conditions, and managing personnel and resources, all the while attending to shifting client and stakeholder needs and priorities. Practice entails somehow managing to simultaneously balance technical quality, client satisfaction, and available resources. If theory and method reflect the science of evaluation design, practice reflects the art of its performance. While theory and method provide the why and how of evaluation, it is practice that ensures that evaluations get done, with quality and in a manner that contributes to a better society.

Within the evaluation profession, issues of practice often are given less attention and are seen as less glamorous than issues of theory or

135

method. Few of the most visible members of the field are famous for being outstanding practitioners; more often it is the methodologists and the theorists who get the attention, journal space, and awards. As Schwandt cautions, however, it is important not to underestimate the significance of practice in understanding the nature of the evaluation enterprise (see Schwandt, Chapter 2).

Furthermore, there are undoubtedly many more people practicing evaluation on a daily basis than are creating theories or developing methods. The importance of issues of practice can be seen, for example, in documents concerning the ultimate quality and social contribution of evaluation. For example, a full third of the standards in *The Program Evaluation Standards* (Joint Committee on Standards for Educational Evaluation, 1994) concern issues of practice. Under the category of Utility, seven standards are listed that "define whether an evaluation serves the practical information needs of a given audience" (p. 5). An additional three standards are listed under Feasibility, which concerns the extent to which evaluations are operable in field settings.

As with many professions, there is a symbiotic but uneasy relationship among theorists, methodologists, and practitioners. There are recurring criticisms that practitioners are not employing the latest theories and methods, with responding complaints that theorists' and methodologists' creations lack contextual relevancy and practical utility. And yet, theories and methods continue to influence the nature of practice, and the practical lessons learned in the field eventually return to reform old theories and shape new methods.

J. Bradley Cousins and Lyn M. Shulha lead off Part III with Chapter 7, "Complexities in Setting Program Standards in Collaborative Evaluation." They address the fundamental issue of deciding how good is good enough—that is, what level of performance must an evaluand achieve for its performance to be considered adequate or satisfactory in a collaborative evaluation? As they note, this is one of the issues that separates evaluation from social science research. (See also Mathison, Chapter 9.)

Cousins and Shulha discuss how to set program standards when conducting formative collaborative evaluations in which stakeholders such as program personnel share more of the responsibility for the evaluation than in traditional evaluations. Under this form of evaluation, power over evaluation decision making is shared equally among the evaluators, who have technical skills, and program personnel, whose understanding of the substance, organization, and daily operations of the program is far greater than that of the program's evaluators. Such evaluations should be ideal for explicitly and carefully deciding how well the evaluated program has to perform. The formative evaluation purpose helps focus evaluators and stakeholders on making recommendations about explicit levels of performance, and the collaborative nature of the study ensures that the process is fair and broad.

Cousins and Shulha state that evaluators and stakeholders deciding how to set standards in collaborative studies are likely to address issues of (1) selecting the bases for comparison, (2) deciding whether to prescribe values or describe them, (3) deciding how to set standards for mixed types of data, and (4) deciding how to ensure cultural sensitivity. They discuss each of these issues at length, and they present a case example that highlights how these issues might be manifested in a collaborative evaluation.

Carlos C. Ayala and Paul R. Brandon continue the focus on formative evaluation in Chapter 8, "Building Evaluation Recommendations for Improvement: Insights from Student Formative Assessments." They consider the case of K–12 student formative assessment that is conducted by the classroom teacher for the purpose of providing immediate feedback to students about how to improve their learning. Approaches to formative student assessment can range from informal assessments to formal assessments embedded within curricula or programs. Ayala and Brandon present a formal approach to assessment called the *Assessment Pedagogy Model*, which uses assessment as an integral part of teaching. They describe the several components of the model and review implications of the model for formative program evaluation in general.

The Ayala and Brandon chapter provides a clear example of how the resolution of a recurring evaluation issue is altered by changing social and political circumstances. Many K–12 educators in the United States have reacted to the federal government's heavy emphasis on the summative testing required by the No Child Left Behind legislation. They have sought to balance the summative emphasis by integrating formative assessment into teaching, thereby inserting evaluation activities more directly into programmatic activities than typically occurs in program evaluations, even those that emphasize the instrumental use of evaluation findings, such as participatory or utilization-focused evaluations.

Both these chapters illustrate how difficulties in evaluation practice not only have resulted in subsequent improvements to that practice but also have led evaluators to reconsider issues of theory and method. For example, does the extensive involvement of stakeholders in standard setting lead to self-serving criteria? Do dual instructional/programmatic and evaluative roles provide teachers and stakeholders with unusual insights into the proper nature and timing of evaluation activities, or do they result in a hopelessly complicated standard-setting process fraught with bias? Both these chapters illustrate the essential contribution of self-reflective practice in producing an effective and useful profession.

REFERENCE

Joint Committee on Standards for Educational Evaluation. (1994). *The program evaluation standards* (2nd ed.). Thousand Oaks, CA: Sage.

CHAPTER 7

Complexities in Setting Program Standards in Collaborative Evaluation

J. Bradley Cousins and Lyn M. Shulha

Program evaluation requires judgment about program merit and/or worth and/or significance, and judgment requires comparison between what is observed, through the systematic gathering of data, and some criterion or set of criteria. In evaluating program quality the question naturally arises, "How good is good enough?" This question not only is central to evaluation, but also, we would argue, it is the essential characteristic differentiating evaluation from social sciences research. To answer the question, a program standard must be set. While this step might be thought to be obvious, some would argue that it is often taken for granted. Nick Smith (personal communication, January 2006), for example, makes the case that program standard setting is assumed in traditional approaches to evaluation and consciously avoided in phenomenological approaches. Program standard setting is as important and relevant in "hard-nosed" external summative evaluations leading to high-stakes decisions about a given program or policy as it is in the context of collaborative approaches to evaluation—participatory and empowerment approaches—that may be program improvement-oriented in intent. If the issue of program standard setting is one that has received unsatisfactory attention in evaluation generally (Brandon, 2005), this is especially the case in collaborative evaluation.

Collaborative approaches to evaluation have been around in the international development literature for a quarter-century (Fernandes &

Tandon, 1981; Friere, 1982) and have found their way into more mainstream evaluation contexts since the late 1980s and early 1990s (e.g.,
Ayres, 1987; Cousins & Earl, 1995; Fetterman, 1994; Greene, 1988).
Most collaborative evaluation aficionados would make the claim that
such methods are comparatively more responsive to the information
needs of members of the program community than are more traditionalist mainstream approaches.

   Given that interest in the theory and practice of collaborative
approaches is on the rise in contemporary evaluation contexts (Cousins,
2003), more needs to be understood about standard setting or modes of
determining whether observed levels of program quality are good
enough. This issue is essential, because the collaborative approaches we
discuss are, after all, approaches to evaluation; hence, they necessarily
involve judgment. Even in decidedly improvement-oriented contexts,
evaluative judgments about program quality are fundamental. Program
developers need to know on which aspects of the program to spend their
time and engage in order to make the program better.

   In this chapter we explore the issue by identifying and examining
conceptual, contextual, and cultural complexities in setting program
standards in collaborative evaluation. We identify these issues through a
review of relevant literature and through reflection on our own evaluation practice. By way of illustration, we draw from a case evaluation of
an educational leadership program in India. In doing so, our intention is
to help frame the discussion in practical terms. But first we briefly set
out our conception of collaborative evaluation, its nature and variations
in application.

CONCEPTIONS OF COLLABORATIVE EVALUATION

Following Cousins, Donohue, and Bloom (1996) we define *collaborative
evaluation* as an umbrella term or as a class of evaluation approaches.[1]
Under this umbrella can be found considerable variations in approach,
including at least the following: practical participatory evaluation (P-PE)
(e.g., Ayers, 1987; Cousins & Earl, 1995); transformative participatory evaluation (T-PE) (e.g., Brunner & Guzman, 1989; Cousins &
Whitmore, 1998); and empowerment evaluation (EE) (e.g., Fetterman,
1994, 2001; Fetterman & Wandersman, 2005). Essentially collaborative
evaluation is a class of evaluation approaches that involves trained evaluation personnel working *with* nonevaluator stakeholders to do evaluation.

   It is important to differentiate among various forms of collaborative
inquiry, since conceptual clarity can foster appropriate application. In

earlier work we identified three primary justifications for collaborative inquiry: *pragmatic*, with a distinct instrumental or problem-solving focus; *political*, which is normative in form and function; and *philosophic*, intended to deepen understanding and enhance the meaning of phenomena under study (Cousins & Whitmore, 1998). We do not mean to imply that a given approach is necessarily exclusively associated with one of these three justifications; it is more a question of emphasis and balance. In our understanding P-PE emphasizes the pragmatic, and T-PE, the political. The aims of EE are somewhat more complicated (see, e.g., Cousins, 2005). While the discourse of EE is decidedly transformative (political), examinations of case examples suggest that it may be oriented toward program problem solving (practical) in focus.

Collaborative forms of inquiry can also be differentiated on the basis of process or form. King and Stevahn (2002) identified as essential dimensions of form the extent to which evaluators and nonevaluator stakeholders are involved in evaluation decision making and implementation. Weaver and Cousins (2004) revised and elaborated on an earlier framework developed by Cousins and Whitmore (1998). The result is five dimensions of form against which any collaborative evaluation project can be compared and described:

- Control of technical decision making (evaluator vs. nonevaluator stakeholder).
- Diversity of nonevaluator stakeholders selected for participation (diverse vs. limited).
- Power relations among nonevaluator stakeholders (conflicting vs. neutral).
- Manageability of the evaluation implementation (unwieldy vs. manageable).
- Depth of participation of stakeholders (involved in all aspects of inquiry vs. involved only in consultation).

COMPLEXITIES OF PROGRAM STANDARD SETTING IN COLLABORATIVE EVALUATION

Collaborative evaluation breaks ranks with traditionalist approaches to evaluation in significant and remarkable ways, especially with respect to goals of evaluation, evaluator roles, and responsibilities for the direct involvement of nonevaluator stakeholders. In this section we consider some of the main problems (or even dilemmas) likely to be encountered with regard to standard setting in collaborative evaluation contexts. Spe-

cifically, we consider as salient the issues of determining the bases
for comparison, perspectives on valuing (prescriptive vs. descriptive),
method choices (quantitative, qualitative, mixed), evaluation purpose
and approach, and cultural sensitivity.

The Basis of Comparison Issue

Evaluation requires judgment and judgment requires comparison. What
will be the basis or bases of comparison? How will they be selected? Will
they be absolute standards or relative? Why and under what conditions?
Framing these questions in the context of collaborative evaluation adds
significant complexity, since in most collaborative approaches members
of the program community have an active role on the evaluation team
and contribute in very direct ways to technical decisions about the evaluation and its implementation. Collaborative evaluation involves new
roles and goals for evaluators that distinguish it from more traditional
forms of evaluation, where evaluators work relatively independently of
program personnel.

In some forms of collaborative inquiry, restrictions may be placed
on the choice of standard by virtue of the constraints of the approach.
The EE approach advocated by Fetterman (2001) is a case in point. In
this approach, through mission-building and stock-taking exercises a
baseline of program operation is defined against which future comparisons of program performance can be made. On the basis of comparisons
using this relative standard, decisions are made about ongoing program
development and improvement of program implementation. Strict adherence to this approach locks the EE evaluation into the *self-referenced
standard* for comparison. Decisions about program development are
based on growth in practice and ongoing assessments of "how the program is doing." Strict adherence to this three-step approach may limit
the responsiveness of the evaluation to local program needs, since some
important evaluative questions, such as "How does this program stack
up against alternative approaches?," which might implicate the use of
other bases for comparison, might never get asked. Having said that, we
acknowledge that the three-step approach represents only one choice on
the EE menu (Fetterman & Wandersman, 1995) and that the essential
EE role of evaluator as critical friend has the potential to ameliorate concerns about restricting the scope for standard setting.

In P-PE, on the other hand, it is typical that the initial planning
phases of the evaluation would involve a good deal of reflection among
evaluators and nonevaluator stakeholder participants about (1) the goals
of the program, (2) the important groups with a stake in the program

and its evaluation and their value position, (3) the important evaluation questions to be asked, and (4) application of evaluation logic in order to answer evaluation questions in terms of developing an evaluation framework that specifies methods, indicators, and bases of comparison. The evaluation plan, in this sense, is emergent and not governed by a prescribed process such as Fetterman's three-step approach to EE. The P-PE approach allows for the identification of self-referenced standards but also for the specification of other *relative standards,* such as comparisons with groups who have not had access to the program or those having access to competing programs. It might also include *absolute standards* and as such would permit comparison with some external yardstick or benchmark.

To conclude, deciding relative or absolute standards for the evaluation of programs in collaborative evaluation contexts ought to be an emergent process, one that involves members of both the program community and the evaluation community. The approach would do well to place a premium on being open-ended and responsive to exigencies identified in the local context rather than to explicitly be guided by a set structure or process. Adherence to the latter approach runs the risk of limiting choices in standard setting and therefore potentially diminishing the authenticity of the approach.

The Prescriptive versus Descriptive Valuing Issue

With the evolution of the traditional social sciences model over the past few decades, evaluation theorists and other social science scholars have made clear the role of valuing in making judgments about program merit, worth, or significance. Forerunning arguments for clean separation of fact and value have been roundly challenged. The evaluator is someone now naturally thought of as having a stake in the program and particularly its evaluation, as do the diverse nonevaluator stakeholder groups. Several evaluation theorists have considered quite deliberately the values component of evaluation theory (e.g., House, 1991; Scriven, 1980; Shadish, Cook, & Leviton, 1991). Building on the work of House and Scriven, Shadish and Leviton (2001) describe the nature and potential use of "prescriptive" valuing and "descriptive" valuing. There are interesting implications for the collaborative evaluation context.

Prescriptive valuing occurs when evaluators promote particular values. Shadish and Leviton use House's (1995) advocacy of Rawl's theory of justice, prioritizing in the interests of the economically and politically disadvantaged. Adopting this stance implies an allegiance to a particular ideology on behalf of the evaluator. On the other hand, evaluators can engage in descriptive valuing, which seeks to systematically investigate and understand the value positions of the array of stakeholders with an interest in the program and its evaluation. The power of collaborative evaluation in descriptive valuing is the additional space it affords evaluation team members, including the trained evaluator member, to probe their own deeply embedded assumptions and understandings. Decisions about standard setting can be made in light of joint understandings of how all value positions are likely to affect the evaluation.

In collaborative evaluation, prescriptive valuing as a basis for standard setting would be most appealing in the context of T-PE, where the goals of the evaluation transcend mere judgments about the merit and worth of the program itself, and seek to have an impact on program community members' awareness of and sensitivity to operative, usually constraining, forces within the local context. T-PE is often implemented within contexts where communities are economically and socially disadvantaged. With its interest in fostering self-determination and the amelioration of social injustice, prescriptive valuing would assist evaluators in the collaborative program standard-setting exercise. The program would be seen as good to the extent that it contributes to the social justice agenda.

Shadish and Leviton (2001) acknowledge challenges to perspective valuing such as the obvious discord between those who speak on behalf of the poor and disadvantaged who are not themselves poor and disadvantaged. In T-PE the evaluator's role is more one of facilitation; yet, operating from a prescriptive stance implies that values are imposed on the evaluation. When members of the disadvantaged program community speak for themselves, Shadish and Leviton observe, the perspective becomes one of descriptive valuing. Another problem with prescriptive valuing is that it is incumbent on the evaluator to justify his or her value choices. This would be increasingly difficult to do in the context of pluralistic or highly diversified value perspectives, as would be the case in many collaborative evaluation settings. That being said, it is important to underscore the need for the evaluation to be self-reflexive, regardless of context. Some would argue that all valuing is prescriptive and that the evaluator's challenge is to be in touch with his or her own deeply embedded understandings so that she does not impose them on others or on the evaluation (B. Whitmore, personal communication, January 2006).

Collaborative evaluations operating from a descriptive evaluation platform are well positioned to ensure that the values diversity inherent within is surfaced and represented within the evaluation, particularly at the level of program standard setting. Nevertheless, in order to develop a deep understanding of such an array of interests, it would be necessary to ensure the involvement of or interaction with a wide array of nonevaluator stakeholder groups. That being said, several approaches to P-PE, for example, tend to limit participation to so-called primary users, those with a vested interest in the program and its evaluation and those in a position to actually use the evaluation findings. Can primary users speak on behalf of other stakeholders and ensure that their interests are represented? Indeed, the question hinges on such considerations as variations in power relationships and the diversity of apparent value positions. We have argued elsewhere that P-PE would not be overly suitable in contexts where such diversity was remarkable (Weaver & Cousins, 2004).

In sum, considerations in standard setting in collaborative evaluation ought to include significant attention to the concept of valuing. The choice between descriptive and prescriptive perspectives will depend substantially on context and the overarching purposes of the evaluation in the first place. However, we suggest that even in cases where such purposes are characterized by and intended to foster self-determinism and empowerment of communities or intended program beneficiaries, evaluators would do well to lean toward creating the space for dialogue and deliberation about what is important to whom and why, rather than adopting a predominantly prescriptive stance.

The Method Choice Issue

Quantitative and qualitative social sciences research methods have evolved considerably over the years, as have deeper understandings of methodological links to epistemological considerations. Many evaluations now embrace the concept of mixed-method approaches openly and warmly; this is particularly the case in collaborative evaluation. In most approaches, the choice to invoke a collaborative evaluation does not imply method choice. Such decisions are made once stakeholder interests are understood and evaluation questions are established. Comparison bases can be selected, and, as is most often the case in our experience, the best methods for answering the questions posed often suggest themselves. They may be quantitative, qualitative, or, as is increasingly the case, both. Certain complications arise from the point of view of standard setting in this context. First, sophisticated preordinate means of setting standards or benchmarks in advance (e.g., Brandon, 2005; Henry, McTaggart, & McMillan, 1992) are not typically available in collaborative evaluation, since reliance on standardized test data or other quantitative methods might not be decided until preliminary collaborative planning exercises are complete.

A related problem is associated with Patton's (1997) suggestion that it is desirable to engage stakeholders in deciding program standards in advance of data collection. He recommends that explicit consideration be given to the explication of indicators of when the program is outstanding, adequate, or poor. An example used was the percentage and number of teachers who have contact with a teacher center. The recommended approach is highly supportable in collaborative evaluation, since stakeholders are forced into such clarification before they see how the program is actually doing, a circumstance under which their judgments about program standards would be susceptible to other influences. But the approach would break down in the context of qualitative data or data that are not in some sense quantifiable. How, for instance, can such standards be set when program participant interview data about program effects on workplace practice are agreed upon as a primary source of evidence? The use of exemplary case and critical incident approaches may be useful for informing an image of good practice in such instances and result in the development and validation of a scoring rubric. The development of key component profiles (Cousins, Aubry, Smith, & Smith Fowler, 2004)—or multidimensional and multilevel representations of program implementation—is a related approach that shows much promise for collaborative evaluation.

Regardless of the approach, collaborative evaluators and non-evaluator stakeholders could engage in the front-end-loaded standard-setting exercise Patton describes. While we appreciate the wisdom inherent in this advice, there would be practical implications to consider. For example, in the case of qualitative methods, the development of scoring rubrics and/or key component profiles as mechanisms for explicit a priori standard setting would carry significant resource implications and may not be particularly feasible, given the many other demands encountered within the collaborative evaluation context. Nevertheless, as would be the case with traditional evaluation approaches, method choices in collaborative evaluation ought to be contingent on the evaluation questions posed. While standard setting might be comparatively easy in the case of quantitative methods, qualitative approaches are available and ought to be given serious consideration.

The Softer–Gentler versus Hard-Nosed Evaluation Issue

It has long been our position that collaborative evaluation is unsuitable in the context of tough-minded, hard-nosed evaluation questions about program continuation, termination, and the like. Optimally, such approaches are suited to program improvement-oriented contexts where evaluation questions are likely to be formative.[2] This is not to say that an accountability function of collaborative evaluation is not important. Indeed, collaborative forms of evaluation are often useful in contexts where funding agencies need assurances that the program is being implemented as intended and that serious self-evaluative reflection and improvement are taking place.

Scriven (1997) has referred to collaborative forms of evaluation as softer-gentler forms of inquiry, and in some instances, though they may be worthwhile developmental activities, they are not at all, he asserts, evaluation. EE, for example, has a strong emphasis on program development, although it does involve a certain element of evaluation (Cousins, 2005). One of the more powerful features of collaborative evaluation, we think, is its potential to foster among members of the nonevaluation program community the capacity for self-evaluation. Program personnel, in essence, become the judges of their own program's performance. In making such judgments, nonevaluator stakeholders compare observations derived through systematic inquiry against self-, norm- or absolute-referenced standards. Such judgment is integral not only to decisions about whether the program is meritorious, significant, and worthwhile but also to decisions about program improvement. So, while collaborative evaluation may be a softer or gentler form of inquiry, it is indeed, in our view, evaluation, and as such the question of how good is good enough remains central.

This being the case, we would argue that nonevaluator stakeholder participation in the standard-setting process should be privileged. It would be incumbent on collaborative evaluators to clarify the essentiality of standard setting to the evaluation process and the choices that are available to nonevaluator stakeholders, and ultimately to engage them in very direct ways in making such choices.

The Cultural Sensitivity Issue

Understanding context and cultural complexity is pivotal in evaluation standard setting. For example, Brandon (2005) argues that programs can only achieve as much as their resources allow, and programs serving economically deprived communities require more resources than those serving communities not so deprived. For this reason, Brandon argues for strong stakeholder participation in standard setting. In collaborative evaluation the trained evaluator brings technical knowledge and expertise, while the contribution made by nonevaluator stakeholders is more aligned with understanding and representing context and program logic. Through working together, the team develops an inquiry that blends local knowledge with professional evaluation practice. Part of the evaluator's role is to ensure that professional guiding principles are maintained. Another important aspect of his or her role is to understand and situate the evaluation within the cultural complexities of the context within which the program is being implemented. Cultural considerations are usefully thought of in terms of values shared among members of the program community or organization (Schien, 2004). Multi- and cross-cultural competency issues in evaluation have attracted considerable attention in the literature of late (e.g., Kirkhart, 1995; Stanfield, 1999; Thompson-Robinson, Hopson, & SenGupta, 2004). This literature, along with a cultural reading of the second edition of the *Program Evaluation Standards* (Joint Committee on Standards for Educational Evaluation, 1994) by the Diversity Committee of the American Evaluation Association will inform the revision of the *Program Evaluation Standards* (Joint Committee, 1994).

Collaborative evaluations are well positioned to introduce evaluators to the complexities inherent in program, organizational, and community culture as they work in partnership with members of that culture. Design decisions can be tailored, reformulated, or rejected outright on the basis of their fit with the organizational and community concerns as represented by the nonevaluator members of the collaborative evaluation team. In deciding program standards in the collaborative context, it is essential that the collaborative evaluator be sensitive to local values and norms. But this challenge is likely to be formidable. Collaborative approaches certainly do make space for the development of deep understandings of culture and context, but some would argue that program, organizational, and especially community cultures are extremely nuanced and complex and that it is not clear that any outsider can fully grasp what is going on (Whitmore, 1998).

Regardless, we would place a premium in the context of collaborative evaluation on taking steps to engage nonevaluator stakeholders in the standard-setting process as full partners, thereby ensuring that the process is informed by the values shared by members of the local community or context. Collaborative evaluation, with its premium on joint participation in the evaluative knowledge production process, is comparatively well suited to attenuate the cultural subtleties in context, subtleties that evaluators in more traditionalistic approaches might be hard-pressed to grasp even as they endeavor to heighten cultural competencies.

Tentative Guidance for Standard Setting in Collaborative Evaluation

The foregoing sections are intended to raise issues concerning program standard setting in the context of collaborative evaluation by way of shedding light on the complexities of the process. Developing a set of principles for standard setting in this context is not warranted at this juncture. Yet, based on the foregoing discussion, we would argue that collaborative evaluators and evaluation teams might benefit from adherence to a set of tentative guidelines. We offer these as tentative, since they would need to be empirically validated and substantiated. In that light we suggest that standard setting in the context of collaborative evaluation is best served when:

- The bases of comparison are jointly decided and informed by the exigencies of the evaluation context.

- There is reliance on descriptive rather than prescriptive valuing.

- Evaluation method choices derive from the evaluation questions posed, and, regardless of choice of quantitative or qualitative methods, the consideration given to standard setting precedes data collection.

- The development of the capacity to self-evaluate is privileged and understood as essential to collaborative evaluation, and evaluators take steps to make this clear to nonevaluator stakeholders and engage them directly in the standard-setting process.

- Cultural competencies are embraced through involving nonevaluator stakeholders as full partners in the standard-setting exercise.

In the interest of considering these rather abstract musings in more concrete terms, we now turn to a case example of P-PE as a basis for reflection. Our intention is to highlight some of the complexities of program standard setting in the context of a cross-cultural evaluation of a South Asian educational leadership program. The evaluation is cross-cultural inasmuch as the trained evaluator participants were Canadian, whereas nonevaluator stakeholder members of the evaluation team were Indian. The case example is not intended to represent an instance of exemplary practice in program standard setting in the context of collaborative evaluation. Rather, it provides a vehicle for showing how the aforementioned issues played out in a practical context.

PARTICIPATORY EVALUATION OF THE EDUCATIONAL LEADERSHIP PROGRAM: CASE EXAMPLE

Case Synopsis

The Educational Leadership Program (ELP), centered in New Delhi, India, has been in existence since 1996. It is a professional development program for school principals and principal aspirants and is intended to promote an ethos of effective leadership for equity and excellence in education, reflective practice, organizational change, and collaboration. Principal foci are the development of personal educational awareness and philosophy, instructional leadership, and systemic organizational management. The program was developed on the basis of mostly American principal training programs such as Harvard's Principal's Course, which leads to qualification for licensure in the state of Massachusetts, and the Danforth Foundation leadership program in Washington State, which leads to certification to practice school leadership in that state.

The impetus for the evaluation came from the ELP's creators, developers, and implementers, specifically the administration and staff of the Centre for Educational Management and Development (CEMD) in New Delhi. Interest in evaluation stemmed from a desire to understand, through systematic inquiry, the program's strengths and limitations; its comparability to other leadership programs, particularly those in Western cultures; and considerations for ongoing development and improvement.

The evaluation was coordinated by the Evaluation and Assessment Group at Queen's University (Kingston, Ontario), of which one of us (Lyn Shulha) is Director, and was contracted by the Aga Khan Foundation, Canada.

For the initial formative phase of the evaluation, we adopted a participatory approach, with external evaluation team members from Canada working in partnership with CEMD staff, the program developers, and implementers. Cousins was contracted as the evaluation team leader. Shulha oversaw the administration of the contract but did not have a direct role in the first major formative phase of the project. Advisory input was provided by a variety of interested stakeholder groups, including ELP alumni, educational consultants and university professors, and representatives of funding agencies.

On the first of three planned site visits, we developed collaboratively a set of guiding evaluation questions and a program logic model and then proceeded to systematically examine program implementation and effects using a mix of quantitative and qualitative methods. Methods employed were an extensive document review of archival information, a questionnaire survey of ELP alumni and a comparison group of nonalumni counterparts, focus groups of alumni and instructional staff, case studies in schools at which ELP alumni were currently located, a cost-effectiveness analysis of financial records and a comparative analysis of the structure and content of the ELP versus that of five other educational leadership programs, mostly situated in Western cultural jurisdictions.

Once planning was complete, data collection, analysis, and reporting responsibilities were decided, with members of the Canadian and Indian teams both contributing. Report segments were sent to Cousins electronically by Indian team members, and he subsequently collated and edited these into a complete draft of the report. This draft served as the basis for the second site visit, where a series of meetings over a 4-day period were used to further develop the draft report, correct inaccuracies, identify and remedy omissions, and most importantly develop a draft set of recommendations for program improvement.

Following the site visit, Cousins revised the report and presented a compilation of the 25 recommendations for ongoing development of the ELP that had been jointly developed during the site visit. Through distance negotiations the list was finalized and the report completed, printed, and bound. The plan was for the CEMD to work with these recommendations for approximately 1 year, at which time an external team from Canada (Shulha and Cousins) would conduct a site visit to examine and report on the extent to which recommendation implementation had been achieved. This final nonparticipative summative component would bring a close to the evaluation. At this writing, CEMD continues to work with the implementation of the recommendations to improve the program.[3]

The Complexity of Program Standard Setting

In the first site visit, considerable time was spent discussing the purposes and mission of the program and its specific objectives. All stakeholder groups with an important interest in the ELP or its evaluation were identified and their interests described. From that point we collaboratively developed a set of questions to guide the evaluation and developed an evaluation framework. We brainstormed a list of available sources of data to assist in this task. As part of the task we identified bases for comparison. However, given time restrictions for the site visit, we were unable to devote a great deal of time to explicit standard setting in advance of the evaluation. In the end, essentially all of the standards were relative, comparing program performance to itself over time or with some sort of comparison group. At no point did we identify absolute standards of program performance.

The bases of comparison took different forms, depending on the question at hand. Several questions relied on self-referenced bases. The extent to which program implementation was successful, for example, could be partially examined through a systematic review of archival data to look for the development of assignment sophistication over time. We wanted to know if the program was leading to observable changes in knowledge, attitudes, and beliefs of candidates, and so we identified a control group of practicing principals and principal aspirants against which to compare ELP alumni, using a common self-report questionnaire instrument.

We wanted to know how the ELP compared with Western principal training programs and so identified several as possible bases for comparison, in terms of course content, activities, hours of instruction, assignment requirements, and other considerations. Although we had identified the principals' courses as a relative program standard, we did not finalize the specific criteria for comparison in advance of the evaluation, nor did we set explicit program standards or specify how closely the ELP needed to approximate these.

For much of our data collection, program standards were emergent in character. That is to say, given the improvement-oriented nature of the evaluation exercise, we wanted to get the views and opinions of alumni and to draw inferences from school case studies about program strengths and weaknesses as grounds for program improvement. We did not explicitly identify bases for comparison for these data, nor did we develop an explicit scoring rubric or other representation on which to judge the results. Essentially, the data (e.g., interviews, focus groups) were judged on an ad hoc basis, and recommendations for program improvement were negotiated on the basis of this input.

From the outset it was made clear to the Canadian evaluation team that the CEMD's interest was in raising the profile of the ELP. At one point, the CEMD director had expressed an interest in having a university from the West accredit the ELP. This challenge appeared to be too daunting, and the evaluation approach described above was adopted instead.

Training opportunities for school principals in India are few and far between. The CEMD was a definite and unchallenged leader in the country in offering such training. In raising the profile of the ELP, it would be possible for the CEMD to garner leverage in the educational policy arena and increase greatly its chances for effecting national policy change with regard to principal development. The program was rooted in principles of leadership theory from the West and naturally it would be useful to use Western leadership programs as the relative program standard.

As the work progressed, questions began to emerge among the stakeholder community as to the appropriateness of this logic. Members of the participatory evaluation team employed by the CEMD raised and questioned assumptions about the comparability of school leadership in

South Asian and Western cultures. Why was it that Western program standards were to be used as the yardstick? The CEMD director, an extremely collaborative and empowering leader herself, was open to discussion and debate on this point. She steadfastly clung to her view, however, that the comparison would be appropriate, given that the program, with its roots in Western culture, was showing itself to be well adapted to the South Asian context. Her primary interest was in receiving explicit acknowledgment from Queen's University that the ELP compares well with standards in the West. This discussion, while not conflict-laden (the CEMD was a highly collaborative work environment), raised some interesting issues around the notion of cultural sensitivity of the evaluation. Ultimately, as a team we carried on and continued to implement the evaluation as had been planned, but the issue left the Canadian evaluation team somewhat perplexed.

Another dimension of this discourse concerned the notion of what is meant by "aligned with Western standards." Members of the Indian evaluation team opined that we did not need to be thinking in terms of raising standards of the ELP to meet those of the West. Rather, the exercise was one of examining the extent to which they were aligned. This issue, although subtle, was culturally grounded and arose from an enormous sense of pride in the ELP held by its developers and implementers.

Further complications arose when it came time to negotiate the recommendations for improvement. Within the 25 draft recommendations, only minor changes in wording were identified. As mentioned, most of the recommendations for program improvement came from the views and opinions of program stakeholders, alumni, and the like, although a significant number of recommendations related to direct comparisons with the Ontario Principals Program Guidelines.[4] Substantively, all of the recommendations except for one were readily agreed to, despite the cultural sensitivity issue mentioned above. The one exception concerned the number of hours of contact time. In the draft recommendations, Cousins had specified that contact time (face-to-face instructional time with candidates) be increased by 50 hours. This augmentation would represent a significant increase for the ELP and would be potentially costly, given travel requirements for some candidates and the added investment in instructor and instructional resources. It would, however, bring the program in line with several other programs in North America, including the Queen's University program. Via email exchanges representatives of the CEMD tried to negotiate this figure downward, but the Canadian evaluators argued vociferously and successfully that it be maintained, pointing to the comparative data in the evaluation report and arguing that this point would be pivotal in the ensuing summative evaluation component.

On a final note, the set of recommendations installed—the product of the formative evaluation component—are, in and of themselves, program standards against which the program may now be judged. These standards may serve a variety of purposes, depending on the source of the impetus for summative evaluation. The developers and implementers of the ELP may benefit from a nonparticipatory evaluation as a vehicle for judging the quality of their improvement-oriented efforts. Should administrators at the CEMD ever wish explicit recognition of the ELP from Queen's University, these recommendations/standards make the task of comparing this program to those accredited in the West relatively straightforward.

DISCUSSION

In summary, on many levels this P-PE has been highly successful. It represents a very sophisticated evaluation that looks at process and outcome data, includes varied methods, and is immersed in the knowledge of program and the cultural context of the local participants. There were relatively few issues of contention concerning the evaluation, and so the power dynamics between evaluator and nonevaluator stakeholder participants or among members of the latter group were not much of an issue, as they can sometimes be (e.g., Whitmore, 1998). The overall evaluation was to combine a formative (participatory) phase with a subsequently more hard-nosed summative (external) component. (That part of the evaluation has yet to materialize, owing to unanticipated circumstances and emergent local exigencies.)

Program standard setting in the present case developed on a fairly ad hoc and emergent basis. Standard setting was very much based on descriptive valuing; no ideological framework was imposed or introduced by the evaluation team as a consideration for standard setting. The Indian team members were clearly involved in judging their own program by comparing evaluation data against expectations that emerged from ongoing dialogue and deliberation. Several bases for comparison were identified, most of which were relative standards. The evaluation inquiry ultimately involved a highly mixed-method approach. This fact, combined with project resource limitations, provided limits on what standards could be set in advance of data collection. There was really no opportunity, for example, to give serious joint consideration to developing scoring rubrics during the planning site visit. The evaluation was very much improvement-oriented, and as such judgments about the focus for change came largely from deliberation and discussion of the interview and observation data collected.

Several complexities regarding standard setting did emerge; these were mostly related to cultural issues having to do with the appropriateness of the fit between Western and South Asian standards. As evaluators working in a cross-cultural setting, these issues have given us considerable pause. It would be interesting not only to examine progress and judge the improved ELP in terms of its alignment with Western standards but also to hold workshops or focus groups with relevant stakeholders to explore in depth with them the meaning of "How good is good enough?" We suspect that such follow-up in this or other projects would lead to more penetrating examinations of the complexities of standard setting in the collaborative evaluation context.

In conclusion, we view this chapter as an exploratory exercise and have found the process to be stimulating and useful. We are persuaded that program standard-setting issues are highly underattended in collaborative evaluation and underscore the need for further conceptual and empirical work in this domain. We used one example of a specific form of collaborative inquiry as a basis for discussion and illustration. It is clear from this retrospective analysis that in the project we were less than successful in adhering to the tentative guidance that we identified above, which begs the questions: What would have been different had we been guided by such advice? How precisely would the evaluation have benefited from such a strategy? These questions are empirical and in our mind speak to the need for further systematic inquiry in this area. It would be useful not only to study the benefits (or drawbacks) of adherence to tentative guidance but also to examine such issues in a variety of collaborative contexts, including case studies employing EE or T-PE approaches. On a theoretical level it would be useful to develop a conceptual framework relating to program standard setting in the collaborative context. Elements of that framework might include bases for comparison, perspectives on valuing (prescriptive vs. descriptive), methodological choices (quantitative vs. qualitative), evaluation purpose and approach, and cultural sensitivity. We think we have made a contribution in this regard, but it is clearly just a beginning.

ACKNOWLEDGMENTS

A prior version of this chapter was presented at the annual meeting of the American Evaluation Association in Reno, Nevada, in November 2003. The evaluation case example described in this chapter was funded by the Aga Khan Foundation, Canada.

NOTES

1. O'Sullivan (2004) uses a more specific definition, one that resonates with our use of the term *practical participatory evaluation*, described below.

2. We define *formative* as improvement-oriented evaluation rather than Scriven's (1991) conception of formative as minisummative evaluations to determine program merit and worth as the program implementation is unfolding and prior to program stabilization.

3. Plans to conduct the summative evaluation were scuttled due to an unrelated emergent and serious conflict between the nongovernmental organization and its principal donor agency.

4. Queen's University offers a training program for principals governed by these guidelines.

REFERENCES

Ayers, T. D. (1987). Stakeholders as partners in evaluation: A stakeholder-collaborative approach. *Evaluation and Program Planning, 10,* 263–271.

Brandon, P. R. (2005). Using test standard-setting methods in educational program evaluation: Assessing the issue of how good is good enough. *Journal of Multidisciplinary Evaluation, 3,* 1–29.

Brunner, I., & Guzman, A. (1989). Participatory evaluation: A tool to assess projects and empower people. In R. F. Connor & M. H. Hendricks (Eds.)., *International innovations in evaluation methodology* (New Directions in Program Evaluation no. 42, pp. 9–17). San Francisco: Jossey-Bass.

Cousins, J. B. (2003). Use effects of participatory evaluation. In D. Stufflebeam, T. Kellaghan, & L. Wingate (Eds.), *International handbook of educational evaluation* (pp. 245–265). Boston: Kluwer.

Cousins, J. B. (2005). Will the real empowerment evaluation please stand up? A critical friend perspective. In D. M. Fetterman & A. Wandersman (Eds.), *Empowerment evaluation principles in practice* (pp. 183–208). Thousand Oaks: Sage.

Cousins, J. B., Aubry, T., Smith, M., & Smith Fowler, H. (2004). Using key component profiles for the evaluation of program implementation in intensive mental health case management. *Evaluation and Program Planning, 27,* 1–23.

Cousins, J. B., Donohue, J. J., & Bloom, G. A. (1996). Collaborative evaluation in North America: Evaluators' self-reported opinions, practices, and consequences. *Evaluation Practice, 17,* 207–226.

Cousins, J. B., & Earl, L. M. (Eds.). (1995). *Participatory evaluation in education: Studies in evaluation use and organizational learning.* London: Falmer Press.

Cousins, J. B., & Whitmore, E. (1998). Framing participatory evaluation. In E. Whitmore (Ed.), *Participatory evaluation approaches* (New Directions in Evaluation no. 80, pp. 3–23). San Francisco: Jossey-Bass.

Fernandes, W., & Tandon, R. (1981). *Participatory research and evaluation: Experiments in research as a process of liberation.* New Delhi: Indian Social Institute.

Fetterman, D. (1994). Empowerment evaluation. *Evaluation Practice, 15,* 1–15.

Fetterman, D. (2001). *Foundations of empowerment evaluation.* Thousand Oaks, CA: Sage.

Fetterman, D., & Wandersman, A. (Eds.). (2005). *Empowerment evaluation principles in practice.* New York: Guilford Press.

Freire, P. (1982). Creating alternative research methods: Learning to do it by doing it. In B. Hall, A. Gillette, & R. Tandon (Eds.), *Creating knowledge: A monopoly. Participatory research in development* (pp. 29–37). New Delhi: Society for Participatory Research in Asia.

Greene, J. C. (1988). Stakeholder participation and utilization in program evaluation. *Evaluation Review, 12,* 91–116.

Henry, G., McTaggart, M. J., & McMillan, J. H. (1992). Establishing benchmarks for outcome indicators. *Evaluation Review, 16,* 131–150.

House, E. R. (1991). Evaluation and social justice: Where are we? In M. W. McLaughlin & D. C. Phillips (Eds.), *Evaluation and education: At quarter century* (pp. 233–247). Chicago: Universtiy of Chicago Press.

House, E. R. (1995). Putting things together coherently: Logic and justice. In D. M. Fournier (Ed.), *Reasoning in evaluation: Inferential links and leaps* (pp. 33–48). San Francisco: Jossey-Bass.

Joint Committee on Standards for Educational Evaluation. (1994). *The program evaluation standards* (2nd ed.). Newbury Park, CA: Sage.

King, J. A., & Stevahn, L. (2002). Three frameworks for considering evaluator role. In K. E. Ryan & T. A. Scwhandt (Eds.), *Exploring evaluation role and identity* (pp. 1–16). Greenwich CT: Information Age.

Kirkhart, K. (1995). Seeking multicultural validity: A postcard from the road. *Evaluation Practice, 16,* 1–12.

O'Sullivan, R. G. (2004). *Practicing evaluation: A collaborative approach.* Thousand Oaks, CA: Sage.

Patton, M. Q. (1997). *Utilization-focused evaluation: The new century text* (3rd ed.). Newbury Park, CA: Sage.

Schein, E. (2004). *Organizational culture and leadership* (3rd ed.). New York: Wiley.

Scriven, M. (1980). *The logic of evaluation.* Inverness, CA: Edgepress.

Scriven, M. (1991). Beyond formative and summative evaluation. In M. W. McLaughlin & D. C. Phillips (Eds.), *Evaluation and education: At quarter century* (pp. 19–64). Chicago: University of Chicago Press.

Scriven, M. (1997). Empowerment evaluation examined. *Evaluation Practice, 18,* 165–175.

Shadish, W. R., Cook, T. D., & Leviton, L. C. (1991). *Foundations of program evaluation.* Newbury Park, CA: Sage.

Shadish, W., & Leviton, L. C. (2001). Descriptive values and social justice. In A. P. Benson, D. M. Hinn, & C. Lloyd (Eds.), *Visions of quality: How evaluators define, understand and represent program quality* (pp. 181–200). Oxford, UK: JAI Press.

Stanfield, J. H., II. (1999). Slipping through the front door: Relevant social scientific evaluation in the people of color century. *American Journal of Evaluation, 20*, 415–431.

Thompson-Robinson, M., Hopson, R., & SenGupta, S. (Eds.). (2004). *In search of cultural competence* (New Directions in Evaluation no. 102). San Francisco: Jossey-Bass.

Weaver, L., & Cousins, J. B. (2004). Unpacking the participatory process. *Journal of Multidisciplinary Evaluation, No. 1*, 19–14.

Whitmore, E. (1998). "We need to rebuild this house:" The role of empowerment evaluation of a Mexican farmers' cooperative. In E. T. Jackson & Y. Kassam (Eds.), *Knowledge shared: Participatory evaluation in development cooperation* (pp. 217–230). West Hartford, CT: Kumarian Press.

CHAPTER 8

Building Evaluation Recommendations for Improvement
Insights from Student Formative Assessments

CARLOS C. AYALA and PAUL R. BRANDON

A recurring topic of discussion among evaluation theorists and practitioners for many years has been the extent to which evaluators should provide recommendations for improvement to the evaluand. This discussion has been about program evaluation, but it applies to other types of evaluation as well. In education, for example, teachers frequently evaluate their students. The teacher's role is inextricably tied to developing recommendations for improving the evaluand—that is, their students. These recommendations are developed from student formative assessment, a form of student evaluation that is currently receiving considerable attention in the educational arena (Black & Wiliam, 1998, 2005; Guskey, 2005). Formative assessment is assessment practice with the purpose of informing instructional decisions about what the teacher and student should do next.

This chapter discusses teachers' development and use of student formative assessments, with specific emphasis on recommendations for improvement. It briefly describes the controversy among program evaluation theorists about the extent to which evaluators should provide recommendations, discusses recent developments in the literature on student formative assessment, and presents a formative assessment model that might illuminate program evaluations requiring recommendations for improvement. We propose that current research in formative assessment practices can further the discussion among program evaluators about formative evaluation practices. Accordingly, we conclude with a section suggesting that, in some instances, program evaluators may find it useful to adopt or adapt features of the model for systematic formative program evaluations.

DISCUSSION ABOUT RECOMMENDATIONS IN THE PROGRAM EVALUATION LITERATURE

Opinions about the extent to which evaluators should provide recommendations for improvement in programs and other evaluands have varied over the years. Several theorists have stated without reservation that program evaluators should always offer any warranted recommendations. These theorists see it as a moral duty to provide recommendations, because evaluations should benefit programs as much as possible, and as a professional requirement, because programs often contract evaluators not only to provide evaluative conclusions but also to help them address deficits and make improvements.

Theorists from a wide range of approaches have advocated for recommendations. Iriti, Bickel, and Nelson (2005, p. 466) concluded that most evaluation textbooks "seem to assume at least the possibility that an evaluation will yield some sort of recommendations." Hendricks and Papagiannis (1990, p. 121) stated that "recommendations are one of the most critical products of any evaluation," and Hendricks and Handley (1990, p. 110) stated that program evaluators "should almost always offer recommendations." Collaborative program evaluation theorists such as Cousins and Whitmore (1998) and Fetterman and Wandersman (2005) support developing recommendations for program improvement. Weiss (1972, p. 26) stated, "Somebody or some body should fill the gap of translating the evaluation research results into explicit recommendations for future programs." Cronbach et al. (1980, p. 238) stated, "The greatest service evaluation can perform is to identify aspects of the course where revision is desirable."

Other theorists have been cautious about advising evaluators to provide recommendations for improvement. For example, Scriven (1991a, 1991b, 1993) has long maintained that program evaluators need not provide recommendations:

> Sometimes recommendations naturally emerge from the evaluation process, but often they do not, and special and distinctly different expertise is needed to generate them. When evaluators are saddled with the expectation

that they are to generate other results besides an evaluation, the evaluation effort is almost always deflected or diluted. (Scriven, 1993, pp. 54–55)

Robert Stake believes that decisions about how to apply evaluation results to program decision making should be delegated to the evaluation user (Shadish, Cook, & Leviton, 1991):

> To an extent, all of us, practitioners or whatever, need to be told what to do. That does not mean that we will do it, particularly not if we see it undermining our standing. . . . I want us, as evaluation specialists, to think of ourselves as facilitators of inquiry but not part of the remediation team. (Stake, 1991, pp. 76–77)

Still others (e.g., Brandon, 1999) have adopted an intermediate position, stating that evaluators who are required to provide recommendations for program revisions should call upon program stakeholders to validate the evaluators' recommendations. This stance requires evaluators to work closely with stakeholders after making recommendations and to obtain stakeholders' concurrence that the recommendations are feasible and appropriate.

FORMATIVE STUDENT ASSESSMENT

Student formative assessment is the evaluation of student performance by a teacher with the ultimate aim of improving student performance (Wiliam, 2005). Formative assessment may be understood as the formative evaluation of student performance for instructional purposes in which the teacher makes day-to-day decisions about what parts of lessons to emphasize, what lessons to implement next, and how to modify lessons to address student misconceptions, as well as how to make long-term decisions about the order of lessons from one implementation plan to the next. Here the evaluation not only determines the quality or worth of the student performance but also contributes to increased student learning via teacher recommendations and actions. Formative evaluation of student performance by a teacher is inescapably linked to the use of formative evaluation results and to recommendations for improvement.

To help understand what a teacher should know and be able to do to use formative assessments to promote student learning effectively, the first author proposed the Assessment Pedagogy Model (Ayala, 2005). Since this model corresponds to program evaluation with recommendations, we believe that the model suggests how a system might be developed for doing some educational evaluations in which one intentionally seeks recommendations. Features of the model might be adapted to formative educational program evaluations in which recommendations are made to program administrators, faculty, and staff.

The model was conceptualized during two National Science Foundation (NSF) research endeavors: *Embedding Assessments in the FAST Curriculum: On the Romance between Curriculum and Assessment (Romance)* (Shavelson & Young, 2001) and *Center for Assessment and Evaluation of Student Learning (CAESL)—FAST Study* (Shavelson & Stanford Educational Assessment Lab, 2004). In both studies, the research team trained teachers to use formal formative assessments that we embedded in the Foundational Approaches in Science Teaching (FAST) (Pottenger & Young, 1992), a middle school inquiry-based science program that has been implemented in 38 American states and in a dozen other countries.

In these research endeavors, our understanding of formative assessment evolved. Our attention moved from assessing a complete and comprehensive understanding of what students were expected to know to assessing a singular understanding of the goal of the unit. Our collection of assessment instruments (*assessment suites*) changed from a comprehensive and intricate collection of assessments to selective assessments at key locations in the curriculum. Our implementation expectations evolved from expecting teachers to be able to use the assessments without support to providing them with scripted assessment tasks and to providing professional development to develop teachers' understanding of the role of formative assessment. Our model of how teachers interpret the assessment results developed from the expectation that teachers would be able to automatically use the assessment information and resulted in frameworks on how to use this information. Although we did not find increased student learning due to the use of formative assessments in these small 1-year experiments, we did learn about the complexity of formative student assessment development and implementation.

The assessment pedagogy model includes six interdependent components that describe how teachers (and students) need to proceed to use formative assessments effectively: (1) knowing the content, (2) designing the tools, (3) using the tools, (4) interpreting the results of using these tools, (5) taking action based on the results, and (6) conducting an evaluation of the entire formative assessment system. Dividing the formative assessment model into components allows us to identify successful strategies and frameworks for each component and helps us understand how these components build toward the actions and recommendations. We describe the six components along with strategies that are important in formative assessment research.

Component 1: Knowing the Content

The first component refers to content or material that is being taught. Pelligrino, Chudowsky, and Glaser (2001) lay out the premise that understanding what one is going to measure is fundamental in the student assessment process. In instructional practice, teachers must know what they want the student to learn. Teachers should also know how student understandings (and misconceptions) in this content area are developed over time. Two content–knowledge frameworks have proven useful in assessment development: knowledge types and progress variables. Knowledge types and progress variables alone are not sufficient for knowing the content, because they lack information on student preconceptions and misconceptions, but these frameworks serve as useful structures when thinking about recommendations for improvement.

KNOWLEDGE TYPES

The Knowledge Type Framework put forth by the Stanford Educational Assessment Lab has been useful in thinking about the targets of learning and assessments. This science achievement framework involves a broad definition of science achievement based on the types of knowledge students are expected to learn in science (de Jong & Ferguson-Hessler, 1996; Li & Shavelson, 2001). The framework includes *declarative* (knowing that), *procedural* (knowing how), *schematic* (knowing why), and *strategic* (knowing when and how knowledge applies) knowledge. Once the important learning and assessment targets have been identified, they can be placed into one of the knowledge types. Placement of content into the knowledge types scaffolds the learning and assessment development processes. For example, if it is known that a content target is procedural knowledge, then it is known how to assess that piece of content. In the case of formative assessment, categorizing the evaluation targets suggests better ways to review and collect information about those targets.

PROGRESS VARIABLES

The Berkeley Evaluation and Assessment Research Center has proposed developing and using progress variables as a method for linking classroom assessments and large-scale summative assessments. These help us lay out how students step through an understanding in a particular content area (Wilson, 2005; Wilson & Darney, 2005). Progress variables can be conceptualized as a set of incremental stages of student understanding in a content knowledge area. For example, in the FAST studies, a progress variable emerged from the curriculum that mapped to what students were expected to know. A student's understanding about density and buoyancy in the FAST curriculum should follow a learning trajectory of "why things sink and float": mass → volume → mass and volume → density → relative density. From the progress variable model, we learned that it is important to use formative assessments that allow for the measurement of student understanding on the whole breadth of the variable and not necessarily only on one particular level. The progress variable helps the teacher locate student understanding and provides a target for a recommendation.

Knowledge types and progress variables have been useful in the construction and use of formative assessments. By using the knowledge types and progress variables frameworks for a particular content area, a teacher can more effectively use formative assessment processes.

Component 2: Designing the Tools

The second component of the assessment pedagogy model is developing quality assessments. Once the content has been selected, assessments can be designed. This is not unlike defining the tools that might be used in evaluations—some tools work better for some situations than others. Only valid, timely, and reliable formative assessments can provide useful information to make midcourse corrections. Important insights about constructing quality assessments that have resulted from this research have been about the application of the Knowledge Type Framework, the Triple, and the Predict–Observe–Explain assessment.

KNOWLEDGE-TYPE FRAMEWORK APPLICATION

The other purpose of the knowledge framework is to allow the identification of assessment types that correspond to the knowledge types; see Table 8.1 (adapted from Li & Shavelson, 2001).

The framework may be viewed as a technology to help teachers and researchers select the most simple and efficient method for constructing an assessment for a particular piece of content. For example, if a piece of content knowledge is deemed as procedural and a teacher wants to find out if student knows it, then the teacher reviews the table and selects from the seven kinds of assessments to test students' procedural knowledge.

TABLE 8.1. Correspondence between Knowledge Types and Assessment

	Knowledge types			
Assessment types	Declarative knowledge (knowing that—facts and concepts)	Procedural knowledge (knowing how—processes)	Schematic knowledge (knowing why—models)	Strategic knowledge (knowing when and how knowledge applies)
Fill in the blank	✓			
Concept maps	✓			
Drawings/diagrams	✓			✓
Multiple choice	✓	✓	✓	
Multiple-choice justified	✓	✓	✓	✓
Observations		✓		
Performance assessments		✓	✓	✓
Portfolios	✓	✓	✓	✓
Predict–observe–explain	✓		✓	
Self-assessment checklist	✓			
Short-answer prompts	✓	✓	✓	✓
Student journals	✓	✓		

THE TRIPLE

Another tool that can be used to help in the assessment development process is the Triple (Shavelson, Solano-Flores, & Ruiz-Primo, 1998). The Triple refers to the three vital components of assessment tasks. The first component is the actual task that the students conduct. The second component is the recording form where the students record their answers. This may be a student's notebook, an answer sheet, or simply a piece of paper. The third component is a scoring system for evaluating the student's responses. The scoring system could be an answer to a multiple-choice item, or it could be the rubric (scoring guide) to rate an open-ended question with a progress variable, enabling the scorer to approximate a student's relative degree of understanding of that variable. When conceptualizing a formative evaluation tool, the teacher considers each of the three pieces.

PREDICT–OBSERVE–EXPLAIN ASSESSMENT

An example of a useful assessment tool that can serve as a formative assessment is the Predict–Observe–Explain Assessment (POE; White & Gunstone, 1992). The POE is useful because it can be carried out quickly and can target student misconceptions. In the Romance and CAESL–FAST studies, we created a soap POE to tap into student conceptions about buoyancy. The soap POE created a situation that elicits a student's incorrect response unless the student has a firm knowledge of buoyancy. In this POE, the teacher places a bar of high-density soap into a clear vessel of water. The soap sinks. The teacher then removes the soap from the water, pats it dry, and then cuts the soap with a knife into two pieces—$\frac{1}{5}$ and $\frac{4}{5}$. The teacher then asks students to predict what will happen when the small piece of soap is placed in the water and then what will happen when the large piece is placed in the water and to explain why they predicted that way. Students with weak understanding about the relationship between density and buoyancy often predict that the small piece of soap will float while the larger piece of soap will sink. Students often state that the small piece will float because it is small, light weight, or of low mass. Students with stronger understandings about density and buoyancy, especially with a solid understanding of density, will predict that both pieces will sink. After the students have predicted, they observe the placement of the soap into fresh water and then reconcile their predictions with their observations. A teacher can quickly evaluate students' buoyancy understandings by reviewing their predictions and explanations.

Selecting the right evaluation tool for formative assessment purposes is important for teachers. Selecting or creating the right evaluation tool becomes important because that tool must be able to provide information on which to base recommendations.

Component 3: Implementing the Assessments

The third component of the assessment pedagogy model refers to the method with which the teachers implement the assessments with their students. We know little about this formative student assessment component, but it might influence the results and subsequent use of the assessments. While one might think that administering an assessment is straightforward, the implementation of the assessment in the classroom is contextualized temporally with the lessons that precede and follow it. For example, if a teacher gives a formative assessment to students to find out what they know about sinking and floating, and he or she just finished a lengthy review of items similar to those in the assessment, students might respond based on their practice and not on what they really believe. Imagine if a teacher were to review the soap POE with students before she administered it. The results would be skewed. Three concepts to consider in the assessment implementation component are (1) summative assessment scripts, (2) making knowledge public, and (3) creating the assessment conversation.

SUMMATIVE ASSESSMENT SCRIPTS

In the FAST studies we identified the problematic way in which one teacher carried out the formative assessments with his students. Rather than viewing the tests as measures of what students know in order to use this information for instruction—a formative purpose—the teacher carried out procedures and routines that would normally precede the summative assessment. Overall, the teacher's action revealed a perception that these formative assessments were actually summative assessments. The teacher reverted from using a formative assessment to using a summative assessment "teaching script." A teaching script can be conceptualized as a formalized teaching pattern consisting of a set of expectations about what events are necessary and about the temporal order of such events (Shavelson, 1986). A summative assessment teaching script might include studying for the tests, taking practice tests, or reviewing lecture notes with the students prior to actually giving the test. A teacher in the FAST studies took as much time with test preparation as with the test itself. In order to avoid the usual summative assessment teaching scripts, the name of the formative assessments in the first FAST assessment project was changed to *Reflective Lessons* (Shavelson & Stanford Educational Assessment Lab, 2004).

MAKING KNOWLEDGE PUBLIC

In another implementation procedure, the teacher has the students commit to an answer to a question and then makes their answers and explanations public. This may promote student learning. In science classes, if students have misconceptions about a particular physical event, and if these misconceptions can be elicited, made public (albeit anonymously), and then compared with other students' conceptions about the physical event, the students might recognize their misconceptions. This might promote conceptual change. For example, in the FAST studies, when students were discussing the results of student understanding about which blocks of soap should sink or float in water, they were able to identify which explanations were productive in predicting the floating and sinking behavior and which explanations were not. Formative assessment researchers are promoting the use of flashcards, electronic devices, signal lights, and colored cups as tools to make information public (Wiliam, 2006).

An important FAST formative assessment component was the discussion that occurs after the students have completed the assessments. While the actual assessments are important, they, in themselves, represent only part of what needs to happen to promote the goals of the assessments— both accountability and learning. The discussions are key because, in them, the teacher helps make student conceptions and reasoning public, emphasizes the importance of supporting one's explanations with evidence, and pushes for universality of the activity—that is, ensuring that the activity relates to the unit goals. This discussion is believed to be key for promoting learning. Ruiz-Primo and Furtak (2004) found that the more of this type of "assessment conversation," the more learning occurred in the classroom. The implementation of the formative assessments provides the moment to begin to carry out the recommendations for improvement. The implementation of an evaluation provides the time to start with recommendations.

Component 4: Interpreting the Results

The fourth component of the model is the interpretation of the formative assessments. Once teachers have successfully implemented the formative assessments, they collect information about what students know and are able to do and then place the student knowledge on some roadmap back to the construct. For example, in the FAST studies, teachers implemented discussions with their students to find out what students understood about some particular activity. The teachers then took this information and placed the students' current model on the buoyancy learning trajectory: mass $\rightarrow$ volume $\rightarrow$ mass and volume $\rightarrow$ density $\rightarrow$ relative density. This model was further developed into a progress variable to help teachers make curricular decisions (Wilson & Darney, 2004). Finding ways to structure this interpretation has not been fully studied.

In the classroom, teachers are faced with the situation where student understanding is not homogeneous across students. At a given point in a curriculum, the teacher presents material to the students, hoping that they will learn the material. In reality, some of the students will learn the material, while other students will not. Darney and Kennedy (2006) found that if progress variables were used to track student learning and understanding after a lesson, most of the students will not have learned what they should. This may suggest that student learning as measured with formative assessments may always be below curricular level and that teachers should just press on with the curriculum because students will catch up. We know little about this, but a rule of thumb that we used in the FAST studies was that if 80% of the students knew the material the teachers were advised to move on without reteaching.

Component 5: Taking Action

The fifth component of the model is closely aligned with development of recommendations for improvement. The teacher in a formative assessment situation uses the information derived from student work to decide on a course of action. The decision about the course of action includes the recommendations for improvement. The teacher might suggest to students that they reread a chapter or revisit an experiment. The teacher might just move on. Based on the FAST studies, these actions may require the most from teachers. Four different taking-action strategies are promising: (1) facet-based instruction, (2) revisiting anchor points, (3) providing feedback, and (4) student self-assessment.

FACET-BASED INSTRUCTION

Minstrell included in his facet-based instruction certain specific methods of taking action (Minstrell & Stimpson, 1996). In facet-based instruction, a teacher asks students a question to get at their initial understanding of a concept, listens to the students' responses, and asks another question or carries out a benchmark lesson in response to this question. Minstrell and van Zee (2003) later argued that, once students' thinking has been exposed with an assessment, teachers must analyze it and consider what they need to do to "challenge problematic thinking and promote deeper thinking" (p. 72). Facet-based instruction requires that teachers have an awareness of the difficulties that students might have in an area and that teachers have a "bag of tricks" into which they reach when they encounter a problem. They argue that this "bag of tricks" can only be acquired by experience.

REVISITING ANCHOR POINTS

Another action-taking method is that of taking students back to some previous lesson and having them revisit the concept. If students are stuck on a misconception and a previous lesson had occurred that allows the students to move on beyond that misconception (in that contextualized situation), it might prove effective to bring the students back to that lesson and have them revisit the misconception. This happened repeatedly in the formative assessments in the FAST studies. It seemed especially valuable when a progress variable was involved. One teacher described how she would ask students to revisit a previous activity to handle a misconception. For example, she asked students if a bottle partially filled with sand would sink or float. The students often considered only the mass of the bottle, even though they had already covered the concept that mass is not the only physical characteristic that matters when considering sinking and floating. When encountering this powerful misconception in later units of FAST, the teacher would ask the students to go to her desk and pick up the materials from a previous lesson where mass was not useful in predicting the sinking and floating event. This revisiting was valuable because the students had already encountered this situation and understood the illustrative nature of the activity. The student conception was pushed again—sometimes it takes more than one exposure for a child to learn.

FEEDBACK

The research focus in this area has been mostly limited to teacher feedback. Ruiz-Primo, Li, Ayala, and Shavelson (2004) found that in the context of student notebooks teachers provided little if any feedback to students, despite the errors or misconceptions found in student responses. Furthermore, the feedback that was found was reduced to grades, checkmarks, or coded phrases ("good job"), and the potential for using feedback as a learning tool was lost. Kluger and DeNisi (1996) found feedback that draws attention to metatask processes (threats or praise to self) lowers performance, while feedback to task motivation or learning processes promotes performance. They concluded that providing quality feedback is important. However, Shepard (2000) noted that we take for granted that providing feedback to students will improve learning. Shepard suggested that studies of expert tutoring reveal how much we have to learn about feedback use. She pointed to studies showing that expert tutors use "indirect forms of feedback" to ameliorate problems both with evaluation and with student motivation and self-confidence. Recommendations for improvement have affective as well as academic components.

In the FAST studies, we proposed to the teachers a series of steps that they could do in order to respond to the formative assessment information. This included moving on if most of the students have mastered the curriculum, having students rejustify their thinking based on activities they already had provided in the assessment conversation, and having students develop experiments to help them answer their questions.

In the FAST studies we also learned that the teachers are not the only ones who can give feedback. The results of a demonstration give feedback, too. When students take assessments such as the soap POE, described above, they can see for themselves whether their predictions are correct. Allowing the assessment to provide feedback directly to the students, as in the case of a physical phenomenon, removes the teacher from the assessment equation and might have positive affective consequences.

STUDENT SELF-ASSESSMENT

The issue about whether or not students should be involved in their own self-assessment is an important matter. On the one hand, having students be self-evaluators to further their learning makes sense. On the other hand, a teacher may provide insights into what a student is missing or doing wrong and provide suggestions for improvement based on their evaluative knowledge and experience. There is more to know about student self-assessment (Atkins & Coffey, 2003).

Formative assessment research suggests that making decisions about what to do next might be the most difficult thing to do. We do know that having clear paths to follow when a student does not know something is important (e.g., with facet-based instruction and revisiting anchor points).

Component 6: Assessment System Evaluation

The final component of the assessment pedagogy model is the metacognitive component of looking at the overall assessment model and deciding whether or not it increases student learning. Borrowing Eisner's (1991) notion that something must be useful to be valid, it becomes important to look back at the whole assessment system, either in a quantifiable or a holistic way, and to decide if it is a valued experience. We must remember that teaching is a very complex and full task, so additional burdens such as "formative assessments," or the use of this model, should not be encouraged if they are not useful in promoting student learning. If new things are going to be added to the curriculum or to teacher pedagogy, then something else must be removed.

IMPLICATIONS OF THE ASSESSMENT
PEDAGOGY MODEL FOR PROGRAM EVALUATION

The description of the formative assessment pedagogy model presented
in this chapter has two primary implications for program evaluators.
First, the model can be adopted without significant revision when planning and implementing careful systematic formative evaluations of educational programs, particularly K–12 programs. It presents a comprehensive system for a thorough and methodologically warranted method
of formative evaluation. The model includes (1) fully understanding the
purpose of the program and the content that is taught, (2) designing
valid and reliable instruments for collecting formative student evaluation
data, (3) implementing the assessments, (4) interpreting the assessment
results, (5) identifying the actions to take (i.e., making and implementing
recommendations for improvement), and (6) conducting metaevalua-
tions of the assessment system. The model can be used iteratively to
improve a program until students' learning proceeds at the desired pace
and results in the intended learning outcomes. Evaluators can apply the
findings from using the model as a formative evaluation tool to modify
the program or project. Data collected on persistent student misconceptions or failure to learn the intended material can help program developers, faculty, and staff revise and improve the program.

   Second, the model suggests a system for formative evaluations of
programs of any sort. We have learned in our FAST studies that teachers
cannot be handed a package of formative assessments and be expected
to implement them without having first built all the components of the
model proposed above. Program evaluators, too, might have to develop
competency in these or related components to effectively create recommendations for improvement. To collect the necessary information for
developing effective suggestions for program improvement, the evaluator should know the material that is being evaluated, know how to
develop the tools, know how to implement these tools, be able to interpret the results of using these tools, and be able to suggest action recommendations to improve the evaluand. A few of examples of how the
model might assist in developing and implementing formative program
evaluation are:

- The assessment pedagogy model can help ensure that program
  delivery addresses the intended program purposes and material.

- Developing valid and reliable instruments for formative evaluations during the development and early implementation of a program helps ensure that evaluation feedback is based on data of
  sufficient quality.

- Adapting the principles of the model's teacher–student assessment conversation can help cement and continue the intensively collaborative interaction among evaluators and program personnel that is necessary if formative evaluation recommendations are to be useful and heeded.

- Acknowledging that a program must not be perfect before its development moves on to the next stage helps ensure that development and early implementation occur in a timely fashion.

- Acknowledging the need to promote deeper thinking among program personnel about how to improve the program, as the assessment pedagogy model endeavors to do with students when using the results of formative assessments, can help make recommendations insightful and useful.

- Avoiding feedback that provides threats or praise and instead focusing on task motivation and learning processes might improve the development of a program.

- Constantly revisiting the formative evaluation process in an iterative formative metaevaluation will continue to improve formative evaluation.

These are a few examples of how adapting the assessment pedagogy model might prove beneficial. Of course, the model is not appropriate or feasible for all evaluation settings. Adapting features of the assessment approach to program evaluation clearly results in a formative evaluation of a much more systematic and thorough nature than most reported in the literature, which often consist of monitoring, consulting, or observing and providing informal feedback. The portion of the program budget devoted to such a formative evaluation might be much greater than usual. It might not be fiscally feasible to conduct an expensive formative evaluation of this nature, or insufficient time might be available to adapt the approach thoroughly. Furthermore, using the approach assumes that program logic is fairly well developed and that evaluators will not have to expend resources simply identifying and describing what the program is about, as is often the case in the evaluation of educational programs, particularly small projects. In addition, adapting the model implies that feedback will be given quickly to program personnel despite the elaborate nature of the model. Nevertheless, we believe that the model holds promise for programs that seek to establish a solid record of improving their efficacy on the basis of a theoretically sound and methodologically warranted formative study. The model is capable of providing the foundation for making sound recommendations. In particular, it deserves further consideration in developing and implementing large educational programs.

REFERENCES

Atkins, M., & Coffey, J. (Eds.). (2003). *Everyday assessment in the science class-room*. Arlington, VA: NSTA Press.

Ayala, C. C. (2005, April). *Assessment pedagogies*. Paper presented at the annual meeting of the American Educational Research Association, Montreal.

Black, P., & Wiliam, D. (1998). *Inside the black box: Raising standards through classroom assessment*. London: School of Education, King's College.

Black, P., & Wiliam, D. (2005). Developing a theory of formative assessment. In J. Gardner (Ed), *Assessment for learning: practice, theory and policy* (pp. 143–181). London: Sage.

Brandon, P. R. (1999). Involving program stakeholders in reviewing evaluators' recommendations for program revisions. *Evaluation and Program Planning, 22,* 363–372.

Cousins, J. B., & Whitmore, E. (1998). Framing participatory evaluation. In E. Whitmore (Ed.), *Understanding and practicing participatory evaluation* (New Directions for Evaluation no. 80, pp. 5–23). San Francisco: Jossey-Bass.

Cronbach, L. J., Ambron, S. R., Dornbusch, S. M., Hess, R. D., Hornik, R. C., et al. (1980). *Toward reform of program evaluation*. San Francisco, CA: Jossey-Bass.

Darney, K., & Kennedy, C. (2006, May). *Designing and using an embedded assessment system to track student progress*. Presentation at the annual conference of the Center for Assessment and Evaluation of Student Learning, Asilomar, CA.

de Jong, T., & Ferguson-Hessler, M. (1996). Types and qualities of knowledge. *Educational Psychologist, 31,* 105–114.

Eisner, E. W. (1991). *The enlightened eye: Qualitative inquiry and the enhancement of educational practice*. New York: Macmillan.

Fetterman, D. M., & Wandersman, A. (2005). *Empowerment evaluation principles in practice*. New York: Guilford Press.

Guskey, T. (2005, April). *Formative classroom assessment and Benjamin S. Bloom: Theory, research and implications*. Paper presented at the annual meeting of the American Educational Research Association, Montreal.

Hendricks, M., & Handley, E. A. (1990). Improving the recommendations from evaluation studies. *Evaluation and Program Planning, 13,* 109–117.

Hendricks, M., & Papagiannis, M. (1990). Do's and don't's for offering effective recommendations. *Evaluation Practice, 11,* 121–125.

Iriti, J. E., Bickel, W. E., & Nelson, C. A. (2005). Using recommendations in evaluation: A decision-making framework for evaluators. *American Journal of Evaluation, 26,* 464–479.

Kluger, A. N., & DeNisi, A. S. (1996). The effects of feedback interventions on performance: Historical review, meta-analysis, and a preliminary feedback theory. *Psychological Bulletin, 119,* 254–284.

Li, M., & Shavelson, R. J. (2001, April). *Examining the links between science achievement and assessment.* Paper presented at the annual meeting of the American Educational Research Association, Seattle, WA.

Minstrell, J., & Stimpson, V. C. (1996). *Instruction for understanding: A cognitive process framework* (final report, NIE-G-83-0059). Mercer Island School District, WA. (Eric Document Reproduction Service No. ED282749).

Minstrell, J., & van Zee, E. (2003). Using questions to assess and foster student thinking. In M. Atkin & J. Coffey (Eds.), *Everyday assessment in the science classroom* (pp. 61–73). Arlington, VA: NSTA Press.

Pelligrino, J., Chudowsky, N., & Glaser, R. (Eds.). (2001). *Knowing what students know: The science and design of educational assessment.* Washington, DC: National Academy Press.

Pottenger, F., & Young, D. (1992). *The Local Environment: FAST 1, Foundational Approaches in Science Teaching,* Honolulu: University of Hawaii at Manoa, Curriculum Research and Development Group.

Ruiz-Primo, M. A., & Furtak, E. (2004, April). *Informal assessment of students' understanding of scientific inquiry.* Paper presented at the annual meeting of the American Educational Research Association, San Diego, CA.

Ruiz-Primo, M. A., Li, M., Ayala, C. C., & Shavelson, R. J. (2004). Evaluating students' science notebooks as an assessment tool. *International Journal of Science Education, 26,* 1477–1506.

Scriven, M. (1991a). *Evaluation thesaurus.* Newbury Park, CA: Sage.

Scriven, M. (1991b). Beyond formative and summative evaluation. In M. W. McLaughlin & D. C. Phillips (Eds.), *Evaluation and education: At quarter century. Ninetieth yearbook of the National Society for the Study of Education, Part II* (pp. 19–64). Chicago: National Society for the Study of Education.

Scriven, M. (1993). *Hard-won lessons in program evaluation* (New Directions for Program Evaluation no. 58). San Francisco: Jossey-Bass.

Shadish, W. R., Cook, T. D., & Leviton, L. C. (1991). *Foundations of program evaluation: Theories of practice.* Newbury Park, CA: Sage.

Shavelson, R. J. (1986). Toma de decision interactive: Algunas reflexiones sobre los procesos cognoscitivos de los profesores. (Interactive decision making: Some thoughts on teacher cognition). In L. M. V. Angulo (Ed.), *Pensamientos de los profesores y toma de decisiones.* Universidad de Sevilla, Servicio de Publicaciones, Seville, Spain.

Shavelson, R. J., Solano-Flores, G., & Ruiz-Primo, M. A. (1998). Toward a science performance assessment technology. *Evaluation and Program Planning, 21,* 171–184.

Shavelson, R. J., & Stanford Educational Assessment Lab. (2004, June). *CAESL and the future of science assessment.* Keynote address at the Center for Assessment and Evaluation of Student Learning Conference, Carmel, CA.

Shavelson, R. J., & Young, D. (2001). *Embedding assessments in the FAST Curriculum: On beginning the romance among curriculum, teaching, and assessment* (NSF grant proposal).

Shepard, L. (2000). The role of assessment in a learning culture, *Educational Researcher,* 294–314.

Stake, R. (1991). Retrospective on "The Countenance of Educational Evaluation." In M. W. McLaughlin & D. C. Phillips (Eds.), *Evaluation and education: At quarter century. Ninetieth yearbook of the National Society for the Study of Education, Part II* (pp. 67–88). Chicago: National Society for the Study of Education.

Weiss, C. (1972). Evaluating educational and social actions programs: A treeful of owls. In C. H. Weiss (Ed.), *Evaluating action programs* (pp. 3–27). Boston: Allyn & Bacon.

White, R., & Gunstone, R. (1992). *Probing understanding.* London: Falmer.

Wiliam, D. (2005, April) *The integration of formative assessment and classroom instruction.* Paper presented at the annual meeting of the American Educational Research Association, Montreal.

Wiliam, D. (2006, April). *Assessment for learning.* Keynote address presented to the annual meeting of the National Association for Researchers in Science Teaching, San Francisco.

Wilson, M. (2005, April) *Building science assessments that serve accountability and student learning: The CAESL model.* Paper presented at the annual meeting of the American Educational Research Association, Montreal.

Wilson, M., & Darney, K. (2004). Some links between large-scale and classroom assessment: The case of the bear assessment system. In M. Wilson (Ed.), *Towards coherence between classroom assessment and accountability. One hundred and third yearbook of the National Society for the Study of Education* (pp. 132–154). Chicago: University of Chicago Press.

PART IV
ISSUES OF
THE PROFESSION

Evaluation is ubiquitous, frequently written about, and even more widely practiced. But, not all evaluation is "professional" evaluation. The focus of Part IV is on evaluation as a professional activity and enterprise.

Thirty years ago, the inaugural issue of one of the major journals in the field of evaluation, *Evaluation and Program Planning*, was published. In the two lead articles of that issue, the editors of the journal, Eugenie Flaherty and Jonathan Morell, summarized the then short history of the field of evaluation, examining both the reasons for and evidence of its growth (Flaherty & Morell, 1978; Morell & Flaherty, 1978). They identified issues relevant to the professionalization of the field, such issues as the development of a specialized body of knowledge, the definition of evaluation tasks, control over who can perform those tasks, the development of professional associations, and problems in the training of evaluators. Morell and Flaherty (1978) made several predictions about the future of evaluation. Notice how their predictions reflect the ongoing fundamental issues the field has subsequently continued to deal with:

- "... we are in for a serious debate on the nature of just what it is that evaluators should be doing" (p. 14).
- "... the evaluation profession will expend considerable effort in developing and laying claim to a specialized knowledge base" (p. 14).
- "... the profession will expend considerable effort in trying to convince the public that its knowledge base is important for the general good" (pp. 14–15).
- "... we are likely to see greater and greater specification of who is allowed to perform specific types of evaluation tasks." (p. 15)
- "... competition with other professions for program evaluation work" (p. 15).
- "... as the field of program evaluation grows it will continually confront the problem of the irrelevance of its professional training" (p. 16).

Morell and Flaherty concluded, "We feel that these problems are not merely by-products of progress in program evaluation but are unavoidable consequences of the process by which evaluation will become an identifiable profession" (Morell & Flaherty, 1978, p. 17). Put another way, these predictions reflect some of the fundamental issues that have arisen and will continue to arise in the profession of evaluation.

Part IV comprises three chapters. Sandra Mathison opens with Chapter 9, "What Is the Difference between Evaluation and Research— and Why Do We Care?," in which she addresses probably one of the most discussed topics in evaluation related to the issue of "just what it is that evaluators should be doing." The editors of this volume recall heated arguments during the 1970s when, as graduate students, we tried to sort out the differences between social science research and evaluation (which is sometimes called *evaluation research*). How do the purposes and methods of these two forms of inquiry differ, and what knowledge and skills sets are required of evaluators versus social science researchers? Our own students continue to raise these questions, as do newcomers to the profession who, wanting to resolve the differences in their minds and distinguish between research and evaluation for their clients, annually raise this topic on the American Evaluation Association's listserv, EVALTALK.

Mathison's discussion of the differences and similarities between evaluation and social science research reflects the nature of fundamental issues: there is no clear, final resolution to them. Her dissection of the caricatured depictions of the differences among the two forms of inquiry, such as the extent to which the findings of studies result in decisions or the extent to which they result in generalizations, shows that the differences depend on the context and the purpose of particular studies.

For example, program evaluations typically use social science methods, but evaluations of other evaluands (e.g., products and sporting events) do not. Research on programs is often very similar to the evaluation of programs, with both resulting in conclusions about how well programs perform, but personnel research is quite different from personnel evaluation. The purpose of some social science experiments is to establish whether causality exists between independent and dependent variables without regard to the merit of the dependent variables, but the purpose of evaluations that use experimental designs is to determine whether a program has more merit than an alternative. Social science research in a laboratory might provide results of interest to academicians only, whereas social science action research in the field is designed, like evaluations, to support social change. Mathison's chapter will help readers move from the overly simple question of what is the difference between research and evaluation to a more sophisticated consideration of the conditions under which research and evaluation share both similarities and differences.

While Mathison's chapter responds to a perennial question concerning an evaluator's professional identity, the two remaining chapters in Part IV address important fundamental issues that have received increasing attention in recent years. With greater appreciation for the diversity within society and the increasing globalization of evaluation, evaluators are now more explicitly dealing with such fundamental issues as: What is the nature of a culturally competent evaluation? and, What is the proper role and means for evaluation in contributing to social justice?

In Chapter 10, "The Impact of Narrow Views of Scientific Rigor on Evaluation Practices for Underrepresented Groups," Elmima C. Johnson, Karen E. Kirkhart, Anna Marie Madison, Grayson B. Noley, and Guillermo Solano-Flores argue that rigorous educational evaluation studies, although internally valid, are often not sufficiently robust, because they do not arrive at conclusions that properly take into account program and evaluation context, particularly the contextual factors that affect communities of peoples of color. Furthermore, studies with rigorous designs are often limited to questions of the comparative effectiveness of programs, ignoring other questions that are worthy of evaluation. The intended purpose of these studies is to identify the most effective methods of teaching and learning; yet, these questions might not be the most relevant to underrepresented groups, for whom contextual factors affect outcomes differentially from the majority group.

Johnson et al. flesh out their argument about rigor versus robustness by focusing on three issues: (1) how definitions of validity determine the operationalization of rigor, (2) how language theory can inform the assessment of second-language learners, and (3) how evaluations can advance social justice by using multiple measures of accountability. Their discussion speaks to the fundamental issue of the proper purposes, roles, and uses of evaluation. They argue that the primary purposes of program evaluations and assessments should be to ensure social justice, enhance fairness, and address inequities in access to power. Their focus on issues of method, discussed in terms of validity, informing assessment with language theory, and the use of multiple measures, ultimately revolves around these purposes.

The final chapter in Part IV is Chapter 11, "Improving the Practice of Evaluation through Indigenous Values and Methods: Decolonizing Evaluation Practice—Returning the Gaze from *Hawai'i* and *Aotearoa*" by Alice J. Kawakami, Kanani Aton, Fiona Cram, Morris K. Lai, and Laurie Porima. These authors, all of whom are part-Hawaiian or part-*Māori*, discuss fundamental issues of ethics and values in the evaluation of indigenous cultures—specifically, Māori (New Zealand) and Kānaka Maoli (Hawai'i) native cultures. The chapter is presented, in part, in a story-telling manner that reflects a historically preferred method of communication among indigenous Polynesian people—the very structure of the manuscript shows the reader how indigenous communication and knowing are practiced in Māori and Kānaka Maoli communities and is meant to be read in more of a *mo'olelo* or storytelling manner than is usually the case in evaluation writing.

The authors make a strong case that many evaluations in Polynesian settings have adapted a "Western approach" that has ignored or disrespected the role of community elders as the arbiters of quality, failed to acknowledge and incorporate indigenous spiritual values, and disregarded cultural practices such as valuing lineage. They argue that these evaluations typically have not benefited the community in which programs occur. They point out that family and geographical identities are central values to indigenous peoples in their cultures. Family comes first in these settings, but this value is ignored by many traditional evaluators.

Kawakami et al. argue that indigenous peoples have a right to evaluation methods that are culturally relevant, not simply because the results will be more culturally and epistemologically valid or because such methods will lead to greater stakeholder support of the resultant findings but because indigenous peoples have a moral right to self-determination. Nonindigenous evaluators are often not capable of discerning cultural violations apparent to indigenous evaluators, and indigenous peoples have a moral right to influence the choice of methods for evaluating the programs that affect their lives.

All three chapters in Part IV illustrate how our understanding of the nature of evaluation as a profession continues to evolve. The latter two chapters draw our attention to especially serious issues about what the generative principles should be that define who evaluators are, what they do, and how—fundamental issues of the profession that Morell and Flaherty predicted we would continue to address.

REFERENCES

Flaherty, E. W., & Morell, J. A. (1978). Evaluation: Manifestations of a new field. *Evaluation and Program Planning, 1*(1), 1–10.

Morell, J. A., & Flaherty, E. W. (1978). The development of evaluation as a profession: Current status and some predictions. *Evaluation and Program Planning, 1*(1), 11–17.

CHAPTER 9

What Is the Difference
between Evaluation and Research—
and Why Do We Care?

SANDRA MATHISON

Offering a definition of evaluation as the process and product of making judgments about the value, merit, or worth of an evaluand does little to answer the perennial question: What is the difference between evaluation and research? Annually, this question is asked on EVALTALK, an international discussion listserv for evaluators. A quick search of the archives illustrates that each year since 1998 there has been a substantial thread in response to this question, posed often by novice evaluators. Indeed, in 1998 there were about 178 messages in response to the question, and the thread was sustained by the contributions of three prominent figures in evaluation: Michael Scriven, Michael Quinn Patton, and William Trochim. Essentially, the two Michaels asserted there is a difference between research and evaluation but that the two overlap, and Trochim argued that evaluation is no different than applied social science. In subsequent years, the threads have been shorter, but the question has not gone away.

 This question about differences between evaluation and research is fueled by the fact that evaluation as a discipline draws on other disciplines for its foundations, and especially the social sciences for its methods. As evaluation has matured as a discipline and profession, this question is sometimes posed to clarify what is distinct about evaluation. This delineation of a profession of evaluation is also tied to a discussion of who is and can be an evaluator. What knowledge and skills does evaluation require, and how do these differ from the knowledge and skills of social science researchers?

This chapter does two things. First, the chapter considers why this question is fundamental, including how the question relates to the development of evaluation as a discipline, a professional practice, and what knowledge and skills evaluators need. Second, I discuss the difference between research and evaluation. This section of the chapter draws on the evaluation literature, including the extensive discussions on EVALTALK. It is often the case that both evaluation and research are caricatured in order to make distinctions between the two. In the search for a simple way of distinguishing research and evaluation, similarities and differences are sometimes masked.

WHY DO WE CARE ABOUT THE DIFFERENCE?

Evaluation practice is ancient, but the discipline and profession of evaluation are quite contemporary. Indeed, evaluation as a profession and the concomitant elucidation of the discipline are only four or five decades old. This newness leads to self-consciousness about what it is we are doing when we say we are doing evaluation (and not research) and an explicit discourse about the fundamentals of evaluation (that differentiate it from research). Disciplines are fields of study having their own logic, often entailing various theories that enable study within the field. For the discipline of evaluation, there is a particular logic (Fournier, 1995; Scriven, 1999) and subtheories, including a theory of valuing, practice, prescription and use. (For a more complete discussion of these subtheories that constitute the discipline of evaluation, see Mathison 2004b.) One might imagine that such questions as "What is the difference between statistics (a newer discipline) and mathematics (a more established discipline)?" were also once asked as the discipline of statistics caught up with the practice of using probability in common-sense ways. The question about the difference between evaluation and research productively pushes evaluation theorists and practitioners to think about and describe the foundations of their discipline, first in comparison to social science research but increasingly in an analytic exploration of evaluation qua evaluation.

Evaluation, especially program evaluation in the United States, had its genesis in the provisions of the Elementary and Secondary Education Act (ESEA), passed in 1965. ESEA's requirement that the expenditure of public funds be accounted for thrust educators into a new and unfamiliar role, and researchers and educational psychologists stepped in to fill the need for evaluation created by ESEA. But the efforts of practitioners and researchers alike were only minimally successful at providing the kind of evaluative information envisioned. The compensatory programs supported by ESEA were complex and embedded in the complex organization of schooling. Research methods that focused on hypothesis testing were not well suited to the task at hand.

The late 1960s through the early 1980s were the gold rush days of evaluation. During this period, models of evaluation proliferated and truly exciting intellectual work was being done. A few traditionally educated educational psychologists experienced epiphanies that directed their thinking toward new ways to do evaluation. For example, Robert Stake, a psychometrician who began his career at the Educational Testing Service, wrote a paper called the "Countenance of Educational Evaluation" that reoriented thinking about the nature of educational interventions and what was important to pay attention to in determining their effectiveness (Stake, 1967). Egon Guba, a well-known education change researcher, abandoned the research, development, diffusion approach for naturalistic and qualitative approaches that examined educational interventions carefully and contextually. Lee Cronbach, a psychometric genius, focused not on the technical aspects of measurement in evaluation but on the policy-oriented nature of evaluation, an idea that led to a radical reconstruction of internal and external validity, including separating the two conceptually and conceptualizing external validity as related to the usability and plausibility of conclusions rather than as a technical feature of evaluation design (Cronbach, 1982).

The failure of social science research methods alone to answer questions about the value of programs spurred this tremendous growth in evaluation as a separate discipline. The matter is not, however, resolved. The debates about how best to determine what is working continue; an example is the current U.S. governmental preference for randomized clinical trials to determine what works. In the past, governmental funding supported the proliferation of evaluation and new ideas in evaluation practice; government agencies now presume to direct how evaluation ought to be done.

For example, the U.S. Department of Education funds very little evaluation because of this narrowed definition of what the government now considers good evaluation. A quick search of the U.S. Department of Education website shows that it funded only 12 evaluation studies in 2003 and 6 in 2004. These are referred to as a new generation of rigorous evaluations. These evaluations must be randomized clinical trials, perhaps quasi-experimental or regression discontinuity designs. Few if any educational evaluations have been of this sort; indeed, much of the work since the 1960s has been directed to creating different evaluation methods and models of evaluative inquiry (not just borrowed research methods) that answer evaluative questions. These are questions about feasibility, practicability, needs, costs, intended and unintended outcomes, ethics, and justifiability.

The question about differences between evaluation and research is also about what knowledge and skills evaluators need, an especially critical matter if there are unique domains of knowledge and skills for evaluators. Evaluators are served well by having knowledge of and facility with most social science research methods, but as illustrated earlier, those alone are not adequate, either in terms of a methodological repertoire or the evaluation knowledge and skills domain. Scriven suggests evaluators must also know how to search for unintended and side effects, how to determine values within different points of view, how to deal with controversial issues and values, and how to synthesize facts and values (Coffman, 2003–2004).

While there are more graduate programs to educate future evaluators, it is still the case that many evaluators come to their work through a back door, often with knowledge of social science methods and statistics but relatively little knowledge about the knowledge domains suggested by Scriven. Given that this is the case, it is natural for this question to be a perennial one, as more and more novice evaluators are acculturated into a profession that requires them to acquire additional knowledge and skills.

In his 1998 American Evaluation Association presidential address, Will Shadish asked a series of questions about basic and theoretical issues in evaluation with which evaluators should be conversant (although they need not necessarily agree completely on the answers) in order to claim they know the knowledge base of their profession. For example, Shadish poses questions like "What are the four steps in the logic of evaluation?" and "What difference does it make whether the program being evaluated is new or has existed for many years?" and "What is metaevaluation and when should it be used?" The point here is not to answer the questions but to illustrate that evaluators are not simply social science researchers practicing in certain applied contexts, but rather they are engaged in a different practice and thus require special knowledge and skills.

The question about differences seems vexing at times, especially to those who have worked through it already. Novice evaluators who venture on to EVALTALK with this fundamental question will likely be met with a slightly impatient suggestion to check the archives, as the question has been thoroughly discussed. However, it is a good question, because it provides an impetus for evaluators to do the philosophical and empirical work of saying what they are doing and how. And as a result, the potential for evaluation practice to be high-quality and to make significant positive contributions to understanding what is good and right is enhanced.

CHARACTERIZING THE ISSUE

It may be helpful to begin with an excerpt from the three evaluation scholars who provided much of the fodder for answering this question in their 1998 EVALTALK discussion. Below is a snippet from each that captures their perspectives.

According to Michael Quinn Patton (1998):

> The distinction between research and evaluation, like most of the distinctions we make, perhaps all of them, is arbitrary. One can make the case that the two are the same or different, along a continuum or on different continua completely.
>
> The purpose of making such distinctions, then, must guide the distinctions made. In my practice, most clients prefer and value the distinction. They want to be sure they're involved in evaluation, not research. The distinction is meaningful and helpful to them, and making the distinction helps engender a commitment from them to be actively involved—and deepens the expectation for use.

According to Bill Trochim (1998):

> Here's the question: Are there any differences between applied social research and *program* evaluation? Between applied social research and *process* evaluation? Between applied social research and *formative* evaluation? How about *summative* evaluation? Is there some combination of evaluation types that has so significant an overlap with the domain of applied social research that the two are hard or impossible to distinguish? My answer is YES—what we do in process–program–formative–summative evaluation (my new term for describing to Michael Scriven what "evaluation" is in my sense of the word!) is that it is virtually impossible to distinguish it (certainly in terms of methodology, less perhaps in terms of purpose) from what I understand as applied social research.

And, according to Michael Scriven (1998):

> Research, in the serious sense (by contrast with what tenth graders call looking something up in an encyclopedia) is extensive disciplined inquiry, whereas evaluation in the serious sense (by contrast with what wine columnists and art critics do) is disciplined determination of merit, worth, or

value. Generally speaking, this involves research, but not quite always since what judges do in assessing the credibility of witnesses or at a skating contest is entitled to be called serious evaluation and only involves the use of highly skilled judgment.

Since disciplined inquiry itself involves evaluation—what I call intradisciplinary evaluation (the evaluation of hypotheses, inferences, theories, etc.)—research is an applied field of evaluation (of course requiring vast amounts of further knowledge and skills besides evaluation skills); and for the reasons in the previous paragraph, much evaluation is a subset of research. So there's a double overlap.

Additionally, in an interview for an issue of the *Evaluation Exchange* reflecting on the past and future of evaluation, Scriven (Coffman, 2003–2004) addresses this question directly:

> Evaluation determines the merit, worth, or value of things. The evaluation process identifies relevant values or standards that apply to what is being evaluated, performs empirical investigation using techniques from the social sciences, and then integrates conclusions with the standards into an overall evaluation or set of evaluations.
>
> Social science research, by contrast, does not aim for or achieve evaluative conclusions. It is restricted to empirical (rather than evaluative) research, and bases its conclusions only on factual results—that is, observed, measured, or calculated data. Social science research does not establish standards or values and then integrate them with factual results to reach evaluative conclusions. In fact, the dominant social science doctrine for many decades prided itself on being value free. So for the moment, social science research excludes evaluation.
>
> However, in deference to social science research, it must be stressed again that without using social science methods, little evaluation can be done. One cannot say, however, that evaluation is the application of social science methods to solve social problems. It is much more than that.

WHAT IS THE DIFFERENCE BETWEEN EVALUATION AND RESEARCH?

Although there are arguments that evaluation and research, especially applied social science research, are no different, in general, evaluators do claim there is a difference but that the two are interconnected. Because evaluation requires the investigation of what is, doing evaluation requires doing research. In other words, determining the value, merit, or worth of an evaluand requires some factual knowledge about the evaluand and perhaps similar evaluands. But, of course, evaluation requires more than facts about evaluands, as suggested by Scriven in his interview with *Evaluation Exchange*. Evaluation also requires the synthesis of facts and values in the determination of merit, worth, or value. Research, on the other hand, investigates factual knowledge but may not necessarily involve values and therefore need not include evaluation.

Even though research and evaluation are interconnected, there is often an attempt to find a parsimonious way to distinguish between the two. For example, research is considered by some to be a subset of evaluation; some consider evaluation to be a subset of research; some consider evaluation and research to be end points of a continuum; and some consider evaluation and research to be a Venn diagram with an overlap between the two. The similarities and differences between evaluation and research relate most often to the purpose of each (that is, the anticipated outcome of doing research or evaluation), the methods of inquiry used, and how one judges the quality of evaluation and research.

The Purpose of Evaluation and Research

The following list illustrates the plethora of pithy ways to capture the distinction between the purpose for and expected outcome of doing evaluation or research.

* Evaluation particularizes, research generalizes.
* Evaluation is designed to *improve* something, while research is designed to *prove* something.
* Evaluation provides the basis for decision making; research provides the basis for drawing conclusions.
* Evaluation—so what? Research—what's so?
* Evaluation—how well it works? Research—how it works?
* Evaluation is about what is valuable; research is about what is.

These attempts at a straightforward distinction between evaluation and research are problematic because they caricature both to seek clear differences. Simple distinctions between research and evaluation rely on limited, specific notions of both social science research and evaluation— social science research is far more diverse than is often suggested, including differing perspectives on ontology and epistemology, and evaluation as a professional practice is often what is portrayed rather than the foundations of evaluation, that is, as a discipline.

Take, for example, the popular distinction between generalization and particularization—neither of which is singularly true for either evaluation or research. While evaluation is profoundly particular in the sense that it focuses on *an* evaluand, evaluation findings may nonetheless and often do generalize. Cronbach's (1982) treatise on designing evaluations specifically addressed the issue of external validity, or the generalization of evaluation findings. The kind of generalization Cronbach described was not a claim about a population based on a sample but rather a knowledge claim based on similarities between UTOS (units, treatments, observations, settings). This suggests the possibility that such a claim might be made by the evaluator or someone completely separate from the evaluation but in a similar setting to the evaluand. (This external validity claim would be represented in Cronbach's notation as moving from utoS [a particular evaluation] to *UTOS [settings with some similarities in uto].) Formulated somewhat differently is Stake's notion of naturalistic generalizations, a more intuitive approach to generalization based on recognizing the similarities of objects and issues in like and unlike contexts (Stake, 1978).

Similarly, research may not be primarily about generalization. A historical analysis of the causes of the French Revolution, an ethnography of the Minangkabau, or an ecological study of the Galapagos Islands may not be conducted in order to generalize to all revolutions, all matriarchal cultures, or all self-contained ecosystems.

While evaluation is primarily about the particular, evaluations also provide the basis for generalization, especially in Cronbach's sense of generalizing from utoS to *UTOS and Stake's naturalistic generalizations. And, while much research is about generalization, especially in the sense of making inferences from a sample to a population, much research is also about the particular.

Another common difference asserted is that evaluation is for decision making, while research is for affirming or establishing a conclusion. But, not all evaluation is about decision making or action. There are contexts in which evaluation is done for the sake of doing an evaluation, with no anticipation of a decision, change, or improvement. For example, evaluations of movies or books can be ends in and of themselves. Most practicing evaluators think first and foremost about the practice of evaluation rather than the discipline of evaluation and therefore focus, appropriately, on the expectation that evaluation will be useful, will lead to improvement, and will help in creating better living. But, of course, evaluation is a discipline, and when one thinks about the discipline of evaluation there is a clear distinction between making evaluative claims and making prescriptions. While these are logically connected, they are in fact distinct forms of reasoning.

In addition, some forms of social science research are closely aligned to social action or seeking solutions to social problems. For example, various forms of action research are about alleviating problems, taking action, determining what is and is not valued, and working toward a social state of affairs consistent with those values. Policy analysis is directly connected to decision making, especially with regard to the alleviation of all sorts of problems—social, environmental, health, and so on. The notion that research is about establishing facts, stating what is, drawing conclusions, or proving or disproving an assertion is true for some but not all social science research.

The link between social science research and action, including decision making, may be looser than for evaluation. Much social science research aspires to influence policies and practices but often does so indirectly and through an accumulation of research knowledge—what might be considered influence at a macro level. In fact, the results from an individual research study are typically considered insufficient to directly determine a decision or course of action since the results of a single study provide an incomplete picture. However, social scientists hope the studies they conduct will affect decision making by raising awareness of an issue, contributing to a body of research that will cumulatively inform decision making, identifying policy alternatives, informing policymakers, and establishing research evidence as the basis for adopting interventions (thus the preoccupation with evidence-based practices).

Evaluation may more directly affect decisions about particular evaluands, that is, affect micro-level decisions. But, the discipline's decades-long preoccupation with evaluation utilization, or lack of utilization, suggests that the connections between evaluative claims and decisions are also tenuous. An obvious example, because of the ubiquity of the program, is evaluations of the effectiveness of the DARE (Drug Abuse Resistance Education) program. Because the DARE program is everywhere, in virtually all schools in the United States as well as many other countries, many evaluations of the program have been conducted. But the results are mixed: early evaluations of DARE concluded it was effective, but more recent evaluations suggest the program does little to decrease the incidence of drug use (see Beck, 1998; and a special issue of *Reconsider Quarterly* [2001–2002] devoted to a critical analysis of drug education, including DARE). Just as an accumulation of research knowledge affects practice, so it is sometimes the case with evaluation, as illustrated by the DARE example. Only over time and with the investment of considerable programmatic and evaluative resources have evaluations of DARE actually resulted in any significant changes in the program.

While evaluation may be more likely to contribute to micro decision making, and research more likely to contribute to macro decision making, this distinction does not hold up so well when analyzed a little more carefully.

Differences in Social Science Research and Evaluation Methods

Evaluation, especially in the infancy of the discipline, borrowed generously from the social sciences for its methods of inquiry. In part, because evaluators were educated within social science traditions, especially psychology and sociology, and to a much lesser extent anthropology, ways of establishing empirical evidence were informed by these traditions. For some evaluators this has not changed, but for many the practice of evaluation has moved far beyond these early days. Because evaluation necessarily examines issues like needs, costs, ethicality, feasibility, and justifiability, evaluators employ a much broader spectrum of evidentiary strategies than do the social sciences. In addition to all the means for accessing or creating knowledge used by the social sciences, evaluators are likely to borrow from other disciplines such as jurisprudence, journalism, arts, philosophy, accounting, and ethics.

While there has been an epistemological crisis in the social sciences that has broadened the repertoire of acceptable strategies for data collection and inquiry, evaluation has not experienced this crisis in quite the same way. While the evaluation profession has explored the quantitative and qualitative debate and is attentive to the hegemony of randomized clinical trials, evaluation as a practice shamelessly borrows from all disciplines and ways of thinking to get at both facts and values. Elsewhere I use Feyerabend's notion of an anarchist epistemology to describe this tendency in evaluation (Mathison, 2004a). Anarchism is the rejection of all forms of domination. And so, an anarchist epistemology in evaluation is a rejection of domination of one method over any or all others; of any single ideology; of any single idea of progress; of scientific chauvinism; of the propriety of intellectuals; of evaluators over service recipients and providers; of academic text over oral and other written traditions; of certainty.

In evaluation practice one sees no singular commitment to social science ways of knowing but rather a consideration of how to do evaluation in ways that are meaningful in the context. There are many examples of this, but two will suffice to illustrate the point—consider the *"most significant change technique"* and *"photovoice."* While both of these methods of inquiry could be used in social science, they have particular salience in evaluation because they focus explicitly on valuing and emphasize the importance of stakeholder perspectives (a perspective unique to evaluation and not shared by social science research).

The most significant change technique

> involves the collection of significant change (SC) stories emanating from
> the field, and the systematic selection of the most significant of these stories

by panels of designated stakeholders or staff. The designated staff and stakeholders are initially involved by "searching" for project impact. Once changes have been captured, various people sit together, read the stories aloud and have regular and often in-depth discussions about the value of these reported changes. When the technique is implemented successfully, whole teams of people begin to focus their attention on program impact. (Davies & Dart, 2005)

The second example is photovoice, a grassroots strategy for engaging stakeholders in social change, that is, in asserting what is valued and good (Wang, Yuan, & Feng, 1996). Photovoice uses documentary photography techniques to enable those who are often the "service recipients" or "subjects" to take control of their own portrayal; it has been used with refugees, immigrants, the homeless, and people with disabilities. Photovoice is meant to tap personal knowledge and values and to foster evaluation capacity building—individuals learn a skill that allows them to continue to be a voice in their community. Hamilton Community Foundation in Canada uses photovoice to evaluate and transform neighborhoods challenged by poverty, unemployment, and low levels of education (see their website *www.photovoice.ca/index.php* for a description of the evaluation).

Particular approaches to evaluation are often connected to particular social science traditions, and so sometimes the unique and broader array of methods of inquiry in evaluation is overlooked. The two examples above (most significant change technique and photovoice) illustrate how evaluators have begun to develop evaluation-specific methods to adequately and appropriately judge the value, merit, or worth of evaluands. There are many other such examples: cluster evaluation, rural rapid appraisal, evaluability assessment, and the success case method, to name a few more.

Judging the Quality of Evaluation and Research

Another difference between evaluation and research—and one stressed especially by Michael Quinn Patton in the 1998 EVALTALK discussion of this question—is how we judge the quality of evaluation and research. In making this distinction, Patton suggested that the standards for judging both evaluation and research derive from their purpose. The primary purpose of research is to contribute to understanding of how the world works, and so research is judged by its accuracy, which is captured by its perceived validity, reliability, attention to causality, and generalizability. Evaluation is judged by its accuracy also, but additionally by its utility, feasibility, and propriety. These dimensions for judging the quality of evaluation are clear in the Metaevaluation Checklist, which is based on the Program Evaluation Standards (Stufflebeam, 1999).

A distinguishing feature of evaluation is the universal focus on stakeholder perspectives, a feature not shared by social science research. And evaluations are judged on if and how stakeholder perspectives are included. While evaluation models are based on different epistemological foundations, all evaluation models attend to stakeholder perspectives—the assessments, values, and meanings of the evaluand's stakeholders are essential elements in any evaluation. Social science research may include the language of stakeholders, but their inclusion is not necessary. When research participants are referred to as stakeholders, it is often a reference to whom the data are collected from rather than a consideration of the stakeholders' vested interests. The following excerpt from the Centers for Disease Control's (1999) *Framework for Program Evaluation* illustrates the essential inclusion of stakeholders in evaluation. No approach in social science research necessarily includes this concept.

> The evaluation cycle begins by engaging stakeholders (i.e., the persons or organizations having an investment in what will be learned from an evaluation and what will be done with the knowledge). Public health work involves partnerships; therefore, any assessment of a public health program requires considering the value systems of the partners. Stakeholders must be engaged in the inquiry to ensure that their perspectives are understood. When stakeholders are not engaged, evaluation findings might be ignored, criticized, or resisted because they do not address the stakeholders' questions or values. After becoming involved, stakeholders help to execute the other steps. Identifying and engaging the following three groups are critical:
>
> 1. those involved in program operations (e.g., sponsors, collaborators, coalition partners, funding officials, administrators, managers, and staff)
> 2. those served or affected by the program (e.g., clients, family members, neighborhood organizations, academic institutions, elected officials, advocacy groups, professional associations, skeptics, opponents, and staff of related or competing organizations)
> 3. primary users of the evaluation (e.g., the specific persons who are in a position to do or decide something regarding the program) In practice, primary users will be a subset of all stakeholders identified. A successful evaluation will designate primary users early in its development and maintain frequent interaction with them so that the evaluation addresses their values and satisfies their unique information needs.

CONCLUSION

Evaluation and research are different—different in degree along the dimensions of both particularization–generalization and decision-oriented–conclusion-oriented, the most common dimensions for making distinctions. But, evaluation and research are substantively different in terms of their methods: evaluation includes the methods of data collection and analysis of the social sciences but as a discipline has developed evaluation-specific methods. And, they are substantially different in how judgments of their quality are made. Accuracy is important in both cases, but the evaluation discipline uses the unique criteria of utility, feasibility, propriety, and inclusion of stakeholders.

As evaluation matures as a discipline with a clearer sense of its unique focus, the question of how evaluation is different from research may wane. However, as long as evaluation methodology continues to overlap substantially with that used in the social sciences and as long as evaluators come to the profession from more traditional social science backgrounds, this will remain a fundamental issue for evaluation. As suggested earlier, fundamental issues provide opportunities for greater clarity about what evaluation is as a practice, profession, and discipline.

REFERENCES

Beck, J. (1998). 100 years of "just say no" versus "just say know": Reevaluating drug education goals for the coming century." *Evaluation Review, 22*(1), 15–45.

Centers for Disease Control. (1999). *Framework for program evaluation in public health*. Atlanta: Centers for Disease Control. Retrieved December 15, 2005, from *www.cdc.gov/eval/framework.htm*.

Coffman, J. (2003–2004, Winter). Michael Scriven on the differences between evaluation and social science research. *The Evaluation Exchange, 9*(4). Retrieved February 26, 2006, from *www.gse.harvard.edu/hfrp/eval/issue24/expert.html*.

Cronbach, L. J. (1982). *Designing evaluations of educational and social programs*. San Francisco: Jossey-Bass.

Davies, R., & Dart, J. (2005). *The most significant change technique: A guide to its use*. Retrieved February 26, 2006, from *www.mande.co.uk/docs/MSCGuide.pdf*.

Fournier, D. (Ed.) (1995). *Reasoning in evaluation: Inferential links and leaps* (New Directions for Evaluation no. 48). San Francisco: Jossey-Bass.

Mathison, S. (2004a). *An anarchist epistemology in evaluation*. Paper presented at the annual meeting of the American Evaluation Association, Atlanta. Retrieved February 26, 2006, from *weblogs.elearning.ubc.ca/mathison/ Anarchist%20Epistemology.pdf.*

Mathison, S. (2004b). Evaluation theory. In S. Mathison (Ed.), *Encyclopedia of evaluation* (pp. 142–143). Newbury Park, CA: Sage.

Patton, M. Q. (1998, January 16). Research vs. evaluation. Message posted to *bama.ua.edu/cgi-bin/wa?A2=ind9801C&L=evaltalk&P=R1418&I=1&X= 15AF91488C1E74BD45&Y.*

Reconsider Quarterly, The Education Issue. (2001–2002, Winter), *1*(4; special issue).

Scriven, M. (1998, January 16). Research vs. evaluation. Message posted to *bama.ua.edu/cgi-bin/wa?A2=ind9801C&L=evaltalk&P=R2131&I=1&X= 2F11357E5870213C59&Y.*

Scriven, M. (1999). The nature of evaluation: Part I. Relation to psychology. *Practical Assessment, Research and Evaluation, 6*(11). Retrieved December 15, 2005, from *pareonline.net/getvn.asp?v=6&n=11.*

Shadish, W. (1998) Presidential address: Evaluation theory is who we are. *American Journal of Evaluation, 19*(1), 1–19.

Stake, R. E. (1967). The countenance of educational evaluation. *Teachers College Record, 68*(7), 523–540.

Stake, R. E. (1978). The case study in social inquiry. *Educational Researcher, 7*(2), 5–8.

Stufflebeam, D. (1999). *Metaevaluation checklist.* Retrieved December 15, 2005, from *www.wmich.edu/evalctr/checklists/program_metaeval.htm.*

Trochim, W. (1998, February 2). Research vs. evaluation. Message posted to bama.ua.edu/cgi-bin/wa?A2=ind9802A&L=evaltalk&P=R503&I=1&X= 089CE94613356B8693&Y.

Wang, C., Yuan, Y. L., & Feng, M. L. (1996). Photovoice as a tool for participatory evaluation: The community's view of process and impact. *Journal of Contemporary Health, 4,* 47–49.

CHAPTER 10

The Impact of Narrow Views of Scientific Rigor on Evaluation Practices for Underrepresented Groups

ELMIMA C. JOHNSON, KAREN E. KIRKHART,
ANNA MARIE MADISON, GRAYSON B. NOLEY,
and GUILLERMO SOLANO-FLORES

> No commentator on evaluation devalues excellence with respect to experimental design, reproducibility, statistical rigor, etc. But we do say that these virtues are purchased at too high a price, when they restrict an inquiry to what can be assessed with greatest certainty.
> —CRONBACH (1988, p. 7)

The quest for scientific rigor has deep roots; it is not a new concern. What makes the issue particularly salient now is the use of "scientific rigor" as a simplistic official stamp of acceptability rather than as a concept marking complex interactions among methods, empirical data, and theory. Using the language of scientific rigor as part of political discourse without understanding the complexities of the scientific process can actually undermine what rigor is seeking to support—validity. This chapter uses the No Child Left Behind Act of 2001 to examine scientific rigor and knowledge-based evidence to support policy decision making. Particular emphasis is placed on how the widespread call for more rigorous research may impact traditionally underrepresented groups in the American society—indigenous peoples, linguistic minorities, and communities of color.[1] The unintended side effect of the current drive to

197

increase methodological rigor may be the reduction or even elimination of a large number of programs designed specifically to benefit traditionally underrepresented groups in society. Though our focus is on K–12 education, the issues raised have relevance for higher education, health care, human services, and other public policy arenas.

Since the passage of the No Child Left Behind Act of 2001 (2002), funding policies have transformed the way in which politicians and the public talk about educational research. *Scientifically based* and *scientific rigor* have become key words in political rhetoric. For many, "scientific" inquiry has come to be equated with experimental methods; state- and federally funded procurements clearly specify the use of randomized trials as the "gold standard" to generate evidence-based knowledge. In support of the policy goals of the No Child Left Behind Act (NCLB), the U.S. Department of Education (DOE) guidelines for external evaluations of Title I of the Act give priority to experimental designs or randomized controlled trials (RCTs). These guidelines have caused concern among education evaluators, who note that although RCTs are the most suitable designs to answer policy questions about effectiveness, there are other significant educational research questions for which RCTs are not appropriate (Ryan, 2002).

The American Evaluation Association (AEA), the National Education Association (NEA), and the American Educational Research Association (AERA) advocate for designs that address a number of questions related to teaching and learning. In its 2003 response to the DOE, the AEA leadership argues that it is impossible for one method to answer all of the relevant questions related to successful teaching and learning. The AEA position statement stresses the importance of understanding both causality and conditionality to explain which methods and practices work in which locales and populations. For this reason, the organization recommends that evaluators choose from a variety of methods for educational evaluations (American Evaluation Association, 2003).

The AERA also supports choosing a variety of methods, stating, "Methods must be selected in light of the problem and questions driving the research, and selected methods must be used rigorously" (American Educational Research Association, 2003). Another concern is that funding based on the limited evidence provided by randomized experiments is more likely to widen the achievement gap rather than to reduce it. The NEA expresses concern that those innovative programs most effective in working with students at risk[2] of failure will not be supported in the future (National Education Association, 2003).

The concerns voiced by educators and evaluators are based on three decades of evaluation research. Education evaluators acknowledge that scientific rigor has played an important role in building a knowledge base about practices that work. Historically, some of the most rigorously evaluated programs addressed low-income students, including the evaluation of Project Head Start by Westinghouse Learning Corporation (1969) and the Follow Through study by Stebbins, St. Pierre, Proper, Anderson, and Cerva (1977). Such evaluations advanced theory and practice in the field and validated the importance of taking variables such as social capital, socioeconomic status, race, ethnicity, and early exposure into consideration when evaluating and assessing academic outcomes. What distinguished these studies is the attention given to robustness.

Strong research designs must be both rigorous and robust. Rigor addresses the extent to which an evaluation adheres to strict standards of research methodology; robustness refers to the degree to which changes can be explained by the program rather than by such other factors as school and student characteristics (Fashola, 2004). Assuring that an evaluation adheres to strict standards of scientific rigor does not necessarily provide a robust understanding of demographic characteristics and contextual factors that may influence change. It is not that these variables are necessarily ignored or excluded by a rigorous design. Rather, we are suggesting that the logic of scientific inquiry leads one to think of such variables as elements whose influence must be removed or "controlled" to achieve the greatest clarity regarding program effects. A complementary stance in which characteristics of students and settings are the focus of exploration and inquiry is important and, in fact, *essential* for a robust understanding of program effects on communities of color and other underrepresented groups.

The scientific rigor debate is fundamental to the role of evaluators in producing knowledge to advance educational theory, practice, and policy. Evaluators have a responsibility and an obligation to ensure that appropriate designs are used to answer complex evaluation questions and that faulty research designs do not harm the students NCLB is intended to benefit. Another fundamental issue is evaluators' commitment to the democratic principles of fairness, justice, and equity (Greene, 1999; Henry, 2001). A growing number of evaluators view themselves as participants in a deliberative process of establishing education system accountability criteria to ensure that these democratic principles are upheld (Ryan, 2002). The NCLB legislation is based on the notion that school systems must be accountable to the public.

Evaluators must ensure that social justice issues related to improving low-performing schools are at the forefront of evaluation research. There are many complex and interrelated issues relevant to this concern. In this chapter, we emphasize three such issues of special importance, each treated in a subsequent section of the chapter: (1) the relationship between scientific rigor and validity, (2) the centrality of theory in scientific rigor (using the assessment of English language learners as a specific example), and (3) the need to advance social justice through multiple measures of accountability.

The perspective presented in this chapter is that scientific rigor is only one aspect of "good science." When emphasis is placed on good science, scrutiny of scientific rigor is not limited to the efficacy of a single methodology. Good science begins with a theoretical construct to observe relationships among phenomena to establish causality. In the absence of sound theoretical constructs, causal explanations cannot be accepted with confidence.

In this chapter we address the role of "good science" in advancing knowledge about the effectiveness of educational practices. We believe "good science" benefits everyone. We also believe that scientific rigor can serve several purposes that advance understanding and ultimately advantage communities of color and other underrepresented groups. First, scientific rigor can clarify the causal explanations for differential educational outcomes. Second, it can provide knowledge to advance theory, focusing empirical exploration linking theory, empirical observations, and practice. Third, it can verify gaps in services and in achievement and can inform policy remedies to address these problems.

Unfortunately, the scientific rigor debate overemphasizes methodology and provides very little discussion of other key elements of good science. Moreover, insufficient attention is given to the deleterious effects of "bad science" when the results are presented as evidence-based knowledge. As we illustrate below, the imposition of evidence-based knowledge derived from "bad science" is likely to be felt disproportionately by members of underrepresented groups. We provide arguments to support a broader, more in-depth exploration of the roles of theory and measurement validity in good science.

Concern with validity is a hallmark of good science. In fact, scientific rigor is valued primarily because it enhances a study's validity. In this chapter, we argue that validity is a cultural construct and that ignoring cultural context distorts scientific rigor. Narrow constructions of validity lead to cultural misrepresentations that have deleterious effects on underrepresented groups (Kirkhart, 2005b; Solano-Flores & Nelson-Barber, 2001). Madison (2004) affirms this position in her cross-cultural experience working in immigrant communities.

In considering the relationship of theory to scientific rigor, we address the consequences of using assessment instruments that do not take into account language theory. Invalid measurement instruments are a major threat to validity. Such research practices fail to allow students to demonstrate accurately what they know (Kusimo et al., 2001). We argue that, particularly in the case of English language learners, the limitations of majority perspective allow mainstream educational researchers to dismiss language theories that could inform testing and assessment practices. The consequence is further stigmatization of English language learners rather than advancing knowledge about how best to measure the academic performance of this group of students.

In the final section, we discuss the potential consequences of the improper use of evidence-based knowledge in policy decision making. Even if the methodology is appropriate and accepted as scientifically rigorous, what are the consequences of policy that does not address social equity issues? Evidence of the effects of social and economic disparities in educational opportunities is critical to understanding contexts in which students perform poorly on standardized measures of academic achievement. Policies that address only educational outcomes, with little attention to access to resources, are more likely to widen the achievement gap, leaving children in the poorest schools trapped at the bottom of the socioeconomic structure. For these reasons, evaluators must advocate for evidence-based knowledge to advance the social justice goals of NCLB.

Three fundamental questions are raised in this chapter: First, how can broader definitions of validity expand the operationalizations of scientific rigor that support it? Second, how can language theory inform educational assessment and testing practices with English language learners? Third, how can multiple measures of accountability be used to improve scientific rigor in advancing the social justice goal of providing a quality education to all children? These questions are examined from the perspectives of validity as the foundation of scientific inquiry, theory as critical to accurate assessment, and evidence-based knowledge as the means to advance socially just policy goals in education.

VALIDITY AND SCIENTIFIC RIGOR

To examine the debate on scientific rigor and its implications for members of underrepresented groups, one must step back from the methodological details and first recognize that scientific rigor is not an end in itself but a means to an end. Scientific rigor is invoked instrumentally to signal that research was conducted in a way that supports credibility, that data reported accurately represent the phenomena of interest, and that interpretations made are trustworthy. It is, in a word, about validity. Validity enjoys a privileged status in conversations about standards of excellence in inquiry (Linn, 1997). It guides what can and cannot be appropriately concluded, marking both the accuracy and the limits of

202 ISSUES OF THE PROFESSION

understandings and evaluative judgments. Because of this gatekeeping role of validity in scientific inquiry, the construct merits iterative examination, affirmation, and, as argued below, expansion.

This section of the chapter explores two assertions regarding the definition of validity itself. First, validity is a culturally defined construct that must be examined and understood within cultural context. Second, narrow definitions of validity reinforce narrow operationalizations of scientific rigor, excluding important questions and restricting ways of knowing. As argued below, these restrictions have a disproportionate impact on people of color, indigenous peoples, and linguistic minorities, whose perspectives are already underrepresented in many empirical conversations.

Validity as a Cultural Construct

To open up conversations about scientific rigor, one must first consider the cultural position of validity itself. The cultural position of legitimizing constructs such as validity has been noted in contexts both international (e.g., Kvale, 1995; Smith, 1999) and domestic (e.g., Kirkhart, 1995, 2005b; Stanfield, 1993).[3] Historically, validity has substantially reflected the perspective of white majority Western thought. With a cultural majority position comes the treatment of minority positions as outgroups. Narrow majority definitions of validity compromise the interests of persons of color and other underrepresented groups by restricting the questions asked, theories considered, designs selected, and measurement strategies employed.

Race-based epistemologies such as Critical Race Theory (CRT), LatCrit, critical race feminism, Asian American CRT, queer theory, and indigenous epistemologies (LaFrance, 2004; Parker, 2003, 2004) challenge the assumption that majority definitions of constructs such as validity are somehow neutral (Pillow, 2003). Scheurich and Young (1997, p. 8) point to the epistemological racism infused in majority research:

> Epistemological racism means that our current range of research epistemologies—positivism to postmodernisms/poststructuralisms—arise out of the social history and culture of the dominant race, that these epistemologies logically reflect and reinforce that social history and that racial group (while excluding the epistemologies of other races/cultures), and that this has negative results for people of color in general and scholars of color in particular.

Recognizing the cultural position of validity directs attention to the location of the validation process as another point of critique. Is validation located within the academy, legislative bodies, governmental agencies, or within tribal governing bodies or the communities of color represented in the evaluation? Historically, focus has been on the academy. For example, Carter (2003) points to the illegitimacy of the academy as the validating site for race conscious research. Rules governing academic discourse, including standards of rigor, protect dominant understandings and preserve traditional modes of inquiry. Recognizing that "static methodological rules render invisible (within the academy) stories that do not or cannot conform" (p. 34), Carter encourages a twofold approach. First, situate validation in the communities outside of the academy. Second, use a peripheral position within the academy as a point of resistance, always considering issues of access and audience in the use of one's work. These strategies are equally relevant to evaluation. The majority position of validity and of the validation process must be recognized and challenged.

In education, federal legislation and priority statements draw similar attention to these as contested sites of validation.[4] The increasing governmental tendency to "prespecify" the characteristics of good evaluation through contract guidelines and standards reflects a bureaucratic shift toward greater predictability and control over evaluation content and process (Norris, 2005). The Committee on Scientific Principles for Education Research argues against legislatively prescribed methodology, noting, "Attempting to boost the scientific basis of federally funded education research by mandating a list of 'valid' scientific methods is a problematic strategy" (National Research Council, 2002, p. 130). Their alternative approach is to develop and nurture a "scientific culture" within the Department of Education, a strategy that itself must be scrutinized for restrictive boundaries.

CONTEXT SPECIFICITY

It is clearly recognized (though not always practiced) that data collection tools must be validated for the context of intended use, that data collection procedures must be adapted in new application contexts, and that the valid use of both tools and procedures must be reestablished with changes in context (Johnson, 2005). Less frequently considered is the fact that the core assumptions underlying inquiry—the evaluative questions asked, the voice in which they are expressed, the choice of success indicators, the operationalization of positive outcomes, etc.—may lose their integrity in translation to new cultural contexts. Rigor must be understood to include asking culturally relevant questions, representing consumer and community voices clearly, and developing mechanisms for recognizing skills displayed in culturally appropriate ways.

To make causal attributions between program intervention and outcomes requires *ceteris paribus*—all things being equal; treatment effects are isolated by comparing the performance of experimental and control groups, initial equivalence between groups having been established through random assignment. As Jolly (2003) points out, however, all things are not equal, nor have they ever been so. This logic of traditional causal attribution assumes an equality that does not exist in the real world. Causal logic may be unresponsive to the important questions of context—controlling for but not really appreciating cultural nuances (e.g., how parent and teacher roles are understood or the value placed on formal education) and masking inequalities of opportunity and resources (e.g., environmental factors such as hunger or the inadequacy of classroom resources and textbooks).

Avoiding Construct Underrepresentation

Construct underrepresentation—operationalization that is too narrow, omitting important dimensions—is one of two core sources of invalidity (Messick, 1995). Not only does this apply to cultural constructs, but it also applies to the construct of validity itself. For validity to retain its relevance, it must be understood broadly. Narrow definitions of validity restrict understandings of scientific rigor. Conversely, creating an inclusive definition of validity opens up opportunities to think more expansively about scientific rigor in cultural context.

CONSIDERING POSSIBLE HARM

Classic psychometric definitions of validity (Cronbach, 1971; Messick, 1981) include actions as well as inferences as objects of validation. The inclusion of actions is particularly significant in evaluation, where evaluators must be held accountable for the judgments and decisions made based upon their understandings.[5] "Validity is an integrated evaluative judgment of the degree to which empirical evidence and theoretical rationales support the *adequacy* and *appropriateness* of *interpretations* and *actions* based on test scores or other modes of assessment" (Messick, 1989, p. 13, emphasis in original). Flowing from this definition of validity, actions taken based upon NCLB's measures of adequate yearly progress must themselves be "adequate and appropriate," raising the bar on validity testing.

Once validity is understood to include the soundness of test-based decisions, one must necessarily consider the consequences of those decisions (Shepard, 1997). Messick (1994, p. 2) lists as one of the perennial validity questions "Are the short- and long-term consequences of score interpretation and use supportive of the general testing aims and are there any adverse side-effects?", noting that the general thrust is to seek evidence and arguments to discount validity threats of construct under-representation and construct irrelevant variance "as well as to evaluate the action implications of score meaning." Hence, validity must acknowledge the possibility of harm emanating from flawed understandings and actions. Harm can occur at individual, organizational, and societal levels—for example, individual trauma associated with classroom student evaluation procedures (Utsey, 2004), racism imbedded in judgments of scholarship within the academy (Carter, 2003), or negative stereotyping of Native American children by indiscriminately associating them with poverty (Noley, 2003). As Cronbach (1988) explicitly acknowledged, validation includes the social consequences of testing, which supports a mandate to examine the impact of inquiry on underrepresented groups.

Including race, ethnicity, or English proficiency as categorical variables is an insufficient solution. For example, Davis (1992) analyzes the use of race as an explanatory variable, noting that it assumes homogeneity of condition and leaves unexamined the complexities of participant experience and social location. Superficial inclusion of race as an explanatory variable may inadvertently reinforce stereotypes by omitting thoughtful discussion of the diversity *within* racial categories or of critical context variables such as poverty (Berliner, 2005). These nuances of inquiry are subtle, but collectively they accrue to give us a distorted view of populations as stereotypes in ways that undermine the validity of our understanding at a societal level.

EXPANDING LEGITIMATION

We must exert caution in our bounding of validity as a construct, lest it be used to delegitimize the worldviews, ways of knowing, and methods of inquiry of nonmajority cultures. Cultural considerations demand a broadening of validity to address multiple epistemologies. No epistemology can be outside the concern for trustworthiness of understanding and action. This includes alternative epistemologies that have risen up in opposition to traditional definitions. For example, Noley's (2003) concern that the worldview of Native American children is poorly represented in mainstream research may be addressed by indigenous evaluation frameworks that draw upon tribal wisdom, community values, and indigenous ways of knowing (LaFrance, 2004). To examine the trustworthiness of understandings and actions under indigenous frameworks requires validity theory that is culturally congruent. Elder epistemology, for example, grounds validity in the core values of respect, reciprocity, and relationship (Christensen, 2003).

Though Pillow (2003) has warned against easy incorporation of race-based epistemologies as add-ons to traditional methods, we would argue that validity must be treated as a capacious construct. Rather than dismissing validity as a tool of the master,[6] the construct must be expanded to encompass all conversations of accurate, trustworthy, and genuine understandings. One approach is to conceptualize validity in terms of multiple justifications, illuminating the cultural intersections of each justificatory perspective (Kirkhart, 1995, 2005b).

The power exercised by validity need not be cast as a zero-sum game in which majority epistemologies lose ground if alternative perspectives are recognized as legitimate. The reality is that majority epistemologies can benefit from the challenges of specificity.[7] Such challenges call us to examine known threats with fresh eyes: for example, *selection* as a factor limiting the ability to appreciate diversity within a sample, leading to essentialism[8] and the perpetuation of stereotypes (Kirkhart, 2005a), versus *selection* as a reason for incorrect inference that the relationship between two variables is causal (Shadish, Cook, & Campbell, 2002). Sometimes, these challenges lead to naming new threats, such as *design incongruence*, that is, selecting a research design that violates cultural norms or applies a time frame inappropriate to the context (Kirkhart, 2005a).

Summary

As a foundational criterion of empirical inquiry, validity exercises power. Historically, it has been infused with majority epistemology and cultural position. Validity must be recognized as a cultural construct and examined through a cultural lens (Kirkhart, 2005b). Multiple, shifting, intersecting cultural identifications make such a lens multifaceted—a kaleidoscope, in the words of Tyson (2003); to appreciate implications for persons of color and members of other underrepresented groups means considering more than race, ethnicity, and language. Validity must be broadened to honor both traditional and alternative paradigms, including those previously marginalized (Rosaldo, 1993). Beyond marking the accuracy of inference, validity must address actions flowing from inference and the consequences of those actions. Consequences for communities of color, linguistic minorities, and indigenous peoples merit explicit attention. Granted appropriate scope, validity has the power to interrupt prejudice and invite rigorous inquiry from specific cultural positions. Narrow conceptualizations of validity constrain how scientific rigor is understood and operationalized. In turn, narrow operationalizations of scientific rigor often marginalize scholarship by and for members of underrepresented groups and undermine genuine understanding of their life experiences.

THE ROLE OF THEORY IN SCIENTIFIC RIGOR

An aspect not sufficiently addressed in the discussions on scientific rigor is the extent to which current funding policies or their interpretation may neglect the important role of theory in scientific research. Narrow views of scientific rigor may lead to emphasizing design and procedural issues over theory in educational research.

The education and testing of English language learners (ELLs), subjects of current debate, is a case in point. Research and practice in the testing of ELLs has poorly addressed three important notions in current thinking about language and culture: that culture and society shape an individual's mind and thinking (Vygotsky, 1978), that constructs measured by tests are not entirely equivalent across cultures (Greenfield, 1997), and that epistemology plays a key role in the ways students interpret test items (Solano-Flores & Trumbull, 2003).

Properly addressing these issues could lead to improved practice in the testing of ELLs through the adoption of more sophisticated methods for test validation, such as those based on the analysis of verbalizations ("think aloud" protocols) made by students as they take tests (Ruiz-Primo, Shavelson, Li, & Schultz, 2001). Inferences can be made about the relationship between the cognitive activity of students and their everyday life experiences (e.g., Hamilton, Nussbaum, & Snow, 1997). While these methods of validation are becoming part of standard practice in test development and have proven to be critical to examining the validity of tests (Baxter & Glaser, 1998), they are not given proper consideration in current testing policies for ELLs, nor are they routinely identified as important task requirements in procurements that involve test adaptation and test development for these students.

Second-language development is another example of how important knowledge that could inform testing practices for ELLs is missing from the discourse on scientific rigor. It is currently accepted within the community of researchers on language and education that the development of academic language takes more time than the development of conversational fluency (see Cummins, 1996; Hakuta, Butler, & Witt, 2000). ELLs cannot reasonably be expected to benefit from instruction in English only and to perform on standardized tests in a way that is comparable to their native English-speaking peers after 1 year of instruction. Yet, as a result of the passage of Proposition 227 and Proposition 203, respectively, in the states of California and Arizona,[9] many ELL students no longer have access to bilingual education programs. Now these students' schools provide "structured English immersion programs" for 1 year (see Gándara, 2000) under the assumption that this time is sufficient for these learners to develop the academic English they need to benefit from education provided in English only. There is no theoretical or empirical evidence to support the way in which this legislation addresses the characteristics of ELLs, the characteristics of academic language, and the conditions in which these students are expected to develop academic English (see Guerrero, 2004). Unfortunately, scrutinizing this legislation is not part of the current discourse on scientific rigor.

The limitations of current testing practices for ELLs can also be examined through the lens of methodology, even without reference to theory. These methodological limitations have been discussed within the measurement community (Linn, Baker, & Betebenner, 2002). School accountability is based largely on standardized test scores, and the indicators of adequate yearly progress of students identified as limited English proficient are a main component of school reporting. But classifications of students as limited English proficient are inconsistent or inaccurate. In addition, the population of ELLs is not stable, since students who attain English proficiency are no longer part of this group. This leaves schools with large enrollments of ELLs with no chance to improve their indicators of adequate yearly progress; yet, they are held accountable to unrealistic and unfair standards (Abedi, 2004).

Unfortunately, the lack of theoretical and empirical support of legislated practice is not a surprise (see August & Hakuta, 1997). As we can see, important knowledge that could improve testing practices for ELLs is not part of what is regarded as scientific. At the same time, policies that are being publicized as scientifically based have serious methodological flaws.

Summary

Limited views on what counts as scientific pose a special danger for linguistic minorities, as they legitimize as "scientifically based" or "evidence based" certain testing practices that are not grounded in theories of language or are seriously flawed. Overemphasis on design and procedures at the expense of theory construction is both scientifically unsound and socially irresponsible. Ultimately, narrow conceptualizations of scientific rigor may limit the access of linguistic minorities to high-quality education and increase their vulnerability due to unfair testing.

SCIENTIFIC RIGOR TO ADVANCE
THE SOCIAL JUSTICE GOALS OF NCLB

Social justice is a complex concept that addresses both equality of opportunity and equity in access to resources. Social justice includes eliminating societal conditions that cause inequalities and making adjustments to take into account the cumulative effects of inequality. The ultimate goals of the No Child Left Behind Act of 2001 are to provide equal educational opportunities and outcomes for all, regardless of demographic background, and to close all educational gaps relating to race, gender, language, socioeconomic status, and other possible background variables.

To achieve the NCLB policy goals, equality and equity in educational opportunity must be addressed. Inequities that create social and economic suffering in depressed communities must be corrected to ensure that families, schools, and communities are capable of providing a quality education. These goals are to be attained through educational system reform. While the reform principles and policy goals of the NCLB Act are clear, the means by which the goals are to be attained are less clearly delineated in the policy and in practice. Improving education in the United States requires more than identifying the most effective teaching and learning methods. Early studies of the effects of NCLB highlight differences in the demographic characteristics of schools identified as needing improvement and schools meeting the federal adequate yearly progress requirements (Kim & Sunderman, 2005).

What role, then, can evaluators play in addressing the social justice issues related to NCLB? One area in which evaluators have an opportunity to advance the social justice goals of NCLB is in broadening the definition of accountability. NCLB defines accountability as adequate yearly progress, measured by performance on statewide achievement tests. This creates a major problem, particularly when one takes into consideration the diversity among learners and learning styles. Not only is the single measure of accountability inadequate to measure performance, but also low performance further disadvantages economically poor communities because provisions to help schools to perform better are not always available (Ryan, 2004). Therefore, multiple measures of accountability must be included in scientifically rigorous studies. These measures should include more than outcome variables. Accountability should include input resources such as social context and environmental variables and the availability of resources required to improve schools.

Evaluators are in a position to engage the community in a deliberative process to broaden the standards for accountability (Ryan, 2004).

Parents, educators, and other stakeholders should be included in defining multiple measures of accountability. The top-down approach should be abandoned for a more democratic process. Ryan (2004) suggests that more democratic approaches to educational accountability serve the public interests of education and provide leverage for accountability across a broad spectrum of stakeholders.

Deleterious Effects of Limited Definitions of Accountability

Evaluators who believe in the principles of fairness should be concerned about the impact of invalid testing and assessment tools that do not measure students' knowledge. Failure to perform well on these tests relegates students to a lifetime of social and economic injustices. Also, the punitive consequences of NCLB for low-performing schools, if they continue not to meet standards of adequate yearly progress, can limit access to education. Consider the following scenarios: Parents are notified of a school's low-performance status; many move their children to other schools. Eventually, the low-performing school's enrollment drops, and the school is closed. The surrounding schools are overcrowded, leaving the students without a neighborhood school to attend. In another case, if a school is closed due to low performance, student use of public transportation to attend other schools may be a problem, or neighboring schools may not be open to accepting low-performing students. In both of these examples, closing the schools may create a hostile environment for the very students for whom NCLB is supposed to provide positive opportunities.

In other cases, highly qualified teachers may choose to transfer to "better" schools in an attempt to retain their jobs and avoid negative consequences, thus leaving fewer highly qualified or seasoned teachers to lift up the low-performing schools. In this scenario, students also are at a disadvantage, because they no longer have access to instructors who are most capable of changing their achievement outcomes. Evaluative research must be used to illuminate cases in which NCLB outcomes impede advancing social justice.[10]

Another negative consequence of NCLB involves the limitations of large-scale experimental designs to identify innovative community-based interventions that target members of underrepresented groups who are at greatest risk of academic failure. Innovative approaches to teaching and learning are often implemented on a small scale to address the particular needs of a specific population. Here, the emphasis is on programmatic intervention rather than large-scale systems change. Case studies are more likely to reveal aspects of the program that improve teaching and learning. However, under the DOE mandates, such innovations are not likely to be considered for funding. In this case, the children that NCLB is intended to benefit are denied access to promising practices.

Another concern for evaluators is that experimental designs are not always feasible in K–12 settings, community-based interventions targeting persons of color, or minority-serving higher education institutions. This also means that innovative teaching and learning interventions that are most likely to benefit underrepresented groups would not be funded by the DOE because they are not suitable for randomized field trials. Priorities given to certain methods create inequities in the support of innovation.

Summary

While scientifically rigorous research is necessary in education, we caution researchers—especially education intervention researchers—to continue to challenge accountability standards, to engage communities in a deliberative process to broaden the definition of accountability, and to understand the potential deleterious effects of NCLB on the communities they study. Scientific rigor for the sake of rigor alone will not fulfill the goals of high educational achievement for all students but can omit certain important variables that address the needs of the students being studied. Scientific rigor must be the means to the end. The end goal must be to achieve fairness and justice in educational opportunities and in the measurement of outcomes.

CONCLUSION

Using the language of scientific rigor as part of political discourse can undermine good science and its value in the evaluation of interventions. More attention needs to be given to the research process and the validity of inferences drawn from evaluations of education interventions. Validity is particularly important to studies of the effects of educational practices on members of underrepresented groups. Practical and political implications for these groups differ from the impact of the debate on majority populations. Put simply, the stakes are higher. For example, superficial inclusion of race as an explanatory variable obscures diversity within communities of color and reinforces stereotypes.

In the case of linguistic minorities, narrow operationalization of scientific rigor may limit access to high-quality education and increase vulnerability as a result of unfair testing. The importance of culturally valid assessment instruments in measuring the learning outcomes of ELLs provides a clear example of the relevance of cultural validity in establishing scientific rigor. Testing practices and policies based on narrow views of scientific rigor, which emphasize method but overlook the relevance of cultural and linguistic specificity in the validation of assessment instruments and procedures, represent a special danger for linguistic and cultural minorities.

Another fallacy is the notion that a single methodology is the essence of scientific rigor. For certain research and evaluation problems, the use of randomized field trials can be a sound approach in education; however, the role of RCTs may be more limited than has been recognized (Murnane & Nelson, 2005). RCTs should not be taken as proof of scientific soundness. In the real world of school districts, there are always contextual variables to be examined and understood (not just controlled for), and this is particularly true when seeking valid understandings about the performance of students of color and members of other underrepresented groups. Causality and conditionality must be considered in the evaluation of educational outcomes.

Scientific rigor must yield trustworthy evidence-based knowledge to improve society. Society must directly attack the issues underlying educational disparities. Evidence-based knowledge is essential to understanding the complex issues that produce the achievement gap. Improving practices is only one component of a very complex social justice issue. As Gloria Ladson-Billings (2006), past president of the AERA, suggests, perhaps communities of color should advocate for addressing the "education debt" rather than the "achievement gap." Education debt is computed based on the cumulative effects of centuries of denial of access to quality education to communities of color. The ledger for other underrepresented groups could be similarly examined.

Evaluators must ask: "What are the differential effects on teaching and learning outcomes of disparities in access to social and economic resources?" "How do family and community circumstances present social and economic barriers to learning?" "How do inequities in school funding lead to differential teaching and learning outcomes?" Answers to these questions are necessary to educate policymakers about educational disparities and the roles that these disparities play in maintaining or sometimes widening the achievement gap. True government accountability demands that policymakers fund educational mechanisms and infrastructures that will deliver the social justice goals of NCLB.

The questions raised in this chapter are ones that members of underrepresented groups and evaluators must continue to ask. The answers will reveal much about the fundamental values, priorities, and commitments of evaluation as a profession.

NOTES

1. We use the term *underrepresented groups* in this chapter to refer to persons who do not hold majority privilege in the United States with respect to race, ethnicity, language, or nationhood. Our examples focus on communities of color, linguistic minorities, and indigenous peoples. Many of the arguments we raise concerning differential impact and inequities also apply to other aspects of minority status—for example, poverty or special education—though the specifics have not been developed here.

2. For a critical discussion of the language of "at risk," see Madison (2000).

3. This characterization is by no means unique to validity. All constructs are cultural products (Cronbach, 1971).

4. For an excellent historical synthesis and analysis of the federal role, see Brass, Nuñez-Neto, and Williams (2006).

5. The *Standards for Educational and Psychological Testing* (American Educational Research Association, American Psychological Association, & National Council on Measurement in Education, 1999) opted for a more restrictive definition of *validity*, excluding actions and focusing attention only on the validity of inference.

6. The phrasing here alludes to Audre Lorde's (1984) well-known quote "The master's tools will never dismantle the master's house."

7. The term *standpoint theories* has often been used to characterize theories that are race- or gender-specific; however, Carter (2003) points to ways in which this label may be used to marginalize such work as narrow or underdeveloped. She prefers the language "epistemology of specificity" (p. 30).

8. As used here, essentialism refers to viewing characteristics such as race and gender as singular defining traits rather than appreciating intersections and variations within groups and individuals. One characteristic is taken as defining the essence of a person.

9. For the specifics of these two propositions, see English Language in Public Schools Initiative Statute, Cal. Ed. Code §300, and English Language Education for Children in Public Schools, Ariz. Rev. Stat. §15-751–756.

10. Though NCLB may exacerbate these consequences, they did not originate with NCLB. Sadly, these consequences that derive from NCLB legislation do not differ much from the vicious cycle of failure in which underrepresented groups are trapped due to poor funding and tracking—a cycle that was described in detail two decades ago (Oakes, 1985, 1990).

REFERENCES

Abedi, J. (2004). The No Child Left Behind Act and English language learners: Assessment and accountability issues. *Educational Researcher, 33*(1), 4–14.
American Educational Research Association (2003, December). American Edu-

cational Research Association response to the U.S. Department of Education, notice of proposed priority, Federal Register RIN 1890-ZA00, November 4, 2003, scientifically based research methods. Retrieved April 29, 2006, from *www.eval.org/doestatement.htm.*

American Educational Research Association, American Psychological Association, and National Council on Measurement in Education (1999). *Standards for educational and psychological testing.* Washington, DC: American Educational Research Association.

American Evaluation Association (2003, November). American Evaluation Association response to the U.S. Department of Education, notice of proposed priority, Federal Register RIN 1890-ZA00, November 4, 2003, scientifically based research methods. Retrieved April 29, 2006, from *www. eval.org/doestatement.htm.*

August, D., & Hakuta, K. (Eds.). (1997). *Improving schooling for language minority students: A research agenda.* Committee on Developing a Research Agenda on the Education of Limited-English-Proficient and Bilingual Students, Board on Children, Youth, and Families, Commission on Behavioral and Social Sciences and Education, National Research Council, Institute of Medicine. Washington, DC: National Academy Press.

Baxter, G. P., & Glaser, R. (1998). Investigating the cognitive complexity of science assessments. *Educational Measurement: Issues and Practice, 17*(3), 37–45.

Berliner, D. (2005). Our impoverished view of educational reform. *Teachers College Record.* Retrieved August 20, 2005, from *www.tcrecord.org/ PrintContent.asp?ContentID=12106.*

Brass, C. T., Nuñez-Neto, B., & Williams, E. D. (2006). Congress and program evaluation: An overview of randomized controlled trials (RCTs) and related issues. Washington, DC: Congressional Research Service, Library of Congress. Retrieved June 25, 2006, from *opencrs.cdt.org/document/RL33301.*

Carter, M. (2003). Telling tales out of school: "What's the fate of a Black story in a White world of White stories?" In G. R. López & L. Parker (Eds.), *Interrogating racism in qualitative research methodology* (pp. 29–48). New York: Peter Lang.

Christensen, R. A. (2003). Cultural context and evaluation: A balance of form and function. In National Science Foundation Workshop Proceedings NSF 03-032, *The cultural context of educational evaluation: A Native American perspective* (pp. 23–33). Arlington, VA: National Science Foundation.

Cronbach, L. J. (1971). Test validation. In R. L. Thorndike (Ed.), *Educational measurement* (2nd ed., pp. 443–507). Washington, DC: American Council on Education.

Cronbach, L. J. (1988). Five perspectives on validity arguments. In H. Wainer & H. I. Braun (Eds.), *Test validity* (pp. 3–17). Hillsdale, NJ: Erlbaum.

Cummins, J. (1996). *Negotiating identities: Education for empowerment in a diverse society.* Ontario, CA: California Association for Bilingual Education.

Davis, J. E. (1992). Reconsidering the use of race as an explanatory variable in program evaluation. In A. M. Madison (Ed.), *Minority issues in program evaluation* (New Directions for Program Evaluation no. 53, pp. 55–67). San Francisco: Jossey-Bass.

Fashola, O. S. (2004). Being an informed consumer of quantitative educational research. *Phi Delta Kappan, 85*(7), 532–538.

Gándara, P. (2000). In the aftermath of the storm: English learners in the post-227 era. *Bilingual Research Journal, 24*(1–2), 1–13.

Greene, J. C. (1999). The inequality of performance measurements. *Evaluation, 5*, 160–172.

Greenfield, P. M. (1997). You can't take it with you: Why ability assessments don't cross cultures. *American Psychologist, 52*(10), 1115–1124.

Guerrero, M. D. (2004). Acquiring academic English in one year: An unlikely proposition for English language learners. *Urban Education, 39*(2), 172–199.

Hakuta, K., Butler, Y. G., & Witt, D. (2000). *How long does it take English learners to attain proficiency?* (Policy Report no. 2000-1). Santa Barbara: University of California Linguistic Minority Research Institute.

Hamilton, L. S., Nussbaum, E. M., & Snow, R. E. (1997). Interview procedures for validating science assessments. *Applied Measurement in Education, 10*, 181–200.

Henry, G. T. (2001). How modern democracies are shaping evaluation and the emerging challenges for evaluation. *American Journal of Evaluation, 22*, 419–430.

Johnson, E. (2005). The use of contextually relevant evaluation practice with programs designed to increase participation of minorities in science, technology, engineering, and mathematics (STEM) education. In S. Hood, R. K. Hopson, & H. T. Frierson (Eds.), *The role of culture and cultural context: A mandate for inclusion, the discovery of truth, and understanding in evaluative theory and practice* (pp. 213–235). Greenwich, CT: Information Age Publishing.

Jolly, E. J. (2003). On the quest for cultural context in evaluation: All things are not equal—they never were. In National Science Foundation Workshop Proceedings NSF 03-032, *The cultural context of educational evaluation: A Native American perspective* (pp. 14–22). Arlington, VA: National Science Foundation.

Kim, J. S., & Sunderman, G. L. (2005). Measuring academic proficiency under the No Child Left Behind Act: Implications for educational equality. *Educational Researcher, 34*(8), 1–13.

Kirkhart, K. E. (1995). Seeking multicultural validity: A postcard from the road. *Evaluation Practice, 16*(1), 1–12.

Kirkhart, K. E. (2005a, June). *Validity, culture, and privilege.* Keynote address, Evaluation Training Institute for Mid-Level Evaluators, Howard University, School of Education, Washington, DC.

Kirkhart, K. E. (2005b). Through a cultural lens: Reflections on validity and theory in evaluation. In S. Hood, R. K. Hopson, & H. T. Frierson (Eds.), *The role of culture and cultural context: A mandate for inclusion, the discovery of truth, and understanding in evaluative theory and practice* (pp. 21–39). Greenwich, CT: Information Age Publishing.

Kusimo, P., Ritter, M., Busick, K., Ferguson, C., Trumbull, E., & Solano-Flores, G. (2001). Focus on assessment for education improvement. *R & D Alert, 3*(3), 1–12. Retrieved January 19, 2006, from *www.wested.org/online_ pubs/rd-01-03.pdf*.

Kvale, S. (1995). The social construction of validity. *Qualitative Inquiry, 1,* 19–40.

Ladson-Billings, G. J. (2006, April). *Presidential address: The education debt.* American Educational Research Association annual meeting, San Francisco.

LaFrance, J. (2004). Culturally competent evaluation in Indian country. In M. Thompson-Robinson, R. Hopson, & S. SenGupta (Eds.), *In search of cultural competence in evaluation: Toward principles and practices* (New Directions for Evaluation no. 102, pp. 39–50). San Francisco: Jossey-Bass.

Linn, R. L. (1997). Evaluating the validity of assessments: The consequences of use. *Educational Measurement, Issues and Practice, 16*(2), 14–16.

Linn, R. L., Baker, E. L., & Betebenner, D. W. (2002). Accountability systems: Implications of requirements of the No Child Left Behind Act of 2001. *Educational Researcher, 31*(6), 3–16.

Lorde, A. (1984). *Sister outsider: Essays and speeches by Audre Lorde.* Trumansburg, NY: The Crossing Press.

Madison, A. M. (2000). Language in defining social problems and in evaluating social problems. In R. K. Hopson (Ed.), *How and why language matters in evaluation* (New Directions for Evaluation no. 86, pp. 17–28). San Francisco: Jossey-Bass.

Madison, A. M. (2004, November). *Culture as a fundamental issue in evaluation.* Plenary panel presentation for Presidential Strand, American Evaluation Association annual meeting, Atlanta.

Messick, S. (1981). Evidence and ethics in the evaluation of tests. *Educational Researcher, 10*(9), 9–20.

Messick, S. (1989). Validity. In R. L. Linn (Ed.), *Educational measurement* (3rd ed., pp. 13–103). New York: Macmillan.

Messick, S. (1994). Foundations of validity: Meaning and consequences in psychological assessment. *European Journal of Psychological Assessment, 10*(1), 1–9.

Messick, S. (1995). Validity of psychological assessment: Validation of inferences from persons' responses and performances as scientific inquiry into score meaning. *American Psychologist, 50*(9), 741–749.

Murnane, R. J., & Nelson, R. R. (2005). Improving the performance of the education sector: The valuable, challenging, and limited role of random assignment evaluations. Cambridge, MA: National Bureau of Economic Research. Retrieved July 1, 2006, from *www.nber.org/papers/w11846*.

National Education Association (2003, December). National Education Association response to the U.S. Department of Education, notice of proposed priority, Federal Register RIN 1890-ZA00, November 4, 2003, scientifically based research methods. Retrieved April 29, 2006, from *www.eval.org/ doestatement.htm.*

National Research Council (2002). *Scientific research in education.* Washington, DC: National Academy Press.

No Child Left Behind Act, 10 U.S.C. 6301 (2002).

Noley, G. (2003). Discussion highlights. In National Science Foundation Workshop Proceedings NSF 03-032, *The cultural context of educational evaluation: A Native American perspective* (pp. 34–37). Arlington, VA: National Science Foundation.

Norris, N. (2005). The politics of evaluation and the methodological imagination. *American Journal of Evaluation, 26*(4), 584–586.

Oakes, J. (1985). *Keeping track: How schools structure inequality.* New Haven, CT: Yale University Press.

Oakes, J. (1990). *Multiplying inequalities: The effects of race, social, class, and tracking on opportunities to learn mathematics and science.* Santa Monica, CA: RAND Corporation.

Parker, L. (2003). Critical Race Theory and its implications for methodology and policy analysis in higher education desegregation. In G. R. López & L. Parker (Eds.), *Interrogating racism in qualitative research methodology* (pp. 145–180). New York: Peter Lang.

Parker, L. (2004). Can critical theories of or on race be used in evaluation research in education? In V. G. Thomas & F. I. Stevens (Eds.), *Co-constructing a contextually responsive evaluation framework: The Talent Development Model of School Reform.* (New Directions for Evaluation no. 101, pp. 85–93). San Francisco: Jossey-Bass.

Pillow, W. (2003). Race-based methodologies: Multicultural methods or epistemological shifts? In G. R. López & L. Parker (Eds.), *Interrogating racism in qualitative research methodology* (pp. 181–202). New York: Peter Lang.

Rosaldo, R. (1993). *Culture and truth: The remaking of social analysis.* Boston: Beacon Press.

Ruiz-Primo, M. A., Shavelson, R. J., Li, M., & Schultz, S. E. (2001). On the validity of cognitive interpretations of scores from alternative mapping techniques. *Educational Assessment, 7*(2), 99–141.

Ryan, K. (2002). Shaping educational accountability systems. *American Journal of Evaluation, 23,* 453–468.

Ryan, K. (2004). Serving public interest in educational accountability: Alternative approaches to democratic evaluation. *American Journal of Evaluation, 25,* 443–460.

Scheurich, J. J., & Young, M. D. (1997). Coloring epistemologies: Are our research epistemologies racially biased? *Educational Researcher, 26*(4), 4–16.

Shadish, W. R., Cook, T. D., & Campbell, D. T. (2002). *Experimental and quasi-experimental designs for generalized causal inference.* Boston: Houghton Mifflin.

Shepard, L. A. (1997). The centrality of test use and consequences for test validity. *Educational Measurement, 16*(2), 5–8, 13, 24.

Smith, L. T. (1999). *Decolonizing methodologies: Research and indigenous peoples*. New York: Zed Books.

Solano-Flores, G., & Nelson-Barber, S. (2001). On the cultural validity of science assessments. *Journal of Research in Science Teaching, 38(5)*, 553–573.

Solano-Flores, G., & Trumbull, E. (2003). Examining language in context: The need for new research and practice paradigms in the testing of English-language learners. *Educational Researcher, 32(2)*, 3–13.

Stanfield, J. H., II (1993). Epistemological consideration. In J. H. Stanfield II & R. M. Dennis (Eds.), *Race and ethnicity in research methods* (pp. 16–36). Newbury Park, CA: Sage.

Stebbins, L. B., St. Pierre, R. G., Proper, E. C., Anderson, R. B., & Cerva, T. R. (1977). *Education as experimentation: A planned variation model: Vol. IV-A. An evaluation of Follow Through*. Cambridge, MA: Abt Associates.

Tyson, C. (2003). Research, race, and an epistemology of emancipation. In G. R. López & L. Parker (Eds.), *Interrogating racism in qualitative research methodology* (pp. 19–28). New York: Peter Lang.

Utsey, S. O. (2004, June). *Advanced statistical analysis for program evaluators: The use of structural equation modeling for decision making related to academic outcomes*. Evaluation Training Institute for Mid-Level Evaluators, Howard University, School of Education, Washington, DC.

Vygotsky, L. S. (1978). *Mind in society: The development of higher psychological processes*. Cambridge, MA: Harvard University Press.

Westinghouse Learning Corporation. (1969). *The impact of Head Start: An evaluation of the effects of Head Start on children's cognitive and affective development* (executive summary). Springfield, VA: Clearinghouse for Federal Scientific and Technical Information.

CHAPTER 11

Improving the Practice of Evaluation through Indigenous Values and Methods
Decolonizing Evaluation Practice— Returning the Gaze from Hawai'i and Aotearoa

ALICE J. KAWAKAMI, KANANI ATON, FIONA CRAM,
MORRIS K. LAI, and LAURIE PORIMA

He 'onipa'a ka 'oiā'i'o. *Truth is not changeable.*
—PUKUI (1983, p. 94)

As is proper in indigenous cultures, we start by telling the audience a bit about ourselves. In *Kānaka Maoli* (Hawaiian) language/culture, one asks "Who is your name? (*'O wai kou inoa*)" and not "What is your name?" In *Māori* language/culture, one asks *"No hea koe?"* ("Where are you from [in a tribal sense]?"). As a group of five indigenous island-dwelling evaluators, we and our *'ohana/whānau* (families) are from *Ngāti Manawa, Tainui, Tuhoe,* and *Ngāti Kahungunu* in *Aotearoa* (New Zealand), from *Waimea* and *Mō'ili'ili* on *O'ahu,* and from *Nāwiliwili* on *Kaua'i.* Among us five authors, some are relatively new to evaluation, and some have more than 30 years of experience in the field. Some of us are steeped in our indigenous cultures; some have less experience. What we have in common is membership in Pacific island indigenous cultures as well as in Western culture, including much of our academic training.

219

Furthermore, we are passionate in our feeling that evaluation, as often currently practiced on indigenous populations, must be decolonized. Concurrently, we honor those who have helped smooth the path we now walk—generations of indigenous professionals who have been mentors to their protégés, standing shoulder to shoulder with us.

> Umia ka hanu! Ho'okāhi ka umauma ke kīpo'ohiwi i ke kīpo'ohiwi. *Hold the breath! Walk abreast, shoulder to shoulder.* Be of one accord, as in exerting every effort to lift a heavy weight to the shoulder and to keep together in carrying it along.
> —PUKUI (1983, p. 314)

As mainstream-trained academics/evaluators as well as cultural practitioners and community advocates, we will describe facets of indigenous life that affect the evolving practices of evaluation. Using a *mo'olelo* (storytelling) approach, we will begin to broach issues of values, theory, practice, and the changing profile of expectations developing in *Māori* and *Kānaka Maoli* communities.

RELEVANCE TO EVALUATORS

In this chapter, we address (1) contextualizing evaluations within culturally appropriate frameworks and (2) meeting the needs of program participants, implementers, and external funding agencies. These two areas of effort are of fundamental importance to the field of evaluation because they ultimately deal with the ethical behavior of evaluators; furthermore, they can help improve evaluations for *Kānaka Maoli*, *Māori*, and other indigenous peoples, as well as for mainstream populations. We caution that although we have noticed many similarities between our *mana'o* (thoughts) and values and those of other indigenous peoples such as Native Americans and First Nations Peoples of Canada, we acknowledge that our indigenous expertise is largely limited to *Māori* and *Kānaka Maoli* considerations.

RELEVANCE TO THE PROFESSION

Our chapter includes suggestions for improving methodological practices within the evaluation profession and explores basic assumptions about the epistemology and values of indigenous communities. Some of the mainstream evaluation profession's propriety standards covering respect strongly imply that methods for conducting evaluations involving indigenous peoples are fundamental issues for the profession (American Evaluation Association, 2004). However, respecting and protecting the rights and welfare of human subjects and respecting human dignity and worth require being familiar enough with evaluation participants to be able to deliver such respect. We will discuss evaluation strategies that focus on access to relevant information and our perspectives, linked to values, beliefs, and worldviews.

RELEVANCE TO SOCIETY

The world of the 21st century is shrinking. Global concerns are common conversation topics, and technological innovations allow for distant individuals and groups to be linked in real time. With these means to gain entry to previously remote and isolated (often by self-choice) communities, evaluators are compelled to face issues of social justice and equity. Awareness of indigenous perspectives, especially values, is critical today, as diversity of culture, language, ethnicity, and national origin continue to be the focus of reclaimed identity and sovereignty for indigenous peoples. We anticipate that our views will resonate with other indigenous peoples who share similar values as well as experiences of colonization and marginalization within their own lands (see Davis et al., 2002). And as eloquently stated in *Principles amd Guidelines for the Protection of the Heritage of Indigenous People*, "The effective protection of the heritage of the indigenous peoples of the world benefits all humanity. Cultural diversity is essential to the adaptability and creativity of the human species as a whole" (Daes, 1995, ¶1).

ADDRESSING THE ISSUES

One definition of *indigenous* is "having originated . . . in a particular region" (*Merriam-Webster's Collegiate Dictionary*, 1993, p. 591). Some key ideas regarding indigenousness include "We were here first. Newcomer, you do not have the right to impose your values on us, even if you have more destructive weapons than we do."

We recognize the changing nature of evaluation for indigenous communities as increasing numbers of indigenous persons are trained in research and evaluation. These communities are no longer solely reliant on nonindigenous evaluators, who must "up their game" if they are to be of service to indigenous peoples. This chapter, while addressing issues of particular relevance to culturally appropriate evaluation conducted by indigenous evaluators, also provides important insights for nonindigenous evaluators about the expectations of, and respect appropriate for (and demanded by), indigenous communities.

As part of a larger group of *Māori* and *Kānaka Maoli* evaluators called the *Evaluation Hui* (Evaluation Team), we have recently spent much effort collectively developing, refining, and disseminating evaluation methods appropriate for indigenous peoples. A notable part of our effort to decolonize evaluation was inspired by the work of Linda Tuhiwai Smith (1999), who wrote eloquently on decolonizing *research* methodologies for indigenous peoples. Smith argued that to begin to undo the negative effects of colonization, which included substantial amounts of research on indigenous peoples, the (Western) research methodology itself has to be decolonized.

By decolonizing *evaluation* methodologies, we aim to recenter ourselves within our own lands. From here we challenge the viewpoints of those outside of our communities who see us as less than a "norm" that is based within their worldview rather than within ours. We are therefore advocating evaluation practices that are "of, for, by, and with us"—that is, *Kānaka Maoli* and *Kaupapa Māori* methodologies (Pihama, Cram, & Walker, 2002; Porima, 2005). Our very survival relies on the acknowledgment, at the very least by our own peoples, that our worldview, culture, and way of being are valid. When this acknowledgment comes within the context of evaluation, we increase the chances that the evaluation methods employed will be decolonized.

LOOKING AT THE WEST

We present some examples of why we are wary of "experts" from prominent Western institutions and academicians. In the first example, we ask a simple question: "Who discovered our lands?" According to the National Maritime Museum in London, the answer for *Hawai'i* is "Captain James Cook," whose efforts are honored in a "medal commemorating the discovery of Hawaii by Captain James Cook" (National Maritime Museum, 2005, ¶1). In a widely used dictionary, a definition for *discover* is "to obtain sight or knowledge of for the first time" (*Merriam-Webster's Collegiate Dictionary*, 1993, p. 331). For sure, only indigenous people can say, with honesty, that their group was there first and discovered their homeland. Even by Western definitions, *Captain Cook did not discover Hawai'i*. Similarly, Abel Tasman absolutely was not the first person to see *Aotearoa*. And yet today one can read on a mainstream New Zealand tourist website words like "First to discover New Zealand in 1642, Abel Tasman annexed the country for Holland . . . " (*Colonisation*, 2006, ¶3). The fact that Westerners continue to be incorrectly credited, for example, by a prominent Western institution as the discoverers of lands in which our ancestors were already living is just one of many reasons why we are wary and even distrustful of many Western experts.

Furthermore, these "discoveries" opened the way for newcomers to arrive on our shores with the expectation that they could acquire large portions of our lands for themselves and their offspring. Regardless of agreements and treaties between them and us, we were subjected to disease, war, illegal overthrows, Christianity, and the sheer weight of numbers of new arrivals. We became the "other" in our own lands, and the ordinariness and normality of "us" became "uncivilized" and "savage" in the constructions of the newcomers.

We know that these constructions happened. The Western "master historians" declared accordingly in their publications, such as in a volume edited by the "renowned American historian" Hubert H. Bancroft in the early 1900s, that in reference to Hawaiian natives, "morally they ranked below other races. . . . The sins of their ancestors have been slowly but surely sapping the vitality of the later generations . . . the barbarian cannot fight against the law which awards the future to the fittest" (Bancroft, 1902, ¶1–2). In indigenous cultures, elders are honored and turned to for serious advisement. They are not accused of being sinners and are not blamed for causing the demise of current generations.

In a visit to *Aotearoa* in 1835, Darwin proclaimed *Māori* as a ". . . fearsome people . . . a more warlike race of inhabitants could be found in no part of the world . . . [whose] shifty looks betrayed a fierce cunning, and tattooed face revealed a base nature" (Desmond & Moore, 1991, pp. 174–175). These descriptions of our ancestors surely helped justify the dispossession of our lands and resources during colonization.

Also in the book by "master historians" is the following tribute to the Christian missionaries who first visited *Hawai'i* in 1820: "The transformation of semi-savages into a remarkably progressive people was mainly accomplished by the efforts of American missionaries . . . who taught the growing generation to read and write" (Bancroft, 1902, ¶3). Tributes were also made to the missionaries in *Aotearoa* for their "civilizing" influence on *Māori*, with Wakefield (1837, p. 29) noting that "these poor savages have a remarkable capacity for being civilized—a peculiar aptitude for being improved by intercourse with civilization."

Those of us from *Hawai'i* find much irony in the condescending attitude of such prominent scholars toward our "semi-savage" ancestors in that the missionaries, supposedly less superstitious and more enlightened than the *Kānaka Maoli*, told the "heathen natives" that Jesus, the son of (the Western) God, was born of a virgin birth, walked on water, and later rose from the dead. The missionaries declared that it was *pono* (proper) to *pule* (pray) to the Christian God but not *pono* to *pule* to the Hawaiian gods, and they told the *Kānaka Maoli* that a man named *Noa*

(Noah) was about 900 years old and saved the world by bringing pairs of animals onto a huge ark in order to survive a flooding rain dumped on earth by an angry God. While doing all this "civilized" proselytizing to the natives, who were viewed as immature, superstitious, naive, and morally destitute in comparison to Westerners, the missionaries and their families acquired much land and wealth in the islands. Those of us from *Aotearoa* find that this all sounds very familiar.

ECHOES OF OUR COLONIAL PAST

The negative legacy of our colonial past remains with us today. Some of the inappropriate writings just described are still being used today to make arguments against the will of indigenous peoples. For example, a 2000 U.S. Supreme Court decision against allowing only Hawaiians to vote for the Office of Hawaiian Affairs trustees was described as follows: "Relying selectively on decades-old historical works written by non-Native Hawaiians . . ., the [U.S. Supreme] Court invoked . . . how the white man 'civilized' the Native savage" (Yamamoto & Iijima, 2000, ¶21). In a major journal of the American Educational Research Association, Kanaʻiaupuni (2004) described several other devastating *hewa* (wrongs) committed against *Kānaka Maoli* by those in power.

These echoes of our colonized past are also found within evaluations that have been conducted on us. *Māori*, for the most part, continue to be the subjects of research and evaluation that are undertaken primarily to assess the impact of government policies on the economic and social position of *Māori* and the extent to which government programs and services "close the gaps" between *Māori* and non-*Māori* (Pipi et al., 2003). Many *Māori* communities have developed an increasing resistance to evaluation for a number of reasons:

1. *Māori* feel overresearched (Smith, 1999) and evaluated too often. It is not unusual for *Māori* individuals or communities to be subjected to several evaluation projects in the same year. One *Māori* provider, closely related to one of the authors, reported that their organization had been subjected to four different evaluations in a 12-month period, as they were part of an interagency funding program.

2. *Māori* are not part of the evaluation decision-making process. For example, decisions about what, when, and why to evaluate are typically driven and managed by government objectives and invariably managed by government officials who in turn contract evaluators.

3. *Māori* are typically portrayed within an evaluation deficit model where *Māori* are identified as the problem, or the problem is deemed to

be within *Māori* communities (Cram, 1997). For example, education statistics report *Māori* as two and a half times more likely to leave school without a formal qualification than non-*Māori*. In contrast the problem or the issues could be redefined as " 'the New Zealand education system is two and a half times more likely to fail *Māori* students than non-*Māori* students,' or again as, 'New Zealand society, through the education system, privileges Pakeha by the time they leave school' " (Robson & Reid, 2001, p. 21).

All too often we continue to be constructed as the "other," then compared to a nonindigenous norm and found to be wanting or judged to be failing to reach acceptable standards (Cram, 1997). Too many nonindigenous evaluators have stood with their feet planted firmly in their own worldviews and have themselves failed to gain any true understanding of our ways, our knowledge, and our world.

PROTECTION OF CULTURAL
AND INTELLECTUAL RIGHTS

In our analysis of widely used mainstream evaluation methods, we have found that the methods themselves include colonialist aspects that result in disrespect of indigenous participants. Although there is acknowledgment in the *Guiding Principles for Evaluators* that they "were developed in the context of Western cultures" (American Evaluation Association, 2004, Preface, ¶1), given that most *Māori* and *Kānaka Maoli* live and work in places dominated by Western culture, we assert that the principles should also fully apply to evaluations involving these indigenous peoples. We also note that conflicts between indigenous and nonindigenous values can occur when projects are developed as well as when they are evaluated.

We acknowledge that some evaluators and funding bodies have been striving for several years to improve evaluation practices through cultural considerations. For example, in her 1994 American Evaluation Association (AEA) presidential address, Karen Kirkhart proposed the construct of multicultural validity as essential to improving evaluation (Kirkhart, 1995), and 3 years later Jennifer Greene argued that advocacy in evaluation is not only inevitable but also supportive of democratic pluralism (Greene, 1997). There are other noteworthy efforts (e.g., Health Research Council of New Zealand, 1998; Patton, 2002; Sen-Gupta, Hopson, & Thompson-Robinson, 2004; Fetterman & Wandersman, 2005); however, our experiences have shown us that evaluation practices are often not aligned with the guidance that has been offered.

We do, however, acknowledge these efforts and the improvements in evaluation practice that they have sometimes brought to our communities, including higher valuing of personal relationships and a higher regard for *mo'olelo* (storytelling or narrative) and other subjective evaluation methods. It is not our intent to disrespect these efforts by nonindigenous evaluators; rather, we wish to push them further in increasing the relevance of their work for our peoples as well as hold back those evaluation practices (such as in the examples that follow) that continue to include inappropriate but widely practiced methods.

VIOLATIONS OF INDIGENOUS VALUES AND MAINSTREAM EVALUATION STANDARDS

When the *Guiding Principles for Evaluators*, together with much of current evaluation practice, are viewed through our *Māori/Kānaka Maoli* lenses, we see violations that are not likely to be apparent to nonindigenous evaluators. For example, we assert that major violations have occurred in evaluations involving indigenous peoples when any of the following have occurred: (1) there were no discernible benefits to the community involved, (2) elders were not considered primary determiners of quality, (3) spiritual outcomes were not highly regarded, or (4) cultural protocols (e.g., sharing family lineage, exchanging gifts, formal inviting to enter into discussion) were not honored. We contend that such evaluations violate the AEA Guiding Principles related to cultural competence and respect for stakeholders.

For an example of an officially approved "evaluation" that we have found disturbing, we turn to a principal at a public elementary school on Hawaiian homestead lands. Following the release of a report as part of a No Child Left Behind (NCLB) review, the principal wrote, "Did you know that . . . PricewaterhouseCoopers did not visit my school? They subcontracted UCLA to do the job, which in turn hired three graduate students (with no background in education) who—after a two-day visit—produced a 26-page report. It is full of inaccuracies" (Theroux, 2004, ¶11).

That aforementioned "evaluation" was regarded by the U.S. federal government and the Hawai'i State Department of Education as an acceptable approach to evaluating a school's efforts to comply with NCLB. Yet, *Guiding Principles for Evaluators* declares that "evaluators should ensure that the members of the evaluation team collectively demonstrate cultural competence" (American Evaluation Association, 2004, B. Competence section, ¶2). Another guideline is "Evaluators respect the security, dignity and self-worth of . . . evaluation stakeholders" (American Evaluation Association, 2004, D. Respect for People section). We did not see any evidence of cultural competence, and certainly the self-worth of personnel at the school was not respected. Quoting the principal at that school again: "When the PricewaterhouseCoopers audit was published, some of my staff were nearly in tears. They felt that their careers . . . were dismissed as meaningless because someone expressed the opinion that they had low expectations of our children" (Theroux, 2004, ¶10). We have also not seen much protesting from the American Evaluation Association that NCLB-sanctioned methods used to evaluate schools violate the association's professional Guiding Principles. We, however, assert that many evaluations conducted following NCLB regulations are culturally and technically invalid.

Another specific example comes from the earlier use of *Kahoʻolawe*, one of the islands of *Hawaiʻi*, for bombing practice by the U.S. military. This island was used from 1920 (officially from 1941) through 1990 as a bombing target for the U.S. Army and U.S. Navy as well as for Pacific Rim allies. Given our Western evaluation training, we can describe what might be a typical approach to evaluating Executive Order #10436, which placed the island "under the U.S. Secretary of the Navy with the assurance that it would be restored to a 'habitable condition' when no longer needed for naval purposes" (Lewis, 2001, ¶4). A common evaluation practice would be to initially conduct a needs assessment covering such things as national security or safety for the bombing personnel. There also likely would be a fiscal analysis that looked at the possible effects on the local economy attributable to increased spending accompanying the military presence. There might even be formative evaluation conducted to improve the situation by making more efficient use of the targeted island or minimizing disturbances to residents within hearing range. An "indigenous evaluation" approach, on the other hand, would simply refer to the fact that in indigenous cultures inanimate things such as *ʻāina* (land) have *mana* (spirit), and of course it is not *pono* (proper) to bomb things that possess spirit.

At times, our Western governments try to provide services for health or education that reflect indigenous cultural values; however, all too often the evaluation of these initiatives reflects mainly the newcomer's "truth." There are now more calls for evaluation methods that reflect indigenous values. Later we describe a project whose planning and evaluation reflect such values.

The United Nations Draft Declaration on the Rights of Indigenous Peoples (United Nations, 1993) speaks to our rights to our identity, to name ourselves, and to maintain our indigenous citizenship alongside our state/country citizenship. In doing so, the Draft Declaration speaks to the dual realities of many indigenous groups. We effectively inhabit two worlds, one of which is our birthright and the other of which is a product of the colonization of our lands (Reid & Cram, 2004). In effect, we bring both Western mainstream and indigenous methods to our evaluation practice.

We have lived under the gaze of newcomers who have evaluated us within their own belief systems, only to find that we are not only different but also deficient compared to their cultural norms. However, this gaze has come to represent a truth about us, a truth that is not of our own making. It is appropriate that the gaze be returned now and that we do our own gazing.

THUS ONE LEARNS

> Nānā ka maka; ho'olohe ka pepeiao; pa'a ka waha. *Observe with the eyes; listen with the ears; shut the mouth.* Thus one learns.
> —PUKUI (1983, p. 248)

Note that the "shut the mouth" part of this traditional *Kānaka Maoli* saying is at odds with much of today's Western teaching practices, in which students are encouraged to speak up and ask questions early in the learning process. *Titiro ki o taringa; whakarongo ki o whatu* (Look with your ears, listen with your eyes). This saying acknowledges *te reo Māori* (the *Māori* language) and an innate ability that indigenous people have in understanding the subtleties of how, what, and when we communicate through the spoken language.

AN INDIGENOUS EVALUATION FRAMEWORK

We now turn to an indigenous framework for evaluation, which we and the *Evaluation Hui* have developed and see as useful in bringing indigenous and nonindigenous evaluators together to improve evaluation practice. Following the description of the framework is a real-life application that illustrates some methods that are consistent with our model of identifying and describing "value" within the community in its own language and its own way as a means of being able to develop comprehensive community plans and set priorities for future initiatives.

Indigenous evaluation seeks to identify the value added by community-based projects imn terms that are relevant to that specific cultural community. Often, indigenous communities do not experience evaluations that are culturally and historically meaningful. Absent are processes for involving the community in discussions to (1) initiate and design projects, (2) determine data collection methods that are respectful and follow cultural norms, and (3) analyze data in ways that include long-standing strategies that are aligned with the cultural context. Usually the process of determining value has been conducted for foreign purposes and reported to external agencies, often focusing on culturally irrelevant outcomes. We propose a framework for discussing indigenous perspectives of community, culture, and value that directly affect evaluation in indigenous communities. We will explore emerging methodologies and challenges as well as assumptions about the nature of data and the honoring of "contextualized realities."

AN INDIGENOUS PERSPECTIVE ON "VALUE"

Identity is central to the concept of value in *Kānaka Maoli* and *Māori* communities (Porima, 2005). Maaka (2004) described the essential connectedness of individuals to their land, their family and ancestors, and their language. Identity is built on perspectives that value proper relationships with spiritual power inherent in every location, ancestral lineage, living family members, and obligations to the collective good of the community (Kawakami, 1999; Kawakami & Aton, 1999; Meyer, 1998, 2003; Osorio, 2004). Value is situated with specific communities and people in a specific time and place and endures in these communities long after the completion of the final evaluation report. Value is viewed in terms of practical and respectful impact on the lives of the people and communities involved (Mead, 2003). In order to tap into data that penetrate below the surface of rigor as defined by Western epistemology, new and expansive paradigms must be considered that include cultural identity, relationships, sense of place, and impact in terms of immediate and long-term contributions and service to the community.

Much of currently accepted evaluation practice takes what we consider to be a narrow cost–benefit perspective, using data that are readily obtained. Data may be limited to a review of financial activity; attainment/nonattainment of stated objectives, benchmarks, and timelines; student test scores; completion of written deliverable products; and dissemination plans. As the core data of many mainstream evaluations, they limit the scope of evaluation and thus inadequately address the community's interest in the determination of value. From the standpoint of the community of individuals who conceive of and carry out work in their own communities, much more than those variables count in describing value (Smith, 1999; Kamehameha Schools, 2003).

If evaluators attempt to document more substantial community processes and outcomes, they may still be at a loss to describe, for example, the spiritual elements at play within a program, or how uplifting program participants' cultural esteem is an important building block to achieving the outcomes desired by a funder (see Cram, Pihama, Jenkins, & Karehana, 2001). What often remains missing is information on culturally significant impacts tied to the context of individuals and groups.

From an indigenous perspective, who we are, where we are, and how we work together are of utmost importance in promoting the values of the community (Porima, 2005). Evaluation from the community perspective is about "value added" to the quality of life that the community cares about. In addition to data that are collected through prevalent mainstream evaluation methodology, insights into cultural value can be found through humble and quiet observation and listening (Cram, 2001).

ASSUMPTIONS ABOUT THE CONTEXT

Evaluation should be based on indigenous epistemology and operate within the following general guidelines:

1. The evaluation must be viewed and implemented as a holistic and contextualized experience with respect to a specific place, time, community, and history.

2. Evaluation of projects in indigenous communities must promote and practice an indigenous worldview, including, but not limited to, consideration of indigenous identity, epistemology, values, and spirituality.

3. Colleagues who have complementary knowledge and skill sets must collaborate to embrace both the cultural and academic perspective during this time of emerging methodology.

Holistic approaches must be used in addition to the more typical methods of gathering and analyzing discrete data. Contextual variables are essential to understanding the value of projects and even for answering seemingly straightforward evaluation questions such as "Who is involved?," "Where are they?," "What was done?," and "How is it perceived?" The impact of projects in the short term and over time should be considered as well. Multiple points of entry into dialogues and gathering and confirming observations and interpretations are necessary to obtain accurate data, draw conclusions, and interpret those data.

In order to promote an indigenous worldview, projects in indigenous communities must be initiated by the community, and evaluations of those projects should focus on variables that the community hopes to change in positive ways. Sometimes these projects are well thought out and planned with evaluation in mind. At other times projects and services are initiated by indigenous communities when they see that there is a need for them, and the first thoughts are to fill this need, rather than attending to the methods of a "scientific intervention" (Pipi et al., 2003).

Evaluations that promote indigenous epistemology must be innovative and creative, including data that extend beyond conventional constructs. Those variables may include certain impacts as proof of attainment of project objectives as well as clarification and strengthening indigenous identity, values, and spirituality. Contextual variables such as location and relationships are features that are essential to understanding and participating in a cultural community. Contextual information and insider views must be used as data to assess value within the realities of the community (Cram et al., 2001).

Both project design and evaluation phases must be conducted by individuals (including community members) with familiarity and competence in cultural and academic realms; however, because of the systematic historical dismantling of indigenous cultures, there is a "gap" generation of indigenous people who have lost much of their language and culture as they gained skills that allowed them to navigate successfully in Western society (Lai, Cram, Kawakami, Porima, & Aton, 2005). These individuals may have been raised by grandparents and parents who had been punished for practicing their culture and speaking their language (Simon & Smith, 2001). Or, as responsible caretakers of the young, they refused to pass on these practices, believing that a successful future for their children lay in assimilation into the dominant culture.

Instead of learning and practicing their culture in the home and community, the "gap group" was groomed for success in the Western world of school and commerce. Many have indeed achieved success in academia and mainstream life and have recently begun to acknowledge the value of their indigenous culture and language. Lost cultural practices are now being acquired as knowledge and skills through formal instruction instead of through family lifestyle and practice.

Conversely, "lucky ones" have learned their mother tongue and native culture through immersion in culture practices with guidance by elders or expert teachers who had the wisdom, foresight, and opportunity to resist Western domination and colonization. In the acquisition and maintenance of cultural knowledge, these "lucky ones" have had the advantage of learning the full range of *nā mea Hawai'i a me ngā mea Māori* (things Hawaiian and things *Māori*), behaviors and skills and, most importantly, understanding of the spiritual dimension of cultural life.

Projects and evaluations in indigenous communities will benefit from collaborations of individuals who bring together both the indigenous cultural and Western perspectives. The "gap group" has the *kuleana* (obligation) to learn about the cultural practices of their ancestors and in return must use their positions and skills in predominantly Western institutions to create a place and space for the practice of indigenous protocols, to acknowledge indigenous points of view, and to promote and protect the value of the "lucky ones," who are obligated to guide and teach the "gap group" so that indigenous ways become standard procedure. Evaluation in indigenous communities needs collaborative teams of indigenous people with both types of knowledge and skills.

In order to empower indigenous communities to determine what is valuable in projects conducted in their midst, evaluation designs need to be viewed in broad and complex ways that begin with the essential cultural factors. Again we acknowledge that not all Western methodologies are as culturally insensitive as the evaluation practice construct we are arguing against; however, there are a plethora of examples of culturally inappropriate evaluations. The following framework is proposed to facilitate discussion of an expanded perspective on evaluation in indigenous communities.

EVALUATION COMPONENTS

At the outset of an evaluation, we must be explicit about who are the "we" during the planning phase. Are we the indigenous *Kānaka Maoli/ Māori* advisor, evaluator, or provider? We need to ensure we have common agreements on the purpose and goals of the evaluation. The purpose and goals of a project or initiative should be determined by the community based on its priorities and needs. Many times projects are imposed on communities by external funding agencies intent on providing services that will "fix" community "needs." True community priorities are essential to promote sustainable benefits over time. The question that evaluations must address is "Has the community been affected in a positive way as a result of the program/project/initiative?"

Methods that are to be used in evaluations involving *Māori/Kānaka Maoli* must be inclusive and appropriate for indigenous communities. Multiple measures and sources of data must be used to capture the impact on the life of the community. In an indigenous perspective, data include information that extends into many facets of the lived experience. Spiritual, cultural, historical, social, emotional, cognitive, theoretical, and situated information all contribute to that understanding. In addition to written reports, methods and media for communicating results of the evaluation may include graphic representations, *mo'olelo* (narratives), culturally created manifestations (e.g., *oli* [chant] and *hula* [dance]) valid to the community, and documentation of *hō'ailona* (naturally occurring environmental conditions or omens). Analyzing and interpreting these data require the team approach mentioned previously. Results must then be viewed in multiple contexts in terms of cultural, historical, political, economic, and environmental significance.

In consideration of respect and courtesy, findings should first be communicated to the community. Findings may be shared as *mo'olelo* (stories) told in community gatherings as well as written as formal reports to funding agencies. These *mo'olelo* must acknowledge the cultural relationships that exist in communities and may be portrayed through photos, DVDs, CDs, and videos. Communication of the data in visual and performance formats may be more effective in depicting the richness of impact than written reports (Lai, Yap, & Dunn, 2004).

The results and conclusions of evaluations should be useful for both the community and the funding agency. The community should see the impact of projects and use that information to revise the community agenda and priorities. Funders should use the information to revisit and inform the development of their own benevolent priorities and goals.

The impact of culturally grounded projects and evaluations should lead to better understanding of strategies and methods. These lessons describe communities' dynamic and unique responses to initiatives. Appropriately conducted projects and evaluations should bring clarity and empowerment to indigenous communities and assist in advancing their agendas toward an improved quality of life.

Table 11.1 provides a summary and comparison of the evaluation methods that are being proposed and discussed.

BARRIERS AND CHALLENGES

Ideally, the model for culturally grounded community projects and evaluations would be implemented easily. However, as an emerging process, many barriers and challenges need to be considered. The following list presents a number of issues:

- How to promote the expansion of paradigms?
- How to develop both cultural capacity and "academic" capacity of individuals involved on community evaluations?
- How to develop alternative models for analysis and data collection?
- How to avoid paralysis due to the fear of being disrespectful in relation to cultural dimensions and protocols?
- In the absence of traditional governance and authority structures, who speaks for the community?

TABLE 11.1. A Conceptual Framework for Indigenous Evaluation Practice

Functions	Methodology: Primarily indigenous (includes some mainstream and adds dimensions)	Methodology: Primarily widely practiced mainstream
Purpose and goals	Set by community agenda.	Externally generated.
Driving question	Has the community been impacted in a positive way as a result of the program/project/ initiative?	Have proposal goals/ objectives been met?
Methodology	Quantitative, qualitative, and more.	Primarily quantitative.
Data	Spiritual, cultural, historical, social emotional, cognitive, theoretical, situated information. Graphics, narratives, culturally created manifestations (*oli* [chant], *hula* [dance]) "valid" to that place.	Objective decontextualized data. Objective validity and reliability. Statistical and practical significance and effect size.
Analysis	Cultural and environmental significance.	Statistical and practical significance and effect size.
Format for findings	Narratives, *mo'olelo* (stories), relationships, photos, DVDs, CDs, videos.	Written reports, charts, tables, graphs, databases.
Conclusions and recommendations	Shared among project, community, evaluator, and funder. Revised community agenda.	Fulfillment of contract. Submitted to funder.
Impact	Value added, lessons learned, clarity, empowerment.	Revised funding priorities.

Indigenous peoples working on new paradigms for projects and evaluation are covering ground that has only recently begun to be chartered in a widely accessible way to indigenous scholars (e.g., Cajete, 2000; Kahakalau, 2004; Smith, 1999). Discussion about variables and perspectives that allow for validation of *nā mea Hawai'i a me ngā mea Māori* (things Hawaiian and things *Māori*) is essential to understanding the value that programs add to the communities. Each project or evaluation that includes these perspectives will advance the understanding of the paradigm that includes indigenous ways of knowing and being. Capacity to conduct these evaluations will increase over time as old methods are adopted and adapted, new methods are developed, and more individuals learn to include new perspectives and tools in their professional repertoire. While cultural aspects are often wrapped in mystique, if cultural practitioners and academics collaborate, progress can be made. Respectful attitudes will help to guide proper behaviors, and guidance from cultural practitioners will mitigate the fear of approaching the cultural realm.

In traditional times, indigenous cultures functioned with governance structures intact. As a result of colonization, traditional leaders no longer can be easily identified, and cultural structures within communities are fragmented and diffused. To begin the dialogue with communities, evaluators and funding agencies need to approach many people in the community and listen carefully to determine who and where to gain access.

Indigenous and nonindigenous evaluators must work together in understanding and developing a more enlightened appropriate approach and a more precise methodology for conducting evaluations in indigenous communities. Indigenous communities are finding their voices in the current context of evaluation and empowerment. Many indigenous professionals have been staunch supporters and advocates for their communities and will continue to raise the issues, create the time and space for dialogue, and speak for their communities.

AN EXAMPLE
SHOWING SOME ASPECTS OF CULTURALLY
APPROPRIATE EVALUATION PRACTICE

He pūkoʻa kani ʻāina. *A coral reef that grows into an island.* A person beginning in a small way gains steadily until he becomes firmly established.

—Pukui (1983, p. 100)

The Institute for Native Pacific Education and Culture's (INPEACE) *Hoʻowaiwai Nā Kamaliʻi (HNK)* initiative provides an example of a community-initiated and culturally based project. INPEACE's mission is to improve the quality of Native Hawaiians' lives through community partnerships that provide educational opportunities and promote self-sufficiency.

Hoʻowaiwai Nā Kamaliʻi can be translated as "valuing the babies" and focuses on *Kānaka Maoli* children prenatal to age 5 on the Outer

Islands of *Hawai'i*. The primary goal of the project is to design and develop a system of data collection and use it to set community priorities that ensure that Native Hawaiian children will be ready to succeed in school. *HNK*'s approach was designed to ensure that the indigenous community did not experience an evaluation that was weak on cultural and historical meaningfulness.

INPEACE staff members serve as Community Based Early Childhood Advocates (CBECAs), who are a part of the target communities. CBECAs work with community stakeholders, such as parents, grandparents, cultural resources, service providers, educators, cultural experts, community leaders, and policymakers, to develop and implement a community-based plan to address critical early childhood education and care issues. Data collection from cultural experts, consumers, and service providers uses several unique, culturally aligned features.

This project strives to empower communities to determine the future of their *keiki* (children) through the use of data that describe their vision for the 5-year-old *keiki,* their desired support system, the cultural resources available, and the gap between desired and available support. With this information, advisory councils are developing an early childhood plan that is community-owned, community-driven, adaptable, culturally based, and sustainable.

At the core of this project lies the vision Hawaiian communities hold for their children at age 5 as being safe, healthy, ready to succeed, and culturally prepared. This vision reflects the overall state of *Hawai'i* vision but has added cultural competence. Focus groups held in *Kānaka Maoli* communities consistently brought up cultural competence as key to defining what readiness for kindergarten is from an indigenous viewpoint.

Data Collection

The data collection procedures took into account the impact on communities, which were leery of providing information because of past efforts that failed to produce positive changes. A clear articulation of purposes was necessary for families to buy into the project. The data collection tools focused on cultural factors that contribute to readiness for kindergarten, informed the well-being of *Kānaka Maoli,* stayed connected to Native Hawaiian values, were usable by Native Hawaiian communities, and added to the statewide early childhood data picture.

An example of the type of data collection tool just described is the INPEACE Consumer Survey (University of Hawai'i, Center on the Family, 2002), which taps into the lives of community members to assess grassroots perceptions of early childhood support in their local area.

Kānaka Maoli communities were able to identify needs and gaps in services as well as comment on the quality of the services and suggest ways to improve. This survey includes questions concerning the availability, accessibility, cost, and quality of services for four key contributors to early childhood well-being: family support, parenting support, health support, and early child-care support.

During the data collection process, one CBECA was assigned to each of the five survey sites. All surveys were completed by parents and caretakers of Native Hawaiian children from prenatal up to 5 years of age. Each advocate gathered surveys from consumers at agencies or programs providing services in each domain, as well as from community events and gathering places such as parks, beaches, laundromats, cultural events, athletic games, grocery stores, and churches. Incentive gifts such as crayons, jump ropes, coloring books, and puzzles were provided to respondents. Because CBECAs are from the communities, they are involved in the daily routines of families in the community and are often present at community events.

CBECAs focused on honoring community and cultural values. The community-based early childhood advocate job position description included a requirement of sensitivity to Hawaiian culture and knowledge about the educational issues that challenge the vulnerable prenatal to age-5 child. Communities were wary of sharing information, but the specialized community knowledge of the CBECAs helped dispel some of the wariness.

Results

Analyses of the 2004 INPEACE consumer survey (University of Hawai'i, Center on the Family, 2005) showed that respondents rated health-support services in their communities the most favorable, followed closely by early-care and education-support services. These results have two main implications. First, more services in each area of support are needed. Specifically, it appears that not only is there a need for more services, but there is also a need for a wider variety of services. This was by far the most frequent suggestion provided by respondents. Second, the results suggested that more publicity and advertising to promote awareness about the availability of these services were needed.

With these community-based data, *HNK* is currently working closely in communities to target identified issues and gaps in services. From the statewide perspective, a pattern of priorities is emerging from the community advisory councils on the numerous early childhood issues. These priorities reflect the results regarding the need for a variety of services and more publicity, as shown in Table 11.2.

TABLE 11.2. Community Priorities and Data Results

Advisory council priority	Data result
Smoothing transitions into kindergarten	Increasing variety of education and care services
Family-focused projects	Increasing variety of family-support services
Supporting children of incarcerated parents	Increasing variety of education and care, family support, parenting-support services
Cultural maps	Increasing the variety of family-support services
Raising early childhood awareness	More publicity
'Ohana (family) resources kits	Increasing access to available services

From the project's perspective, a notable result is the statewide creation of community-based advisory councils, which will continue to advocate at executive/legislative/local policymaking levels, at education institutions (Department of Education, university, private/public schools), and at the family level for referrals to appropriate social services. Also noteworthy are community-based capacity-building efforts through the *HNK* first-ever Native-Hawaiian Early Childhood Summit and the synthesis of all the community-based plans. Finally, the *HNK* project developed an extensive network of supporting partnerships and relationships that will continue to help to close service gaps in communities. Ultimately, *HNK* communities have been able to determine their needs in ways that are important to them and respect their cultural protocols. *HNK* provided a viable venue to do this.

Although this example may be more of a needs assessment than a full external evaluation, it provides us with instances of how the indigenous perspective may be honored within a community-based self-evaluation that respects who we are and what we value and leads to the identification of fully functioning (valuable) support systems currently working in the community. As a needs assessment, it provides the community with data to develop community plans and to identify its priorities to increase the value of culturally and community-based support for the future.

This traditional Hawaiian saying speaks well to the overall *HNK* project:

E kaupē aku no i ka hoe a kō mai. *Put forward the paddle and draw it back.* Go on with the task that is started and finish it.
                                                    —PUKUI (1983, p. 39)

This culturally and community-based project was a valuable effort that was in sync with national initiatives focused on making sure our most vulnerable populations of young children are prepared to succeed in school. Of value in this project is the way this synchronicity stemmed from the family, up to the community, to the island, to the state, and to the nation.

CONCLUDING REMARKS

We began this paper by introducing ourselves and talking about our shared histories of "discovery," colonization, and misrepresentation. These histories have made the indigenous peoples of our lands both wary and weary of evaluation practices that disregard our worldviews and our place as *kama'āina* and *tangata whenua* (peoples of the land). Such practices are an offense to our *mana* (spirit). They also further marginalize us when our own aim is to improve our life circumstances within the societies we now know. New evaluation practices are therefore sought that honor the dreams and aspirations of indigenous peoples in *Hawai'i* and *Aotearoa.*

The time for this is long overdue. As our understandings of our own cultures and our training in mainstream approaches to evaluation come together, the opportunities for synergies are many and exciting. At their core, these synergies are about valuing and respecting the voices of indigenous peoples and ensuring that interventions and evaluations speak to those who are most involved—our communities. Tied to this is the recognition that our worldviews, our ways of knowing, and our knowledge are fundamentally valid and legitimate.

Even though the processes of colonization have marginalized us within our own lands, we remain sovereign people who insist on the right to find our own solutions and our own ways of evidencing social transformations. Evaluations that support us in this effort must exhibit both academic and cultural validity. We look forward to the day when this approach becomes the norm of our evaluation experience.

He 'a'ali'i ku makani mai au; 'a'ohe makani nana e kula'i. *I am a wind-resisting* 'a'ali'i; *no gale can push me over.* . . . I can hold my own in the face of difficulties. The *'a'ali'i* bush can stand the worst of gales, twisting and bending but seldom breaking off or falling over.
                                                    —PUKUI (1983, p. 60)

ACKNOWLEDGMENTS

We acknowledge our other colleagues in the *Evaluation Hui* for developing with us much of our *mana'o* (thinking) presented in this chapter. We also thank the W.K. Kellogg Foundation for supporting the *Evaluation Hui* and also for supporting our attending and presenting at the 2005 conference of the American Evaluation Association held in Toronto and at the 2005 World Indigenous Peoples Conference in Education (WIPCE) held in Hamilton, Aotearoa. And finally, to our families and predecessors, in the *mo'oku'auhau* and *whakapapa* (genealogical) sense as well as in the academic sense, we express our deepest gratitude and *aloha/aroha*.

REFERENCES

American Evaluation Association. (2004). *Guiding principles for evaluators.* Retrieved February 16, 2005, from *www.eval.org/Publications/Guiding-Principles.asp.*

Bancroft, H. H. (Ed.). (1902). *The great republic by the master historians: The annexation of Hawaii.* Retrieved January 2, 2006, from *www.humanities-web.org/human.php?s=s&p=h&ID=1005.*

Cajete, G. (2000). *Native science: Natural laws of interdependence.* Santa Fe, NM: Clear Light.

Colonisation. (2006). Retrieved January 3, 2006, from *www.newzealand.com/travel/about-nz/history/history-colonisation.cfm.*

Cram, F. (1997). Developing partnerships in research: Māori research and Pakeha researchers. *SITES, 35,* 44–63.

Cram, F. (2001). Rangahau Māori: Tona tika, tona pono. In M. Tolich (Ed.), *Research ethics in Aotearoa* (pp. 35–52). Auckland, NZ: Longman.

Cram, F., Pihama, L., Jenkins, K., & Karehana, M. (2001). *Evaluation of programmes for Māori adult protected persons under the Domestic Violence Act 1995.* Wellington, NZ: Ministry of Justice.

Daes, E.-I. (1995). *Principles and guidelines for the protection of the heritage of indigenous people.* Elaborated in conformity with resolution 1993/44 and decision 1994/105 of the Sub-Commission on Prevention of Discrimination and Protection of Minorities of the Commission on Human Rights, Economic and Social Council, United Nations. Retrieved January 15, 2006, from *www.ankn.uaf.edu/IKS/protect.html.*

Davis, J. D., Erickson, J. S., Johnson, S. R., Marshall, C. A., Running Wolf, P., & Santiago, R. L. (Eds.). (2002). *Work Group on American Indian Research and Program Evaluation Methodology (AIRPEM), Symposium on Research and Evaluation Methodology: Lifespan issues related to American Indians/Alaska Natives with disabilities.* Flagstaff: Northern Arizona University, Institute for Human Development, Arizona University Center on Disabilities, American Indian Rehabilitation Research and Training Center.

Desmond, A., & Moore, J. (1991). *Darwin.* London: Penguin.

Fetterman, D. M., & Wandersman, A. (Eds.). (2005). *Empowerment evaluation principles in practice.* New York: Guilford Press.

Greene, J. C. (1997). Evaluation as advocacy. *Evaluation Practice, 18*(1), 25–35.

Health Research Council of New Zealand. (1998). *Guidelines for researchers on health research involving Māori.* Auckland, NZ: Author.

Kahakalau, K. (2004). Indigenous heuristic action research: Bridging Western and indigenous research methodologies. *Hūlili, 1*(1), 19–34.

Kamehameha Schools, Policy Analysis & System Evaluation. (2003, March). Evaluation Hui: Toward guidelines for culturally responsible evaluation and research. *InfoBrief,* Report No. 02-03-17, 1–4.

Kanaʻiaupuni, S. M. (2004). Kaʻakālai kū kānakā: A call for strengths-based approaches from a Native Hawaiian perspective. *Educational Researcher, 33*(9), 26–32.

Kawakami, A. J. (1999). Sense of place, culture and community: Bridging the gap between home and school for Hawaiian students. *Education and Urban Society, 32*(1), 18–40.

Kawakami, A. J., & Aton, K. K. (1999). *Na Pua Noʻeau curriculum guidelines.* Hilo: University of Hawaiʻi at Hilo, Center for Gifted and Talented Native Hawaiian Children.

Kirkhart, K. E. (1995). Seeking multicultural validity: A postcard from the road. *Evaluation Practice, 16*(1), 1–12.

Lai, M. K., Cram, F., Kawakami, A. J., Porima, L., & Aton, K. K. (2005). *Brackish waters: Going with the flow in the space between indigenous cultural identities and Western professional evaluation roles.* Presentation at the annual meeting of the American Evaluation Association, Toronto.

Lai, M. K., Yap, M., & Dunn, H. (2004). *Developing Moʻolelo evaluation methods for Pihana Nā Mamo.* Presentation at the Kamehameha Schools Research Conference on Hawaiian Well-Being, *Keaʻau,* HI.

Lewis, C. (2001). *ICE case study: Kahoʻolawe and the military.* Retrieved February 21, 2005, from *www.american.edu/ted/ice/hawaiibombs.htm.*

Maaka, M. J. (2004). E kua takoto te mānuka tūtahi: Decolonization, self-determination, and education. *Educational Perspectives: Indigenous Education, 37*(1), 3–13.

Mead, H. M. (2003). *Tikanga Māori: Living by Māori values.* Wellington, NZ: Huia.

Merriam-Webster's collegiate dictionary (10th ed.). (1993). Springfield, MA: Merriam-Webster.

Meyer, M. A. (1998). Native Hawaiian epistemology: Sites of empowerment and resistance. *Equity and Excellence in Education. 31,* 22–28.

Meyer, M. A. (2003). *Hoʻoulu: Our time of becoming.* Honolulu, HI: ʻAi Pohaku Press.

National Maritime Museum. (2005). Medal commemorating the discovery [*sic*] of Hawaii by Captain James Cook—obverse. Retrieved February 19, 2005, from *www.nmm.ac.uk/server/show/conMediaFile.3188.*

Osorio, J. K. K. (2004). Gazing back: Communing with our ancestors. *Educational Perspectives: Indigenous Education, 37*(1), 14–17.

Patton, M. Q. (2002). *Qualitative research & evaluation methods* (3rd ed.). Thousand Oaks, CA: Sage.

Pihama, L., Cram, F., & Walker, S. (2002). Creating methodological space: A literature review of Kaupapa Māori research. *Canadian Journal of Native Education, 26,* 30–43.

Pipi, K., Cram, F., Hawke, R., Hawke, S., Huriwai, T. M., Keefe, V., Mataki, T., Milne, M., Morgan, K., Small, K., Tuhaka, H., & Tuuta, C. (2003). *Māori and iwi provider success: A research report of interviews with successful iwi and Māori providers and government agencies.* Wellington, NZ: Te Puni Kokiri.

Porima, L. (2005). *Cultural well-being through tikanga Māori: A grounded interpretation in relation to the practice of evaluation.* Whitby, Porirua, NZ: LLE Research.

Pukui, M. K. (1983). *'Olelo no'eau: Hawaiian proverbs and poetical sayings* (collected, translated, and annotated by M. K. Pukui). Honolulu, HI: Bernice P. Bishop Museum.

Reid, P., & Cram, F. (2004). Connecting health, people and county in Aotearoa/New Zealand. In K. Dew & P. Davis (Eds.), *Health and society in Aotearoa New Zealand* (2nd ed., pp. 33–48). Auckland, NZ: Oxford University Press.

Robson, B., & Reid, P. (2001). *Ethnicity matters: Review of the measurement of ethnicity in official statistics.* Wellington, NZ: Statistics New Zealand.

SenGupta, S., Hopson, R., & Thompson-Robinson, M. (2004). Cultural competence in evaluation: An overview. In M. Thompson-Robinson, R. Hopson, & S. SenGupta, *In search of cultural competence in evaluation* (New Directions for Evaluation no. 102, pp. 5–19). San Francisco: Jossey-Bass.

Simon, J., & Smith, L. T., with Cram, F., Hōhepa, M., McNaughton, S., & Stephenson, M. (2001). *A civilising mission? Perceptions and representations of the native schools system.* Auckland, NZ: Auckland University Press.

Smith, L. T. (1999). *Decolonizing methodologies: Research and indigenous peoples.* London: Zed Books.

Theroux, J. (2004, March 9). *Understanding our "broken" schools.* Retrieved February 1, 2005, from *the.honoluluadvertiser.com/article/2004/Mar/09/op/op04a.html.*

United Nations, Commission on Human Rights, Sub-Commission on Prevention of Discrimination and Protection of Minorities. (1993). *Draft declaration on the rights of indigenous peoples.* Retrieved February 11, 2005, from *www.usask.ca/nativelaw/ddir.html.*

University of Hawai'i, Center on the Family. (2002). *Native Hawaiian young children: Data, information, and services report to Ho'owaiwai Nā Kamali'i, the Native Hawaiian Early Childhood Education and Care Consortium.* Honolulu, HI: Author.

University of Hawai'i, Center on the Family. (2005). *Community perceptions of services for Native Hawaiian young children: 2005 INPEACE Report.* Honolulu, HI: Author.

Wakefield, E. G. (1837). *The British colonisation of New Zealand.* London: J. W. Parker.

Yamamoto, E., & Iijima, C. (2000). The colonizer's story: The Supreme Court violates Native Hawaiian sovereignty—again. *ColorLines, 3*(2). Retrieved January 2, 2006, from *www.arc.org/C_Lines/CLArchive/story3_2_01.html.*

Author Index

Subject Index

"n" following a page number indicates a note;
"t" following a page number indicates a table.

Committee on Scientific Principles
for Education Research,
203
Compensatory equalization, 83n–84n
Competence, practical knowledge and,
33–35
Comprehensive Dynamic Trial Designs,
103
Concurrent bias assessment, 76
Congressional Research Service, 17
Construct underrepresentation, validity
and, 204–206
Contamination in research, biasing
social interactions and, 72–75,
73t
Context specificity
indigenous cultures and, 230–232
validity and, 203–204
Credibility, scientific rigor and, 201–
207
Critical analysis of evaluation practice,
transformative paradigm and,
44–46
Critical race feminism, validity and,
202
Critical Race Theory (CRT), validity
and, 202
Cross-cultural, 34, 149, 155, 200
Cross-Design Synthesis, 89–90, 93t,
94–100, 98. See also Research
synthesis
Cultural competence
Center for Research on Education of
Students Placed at Risk
(CRESPAR) and, 50
indigenous cultures and, 227
overview, 38n, 47, 48–49
practical knowledge and, 33
transformative paradigm and, 46–48,
48–49, 56, 56–57
Cultural diversity, transformative
paradigm and, 42–44, 43t, 45.
See also Diversity
Cultural knowledge, indigenous
cultures and, 231–232
Cultural rights, indigenous cultures
and, 225–226

Cultural sensitivity. See also Indigenous
cultures
program standard setting and, 147–
148
scientific rigor and, 211–212
validity and, 202–204, 205–206
Culturally appropriate evaluation
barriers and challenges and, 233–235
colonial past of, 224–225
context and, 230–232
evaluation components, 232–233,
234t
evaluation framework and, 228–229
example of, 235–239, 238t
introduction to, 219–221
overview, 221–222, 239
protection of cultural and intellectual
rights in evaluation, 225–226
values and mainstream evaluation
standards and, 226–228, 229–
230
Western culture and, 222–224

DARE (Drug Abuse Resistance
Education) program, 191
Data collection
alternative strategies to minimize
bias, 78, 79
indigenous cultures and, 228–229,
232–233, 234t, 236–237
validity and, 203–204
Decision making. See also Policy
decision making; Rigor,
scientific; Scientific rigor
differences between evaluation and
research and, 191
Declaration on the Rights of
Indigenous Peoples, draft, 227–
228
Declarative knowledge, 163, 165t
Delinquent behavior, bias and, 74, 84n
Department of Education. See also U.S.
Department of Education
differences between evaluation and
research and, 185–186
disability and, 52
inclusion criteria and, 91–92

Religion, indigenous cultures and, 223–224
Research and Evaluation on Education in Science and Engineering program, 126–127
Research on evaluation. *See also* Differences between evaluation and research; Research synthesis
calls for increasing, 113–116
framework for, 116–126, 117*t*, 122*t*, 123*t*
as a fundamental issue, 111–113
overview, 64, 126–130
Research synthesis. *See also* Broad-based research synthesis; Cross-Design Synthesis; Evaluation Synthesis; Prospective Evaluation Synthesis; Qualitative review; Research on evaluation
existing primary research and, 100–104
further specification of, 94–100
inclusion criteria of, 91–92
overview, 89–90, 104–105
taxonomy of research and, 116
types of reviews, 92–94, 93*t*
Rigor, scientific
evidence-based knowledge and, 201
No Child Left Behind Act of 2001 and, 198, 201, 204, 209–211, 212
overview, 197–201, 211–212
policy decision making and, 201, 209–211
social justice goals and, 209–211
theory and, 200–201, 207–208
validity and, 200, 201–207

Saturation trial, 102–103
Schematic knowledge, 163, 165*t*
Scientific rigor
evidence-based knowledge and, 201
No Child Left Behind Act of 2001 and, 198, 201, 204, 209–211, 212
overview, 197–201, 211–212

policy decision making and, 201, 209–211
social justice goals and, 209–211
theory and, 200–201, 207–208
validity and, 200, 201–207
Selection bias
overview, 83*n*
randomized studies and, 66
Self-assessment, student, 171
Self-fulfilling prophecy, differential reactivity and, 69
Self-referenced standard, in collaborative evaluation, 142
Self-reports, bias assessment using, 76–80
Significant change technique, differences between evaluation and research and, 192–193
Social interactions, biasing
assessments of, 75–82
minimizing, 80–82
overview, 63, 66–67, 68–69, 68*t*, 82–83
subcategories of, 72–75, 73*t*
Social interactions, practical knowledge and, 31–32
Social justice perspective
scientific rigor and, 209–211
transformative paradigm and, 56
Social science research, differences between evaluation and research and, 191, 192–193, 194
Societal values, profession and, 18–19
Society for Research on Educational Effectiveness (SREE), 18
Specificity, validity and, 205–206
"Stable unit treatment value assumption" (SUTVA), 67
Stakeholders
cultural competence and, 47
differences between evaluation and research and, 194
involvement of, 119
overview, 41–42
program standard setting and, 145–146

About the Editors

Nick L. Smith, PhD, is Professor in the School of Education at Syracuse University and 2004 President of the American Evaluation Association. The primary focus of his writings is the nature of applied field research and evaluation methods, and the theory of evaluation.

Paul R. Brandon, PhD, is Professor of Education and Director of the Program Research and Evaluation Office at Curriculum Research & Development Group, University of Hawai'i at Mānoa. His current scholarly interests include the evaluation of program implementation and standard setting in evaluations.

About the Authors

Kanani Aton, MEd, is a private consultant. She coordinates a statewide collaboration to improve outcomes for Native Hawaiian students, supports the use of a web-based evaluation tool designed specifically for Hawaiian charter schools, and serves the Native Hawaiian Education Council of Hawai'i Island as their facilitator.

Carlos C. Ayala, PhD, is Associate Professor of Science Education and Assessment at Sonoma State University. He is a former middle and high school science teacher and principal. He has performed evaluations of science curriculum and carried out assessment projects.

Paul R. Brandon, PhD (*see* "About the Editors").

J. Bradley Cousins, PhD, is Professor of Educational Administration at the Faculty of Education, University of Ottawa, Canada. His interests are evaluation capacity building and the organizational impact of evaluation. He has practiced predominantly participatory approaches to evaluation in education, public health, and community mental health.

Fiona Cram, PhD, Ngāti Kahungunu (indigenous tribe of New Zealand), mother of one son, is Director of Katoa Ltd., a small research and evaluation company. Most of her evaluation work is with *Māori* and *Iwi* (tribal) organizations and social service providers.

Judith A. Droitcour, PhD, is Assistant Director, Center for Evaluation Methods and Issues, U.S. Government Accountability Office. Her previous work includes developing and applying a "cross-design synthesis" approach combining meta-analysis of RCTs with database analyses that reflect day-to-day medical practice.

Elmima C. Johnson, PhD, is Senior Staff Associate and Program Director at the National Science Foundation. She serves as the American Evaluation

Association (AEA) representative to the Joint Committee on Standards for Educational Evaluation and chairs the AEA Multicultural Issues Topical Interest Group.

Alice J. Kawakami, PhD, is Associate Professor of Education at the University of Hawai'i at Mānoa, and one of three founders of the Institute for Native Pacific Education and Culture, a private nonprofit organization determined to improve the quality of life for Native Hawaiians through educational and economic partnerships.

Karen E. Kirkhart, PhD, is Professor, School of Social Work, College of Human Services and Health Professions, Syracuse University. Her work on multicultural validity examines ways in which culture bounds understanding, particularly judgments of program merit and worth. Her work on evaluation influence examines intersections of power, ethics, and validity.

Mary Grace Kovar, DrPH, is a consultant to the National Opinion Research Center. She has published 125 peer-reviewed journal articles and is a Fellow of the American Statistical Association, the American College of Epidemiology, the American Association for the Advancement of Science, and the American Public Health Association.

Susan N. Labin, PhD, is an independent consultant with 20 years of evaluation experience in various substantive areas. She uses collaborative planning and evaluation frameworks, and recently has focused on the health effects of workplace practices. She has worked for university research institutes and federal agencies, including the U.S. Government Accountability Office.

Morris K. Lai, PhD, is an educational associate with Curriculum Research & Development Group, University of Hawai'i at Mānoa. Much of his recent work has focused on culturally appropriate evaluation methods for Native Hawaiians.

Anna Marie Madison, PhD, is Associate Professor, Human Services, College of Public and Community Service at the University of Massachusetts, Boston. Her primary evaluation focus is evaluation policies and practices affecting people of color, community-based evaluation, capacity building, and participatory evaluation methods.

Melvin M. Mark, PhD, is Professor of Psychology at Pennsylvania State University. His interests include the consequences of evaluation. He has been involved in evaluations in a number of areas, including prevention programs, federal personnel policies, and various educational interventions.

Sandra Mathison, PhD, is Professor of Education at the University of British Columbia. Her research is in educational evaluation and focuses especially on the potential and limits of evaluation to support democratic ideals and promote justice. She has conducted evaluations of traditional schools, informal educational contexts, and postsecondary education.

Donna M. Mertens, PhD, is Professor of Educational Research and Foundations at Gallaudet University in Washington, DC. Her major contributions focus on social justice and evaluation's role in the transformation of society, based on her work in culturally complex communities.

Grayson B. Noley, PhD, is Chair of Educational Leadership and Policy Studies at the University of Oklahoma. He studies mostly issues about the improvement of education for American Indians.

Laurie Porima, BA, BCA, Ngāti Manawa (indigenous tribe of New Zealand), is Director of LLE Research Ltd., a research and evaluation company. He is the happily married father of three girls and one son.

Thomas A. Schwandt, PhD, is Professor of Education at the University of Illinois at Urbana–Champaign, and Distinguished University Teacher/Scholar. His scholarship focuses on issues in the philosophies of interpretive methodologies and theory of evaluation.

Lyn M. Shulha, PhD, is Director of the Assessment and Evaluation Group, Queen's University at Kingston, Canada. She is primarily a participatory evaluator with a focus on professional learning and evaluation use. She has done evaluation primarily in schools (pre-K–12).

Nick L. Smith, PhD (*see* "About the Editors").

Guillermo Solano-Flores, PhD, is Associate Professor of Bilingual Education and English as a Second Language at the School of Education of the University of Colorado at Boulder. He specializes in educational measurement, assessment development, and the linguistic and cultural issues that are relevant to testing.